GERARD STAMP
AT THE STILL POINT

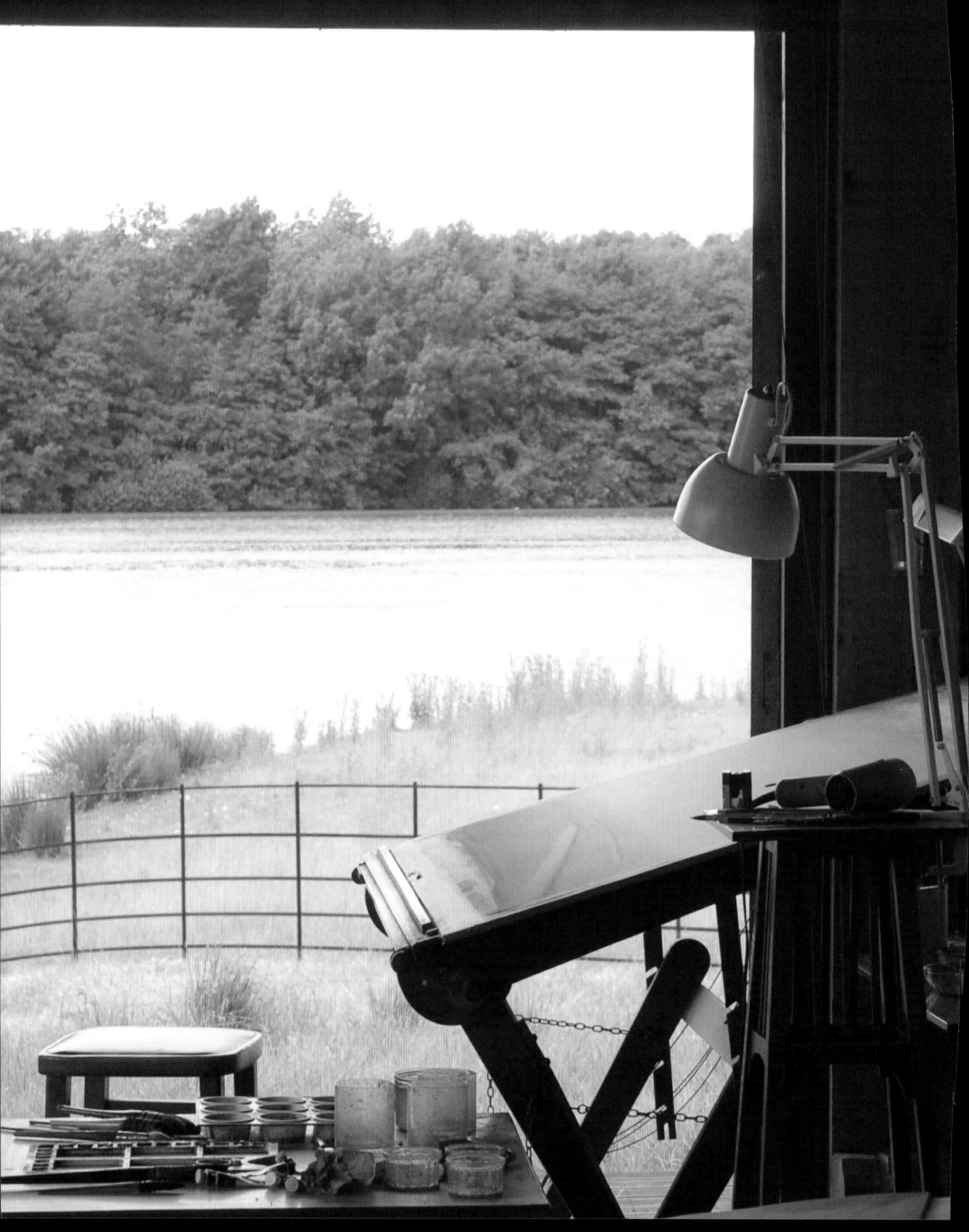

GERARD STAMP
AT THE STILL POINT

Ian Collins

Published in 2026 by Unicorn
an imprint of Unicorn Publishing Group
Charleston Studio
Meadow Business Centre
Lewes BN8 5RW
www.unicornpublishing.org

Designed by Gerard Stamp
Typeface: Freight text, sans and display

Printed by Publikum, Beograd, Serbia

ISBN 978-1-918271-10-2
10 9 8 7 6 5 4 3 2 1

(Frontispiece)

Great Water from the Boathouse studio Gunton Park, Norfolk

Contents

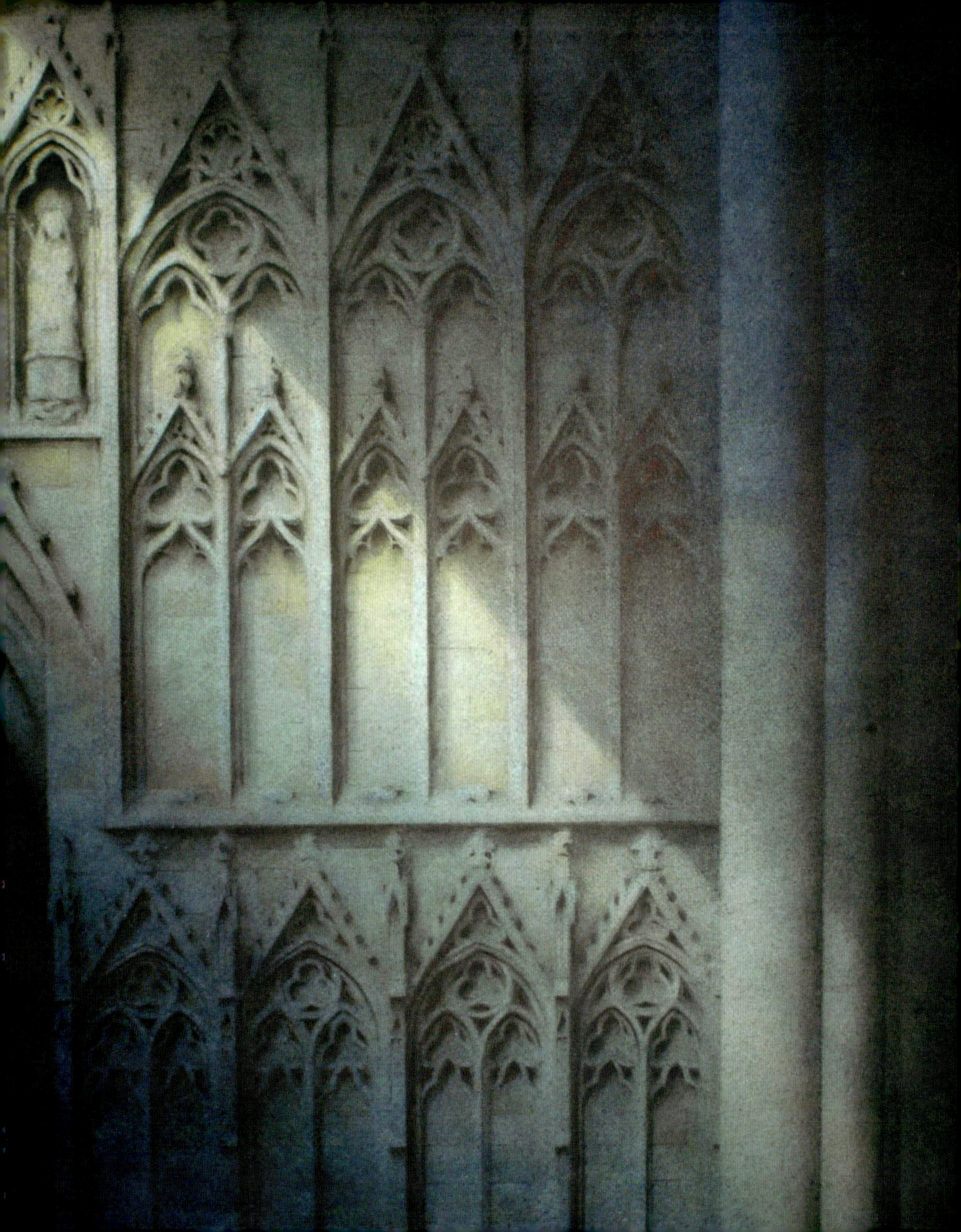

Foreword

by Dame Judi Dench

I was lucky enough to be born and bred in York – from a very young age, I was taken to York Minster on a regular basis and it made an indelible impression on me. Whatever the weather, the moment you enter the doors you are in a place of serenity and calm and extreme beauty.

This is the effect that Gerard Stamp's pictures had on me the first time I saw them – the great vaulted ceilings, the cool naves and the soaring architecture which he captures so magnificently. The very English view across a ploughed field to a misty church in the distance epitomises for me all that I have learned to love about English cathedrals and architecture.

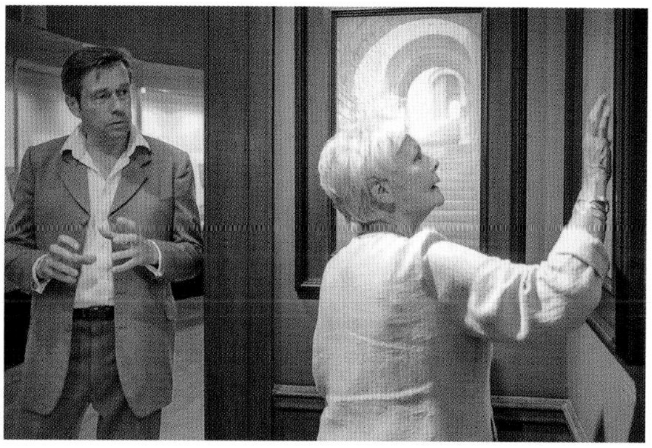

Gerard Stamp and Dame Judi discuss a painting in Norwich Castle Art Gallery at his exhibition, *Conquest,* in 2013

Not only does he evoke the beauty of these buildings, but Gerard Stamp manages to instil them with age and atmosphere. At the same time, there is a sense of timelessness about his paintings and you feel drawn into them, as if you could walk through the frame straight into the church or cathedral. The peace and tranquillity is overwhelming and I could sit and look at them for hours.

I envy anyone coming across these paintings for the first time. They take your breath away.

Written by Dame Judi Dench in 2012

York Minster Moonlight

(detail)

Watercolour and charcoal

2006

31 x 21 ins | 79 x 53 cm

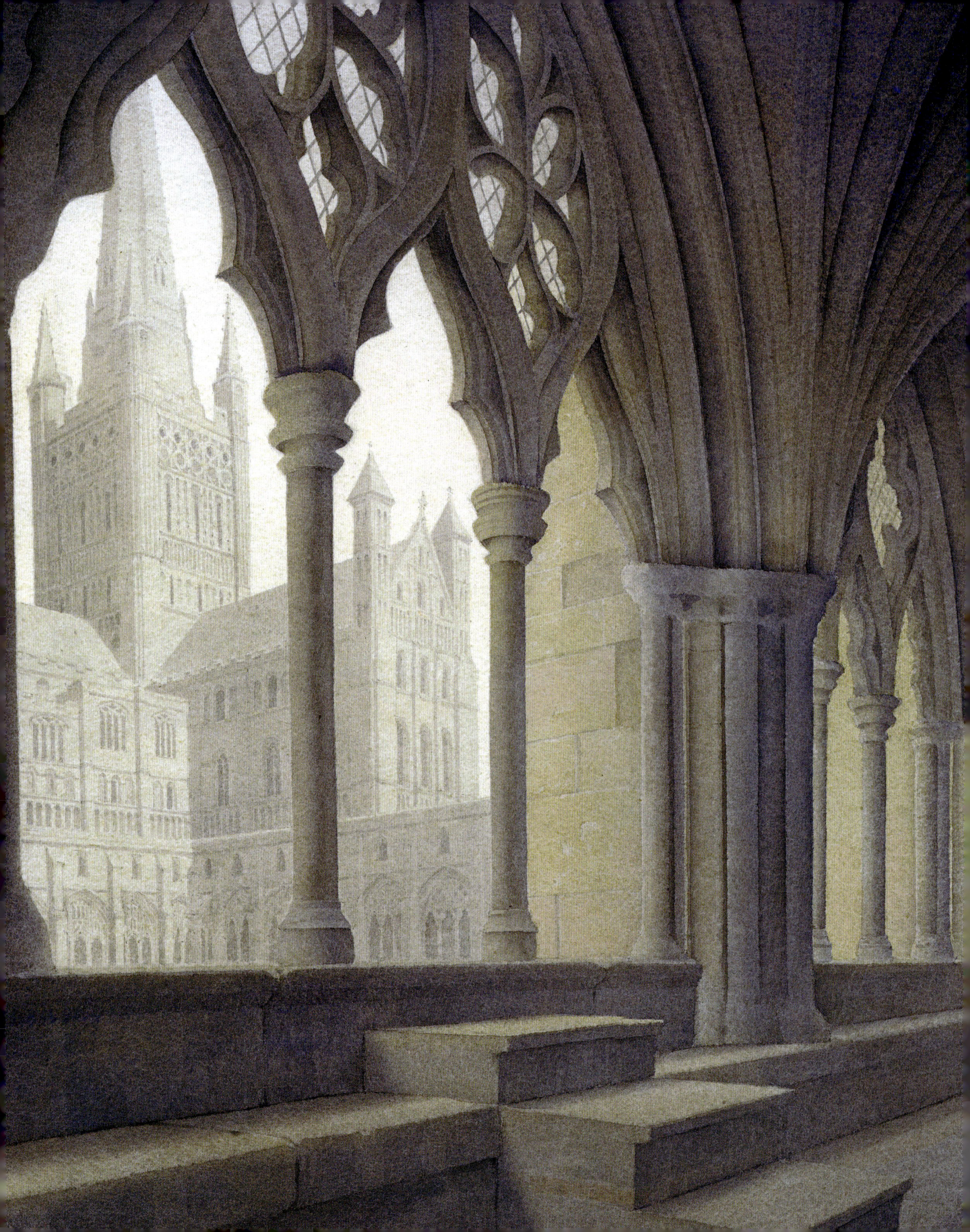

Introduction

Gerard Stamp and I have been friends for close on twenty-five years. I had the pleasure and honour of writing the catalogue essay for his first exhibition as a watercolour painter, also championing him in *Eastern Daily Press* features and a chapter in my book *Water Marks: Art in East Anglia.*

His charcoal drawings featured prominently in my seventy-artist *SEAhouse LIGHThouse SPIRIThouse* exhibition in Salthouse church, to the delight of show-opener Sister Wendy Beckett, on the North Norfolk coast in 2008. Now the chance to write this monograph was not to be missed. My joke title for this volume-in-progress was the 'Stamp Album', because Gerard excels in two creative fields – in both of which he is essentially self-taught. He happens to have one of the most beautiful artist's studios in Britain where, in rural quietude, every picture of his professional career has been painstakingly drawn and painted. It is a perfect base for peaceful solitary labour and tuneful social life.

'At the still point of the turning world... there the dance is.'

Playing keyboards by ear, having given up on piano lessons early in childhood due to the tedium of practising scales, he performs with the Boat House Blues Band against a backdrop of studio, parkland and lake, sheep-bleat and birdsong.

In many ways the musical painter is an unassuming man, but he can't help a stamp of style. His two local bars, the Gunton Arms and Suffield Arms, are the best food-serving pubs in the county – thanks to art-dealer Ivor Braka, his friend and neighbour, who also helped to provide the park. Gerard and Jacqui live in Georgian former kitchens, but what a temptation not to cook.

While both of us are firmly rooted in Norfolk, Gerard and I have come upon our lives in art via very different and far-flung fields. Just about the only pictures in my boat-building family were Victorian and Edwardian watercolours of Broadland which had faded virtually to blank sheets of paper by the time they passed to me. I failed Art O-level.

Looking at art and reading art books became my consolation after the shocking discovery that studies in Economics at Manchester University assumed an aptitude for maths. Grabbing the offer of a graduate trainee journalist post on the *Eastern Daily Press*, since unsure of any other employment offer ever after, I wrote for the regional paper for thirty-five years. Early postings to Lowestoft and Fakenham offices led to fine swathes of East Anglian coast, and to my future home in Southwold. I also found there, and then pursued the theme in Norwich and London, that what I loved most was the company of artists – people who re-invent the world every day through a peculiarly personal vision. For me, the stuff of joy.

But beware what you wish for if a practising artist. Brilliant creativity may entail less observation than obsession and more perspiration than inspiration. Making good new art is a rum – mind-racking, soul-wrenching – old business. It can be a great way of life but a grim means of making a living. My life as an artists' groupie fixated me on Suffolk via the likes of Margaret

Norwich Cathedral from the Cloister
(detail)
Watercolour 2009
26 x 17.5 ins | 66 x 44 cm

Mellis, Mary Newcomb and Prunella Clough. At the latter's funeral, I met John Craxton, visiting from Greece. In a Soho pub that evening, I asked to write his biography. 'Over my dead body,' he said. Sadly, that is what happened, though he had long since agreed to a book.

What Craxton hated was the bitterness in failed painters turned art critics. He plotted a book on them called *Manqué Business*. And he fumed: 'I refuse to allow my carefully orchestrated pictures to play second fiddle to anyone else's art theories.' Points that every art writer should heed. It's all about the artist, not the critic. The groupie in me got Ronald Blythe, self-made giant of East Anglian letters, to write the foreword to my first art book, *A Broad Canvas*. Our ensuing thirty five-year friendship also flowed from my maternal grandmother having been postmistress in the Suffolk village recast by Ronnie as *Akenfield*. Naturally, in the end, I wrote his biography too.

Gerard Stamp was lucky to know early on that his vocation would be in the visual arts – even if for a while as a teenager that meant designing buildings or directing movies. It all rested on the lightning bolt, striking him when aged nine while executing a drawing, that here was something he could do. We – and John Craxton and Ronald Blythe – have fellow feeling here. Lack of broader talent focuses the mind wonderfully. Or, at times, woefully. I can only write and curate exhibitions. Gerard was all the luckier since aware that music could be a balm in testing times.

'it is in that golden stain of time, that we are to look for the real light...'

Untrained can also mean unconstrained, as it was for Stamp, Craxton and Blythe. Gerard studied design and illustration, and carved a major career in advertising, knowing all the while that his true loves lay in architecture and art. He needed the means of melding them together and the funds to buy time. But the key task was to advance beyond technical proficiency to that mysterious point where magic is made.

It is thrilling and terrifying that our lives hinge on a handful of accidental moments, as well as a few facts beyond our control. In a family of high-fliers, Gerard was most fortunate to have an elder brother as a mentor. Gavin, the architectural historian and campaigner, complained, at least partly in jest, that they could easily be confused since they even shared the same initials. But the seven years between them was also a chasm.

When a job move took Gavin and Gerard's restless father to Norwich, back in 1964, only the younger brother went with him. As a pupil at Norwich School, his closest companion was a cathedral. He found himself in a city with more medieval churches than any settlement north of the Alps – surpassing the combined tally in London, York and Bristol. The 650-strong congregation across Norfolk is greater than anywhere else. He absorbed the eroding details and eternal spirit of these spectacular survivals into his very being.

But alchemy can be a slow burn, and Gerard Stamp had turned fifty when presenting in a new light what art critic John Ruskin called 'the golden stain of time'. After that, he never looked back – always aiming for, in T.S. Eliot's phrase, 'the still point of the turning world'. The line from *Burnt Norton*, first of the poet's *Four Quartets*, evoking spiritual peace amid the chaos of constant movement, gave us the title for this book.

As Gerard has said: 'This fascination with decay, romance and echoes in the wind are all tangled up with my love of Norfolk.

'There is a wonderful chapter in Lilias Rider Haggard's *Norfolk Notebook* in which, referring to the area around Binham but summing up the entire county for me, she writes: "The whole place is so heavy with history that in certain moods it gives you the feeling that you have but to put out a finger to touch the past." '

Having touched (and even climbed) Norwich Cathedral in boyhood, he returned in 2010 with a stupendous exhibition to celebrate the completion of the Hostry and its opening by Queen Elizabeth II. I was fund-raising for a suite of three stained-glass windows by the Scottish abstract artist John McLean; profits from Gerard's show helped to clinch an intervention which colours the air of the north aisle as if in celestial light. I would watch as astonished visitors suddenly found themselves bathed in orange and purple. The impact, reflecting the glittering jewel boxes of medieval churches, has been best captured in a Stamp painting.

The sense of revelation, and epiphany, I get from a Stamp picture may also be best expressed, by way of introduction, in my response to another work of art. On a sunny day in May, during a Norfolk and Norwich Festival, I wandered through an overgrown city centre graveyard into the 'redundant' church of St Peter Parmentergate.

A forlorn building remained deserted, but a ring of forty large speakers stood in a nave cleared of pews. As I walked around them, one whispered. Others coughed, sighed or rustled. And then, when I stood in the centre of the circle, they began to sing out *Spem in Alium* by Thomas Tallis – for *The Forty Part Motet* installation by Canadian artist Janet Cardiff. I sat on the floor, literally swept off my feet.

A while later, escaping a snowstorm in New York, I entered the Museum of Modern Art and heard the sound of Tallis and Cardiff in a distant gallery. It was no less evocative. All the art in the building, and towering Manhattan beyond, seemed to be singing.

Gerard Stamp has already travelled from Norfolk to Venice in his radiant watercolours, and I am sure he would go down a storm in America. No artist cares more about the spirit of place, but he also transcends space and time, making the specific universal and the past immortal. As with another great artwork – Stanley Spencer's *The Resurrection, Cookham* – the stamp of genius is to restore everyone and everything to life.

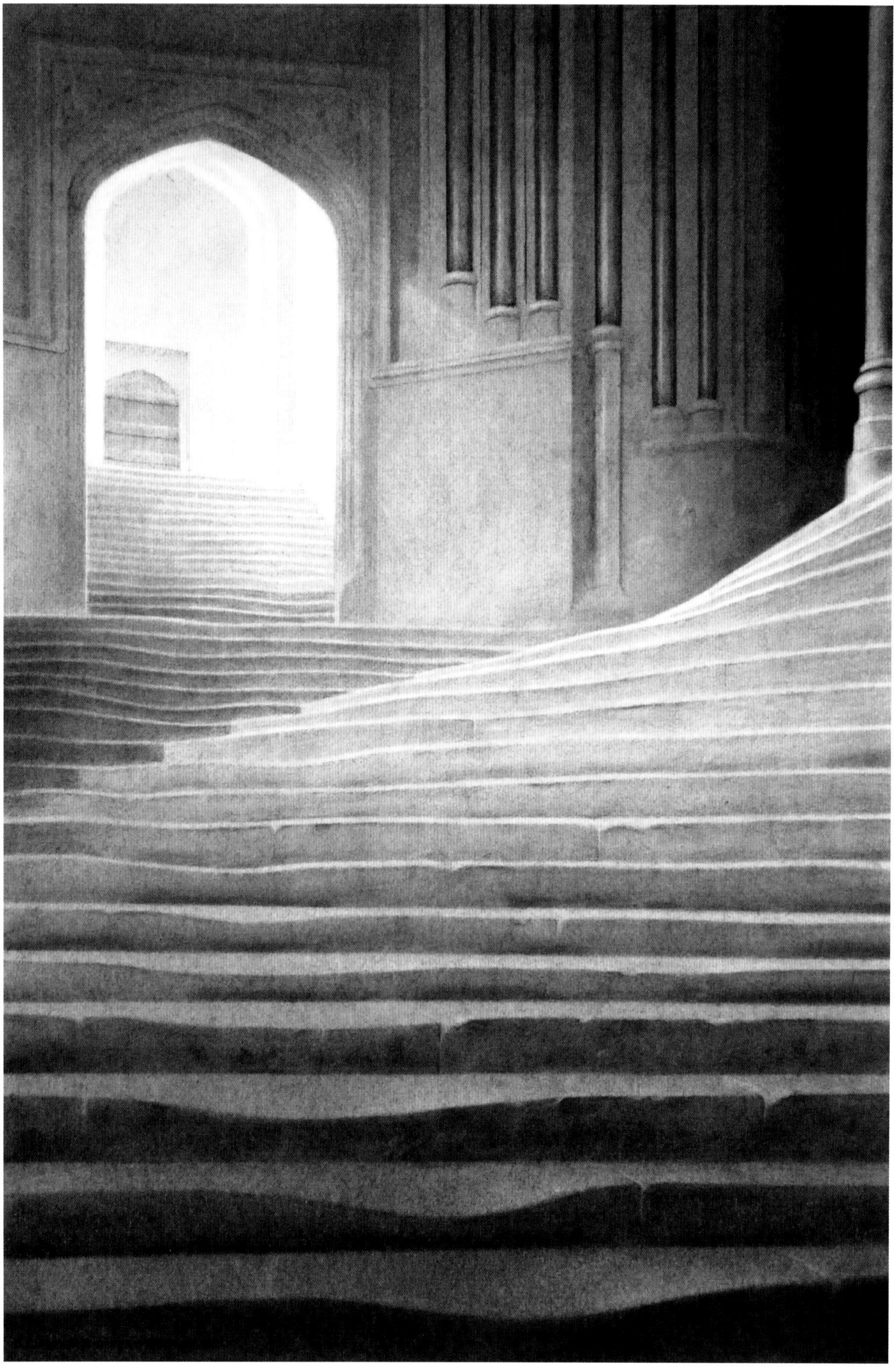

Chapter House Steps

Wells Cathedral

Charcoal 2012

41 x 28 ins | 104 x 71 cm

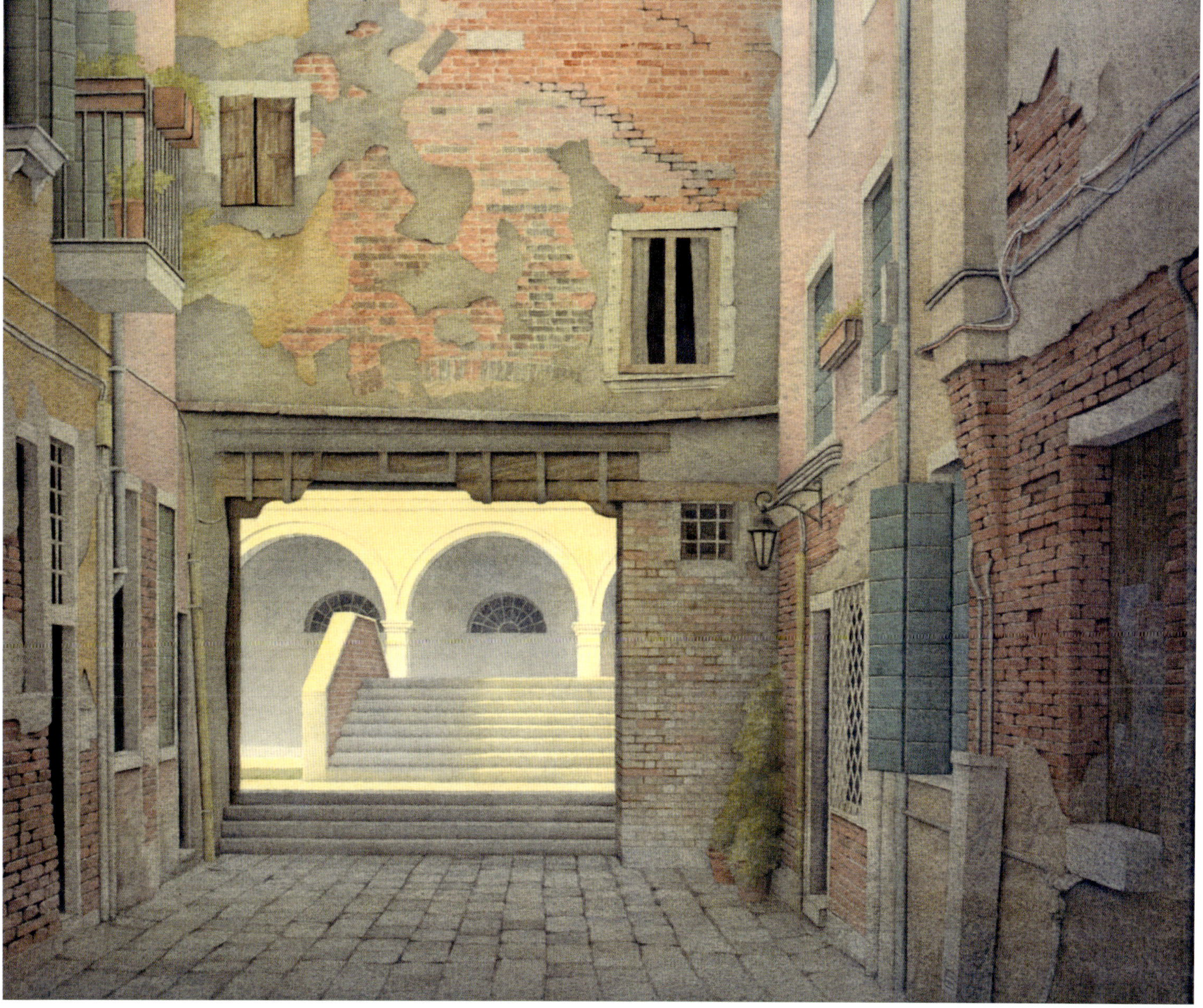

Towards Ponte de la Corte Nova

Watercolour 2025

25 x 30.5 ins | 63 x 78 cm

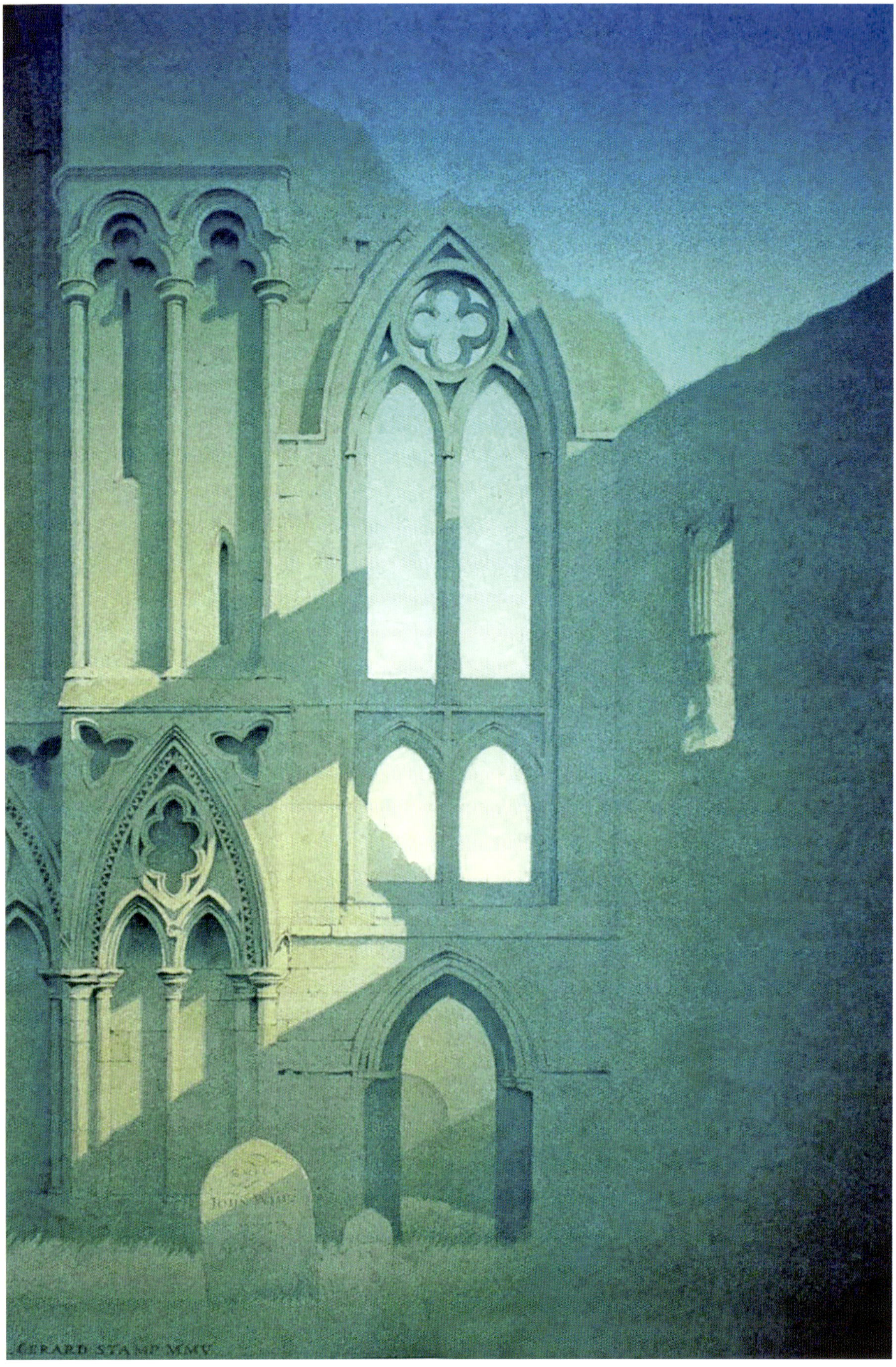

Binham Priory

Shadows

Watercolour 2005

24 x 16.5 ins | 61 x 42 cm

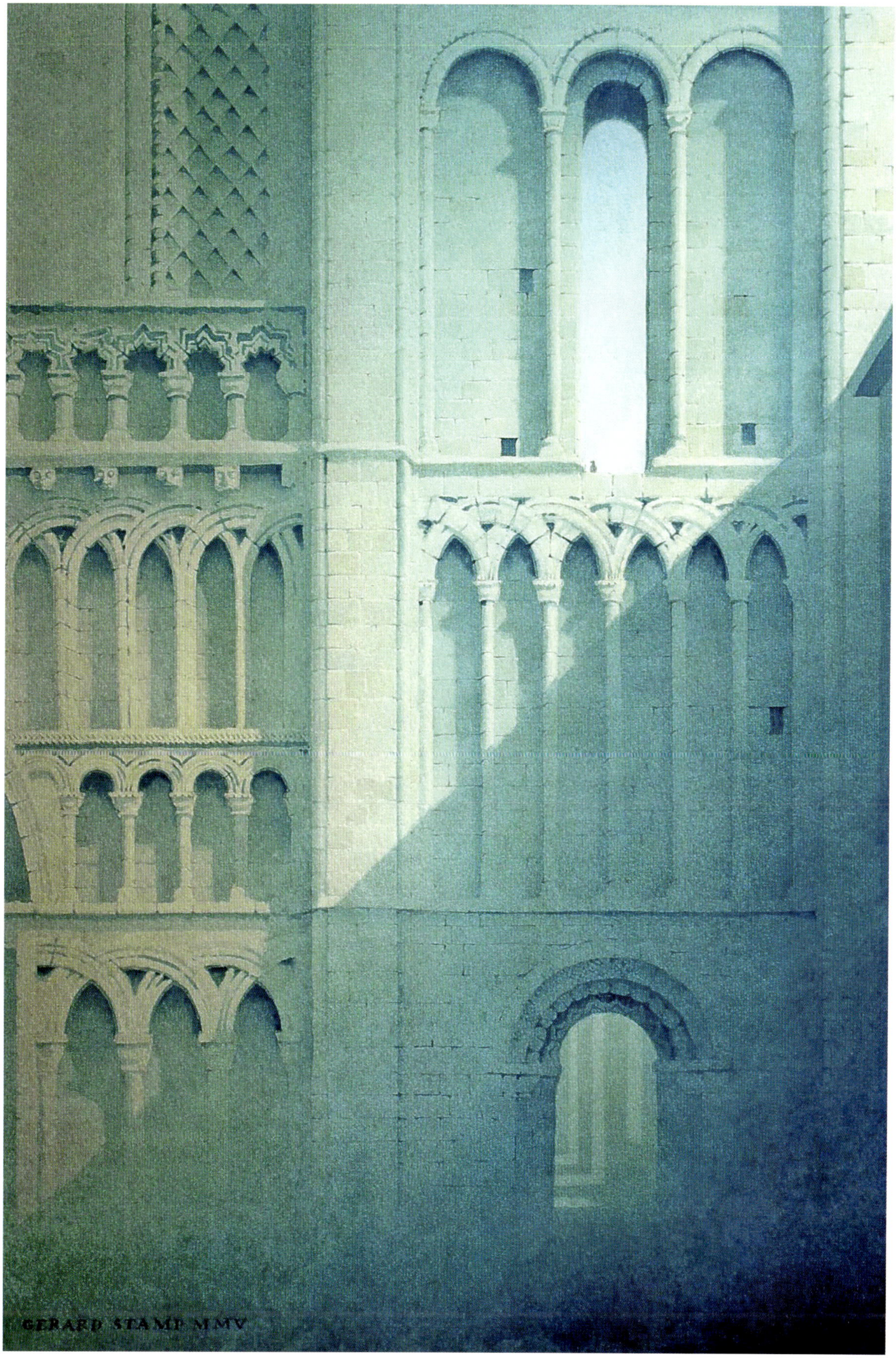

Castle Acre Priory

Shadows

Watercolour 2005

24 x 16.5 ins | 61 x 42 cm

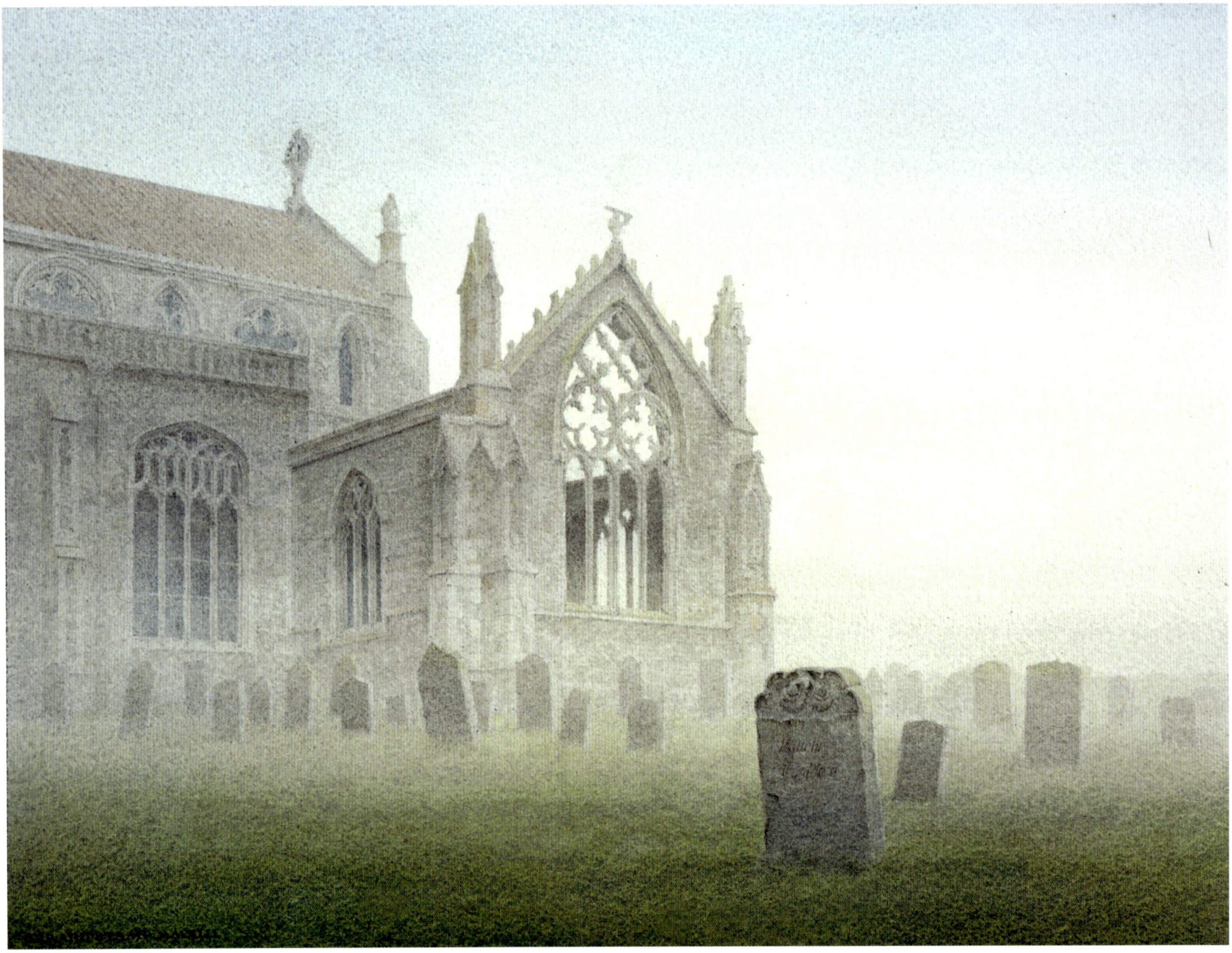

Ruined Transept, Cley

Watercolour 2013

16 x 24 ins | 41 x 61 cm

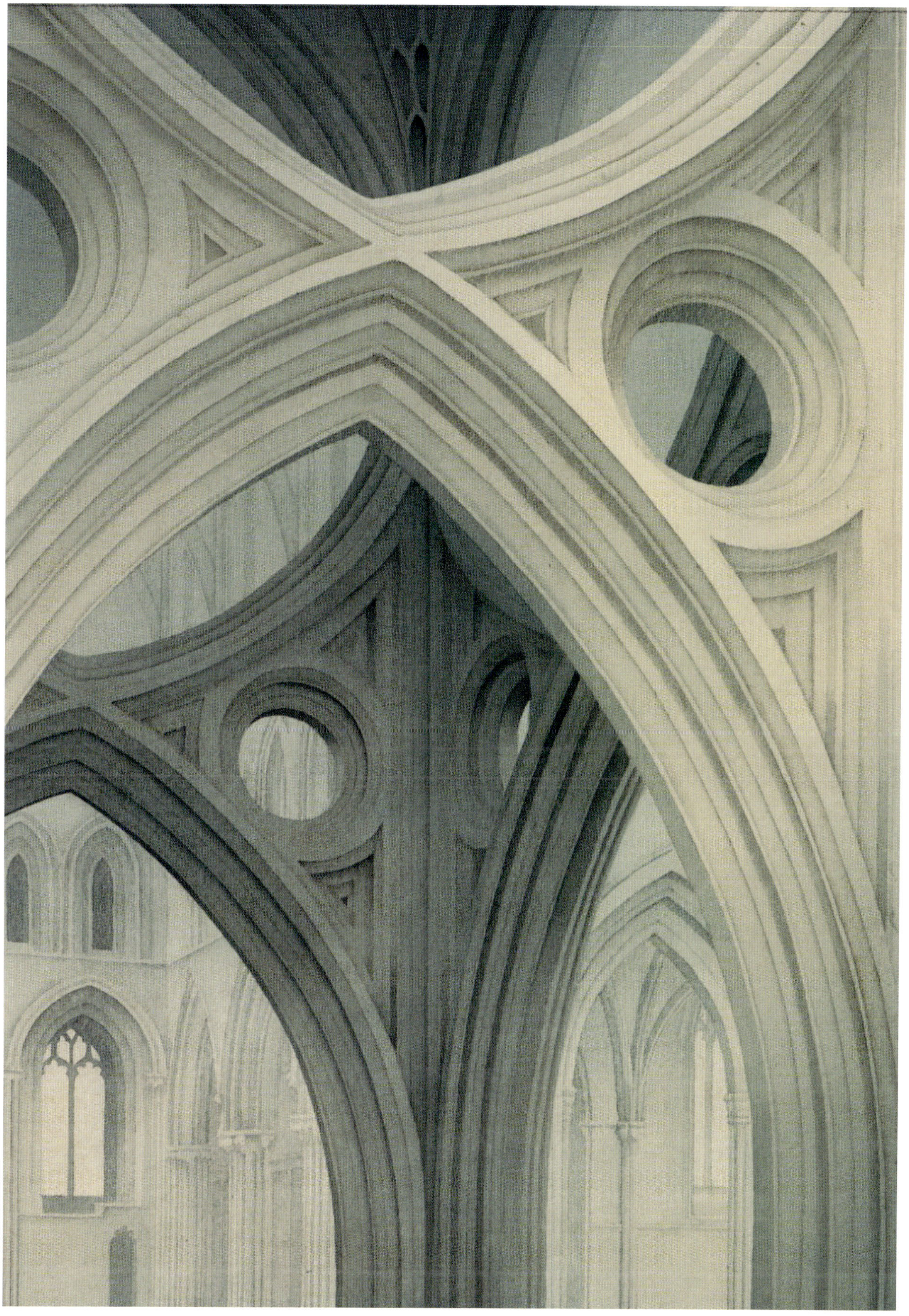

Scissor Arches

Wells Cathedral

Watercolour 2020

24.5 x 17.5 ins | 63 x 45 cm

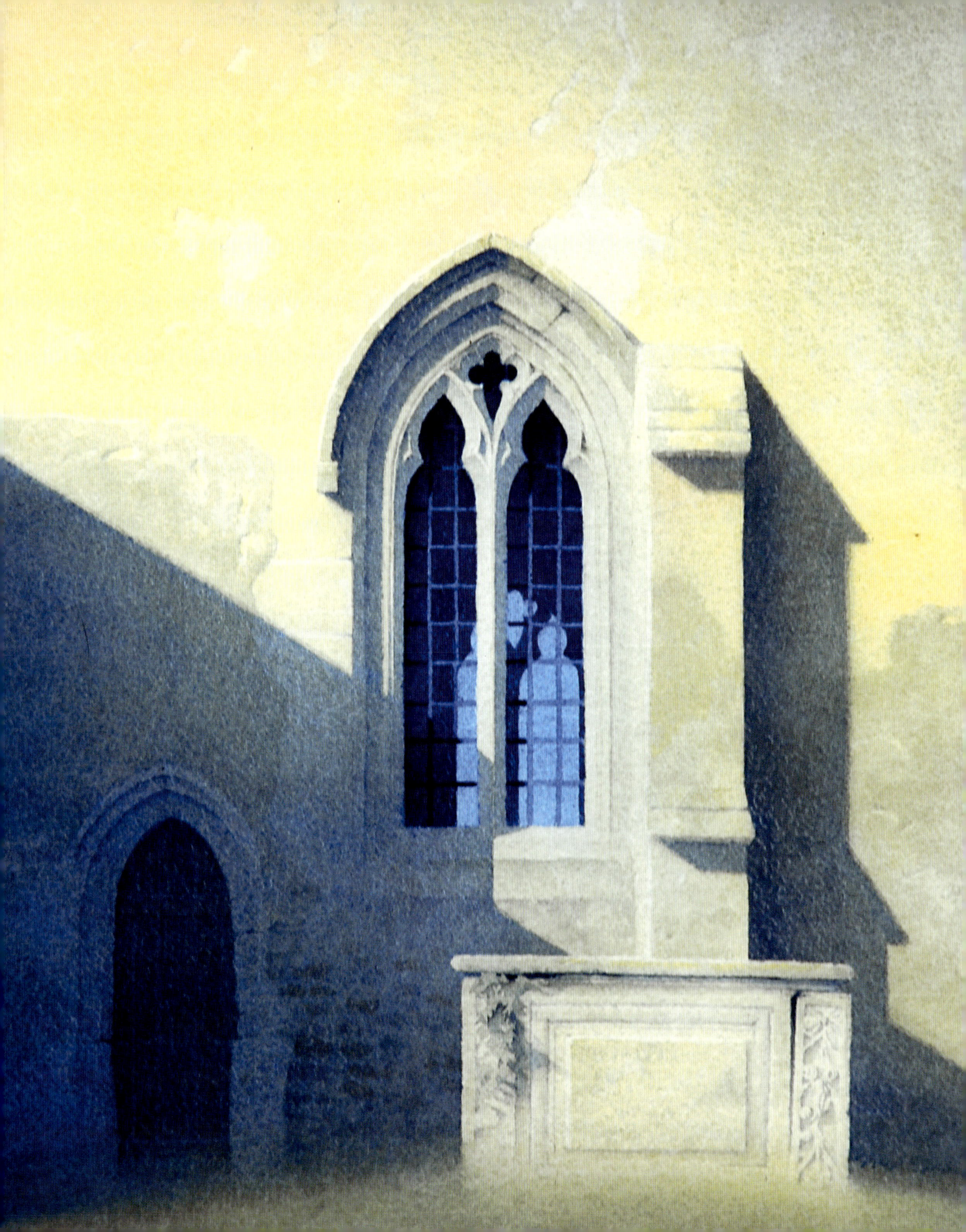

I Family Affairs

In the London census of 1871, Charles Stamp was intriguingly listed as a 'writer on glass' and 'painter'. A decade on, the erstwhile artist – Gerard Stamp's great-grandfather – had picked a more profitable pursuit. He was a Kilburn cheesemonger, living over the shop with his wife, Clara Jane.

This lowly start in commercial life was a cut above fellow London retailers John James and Mary Ann Sainsbury, who shared rooms over their first dairy store, in Covent Garden, with three other families. Both fledgling traders were bent on expansion through the twin operating principles of fine quality at fair prices.

A family flair for visual art was continued via Bertha Stamp, one of Charles and Clara's seven children. She was to prove a gifted and prolific landscape and architectural watercolourist, as well as a writer and illustrator whose books and pictures are still in circulation today.

'You will get on well in Norfolk. They're all backward there'

In 1896 the Stamp cheese and general provisions business was among several enterprises – grocers, tea importers, wine and spirit merchants – incorporated as a Cave Austin and Co public company. Charles Stamp was one of seven directors for an expansive concern with grocery-store and café divisions.

The wholesale tea business of the former Lindoo Valley Tea Company was abandoned in 1903 in a prediction of evolving public taste for coffee – with popularity to be assisted by a striking promotional campaign. All coffee served and sold was to be roasted, blended and ground on company premises, with the spectacle of grinding machines prominent in every window. By the 1930s, in the depths of the Great Depression, the focus was on developing 'high-class' grocery and café chains across south-east London, Kent, Sussex and Surrey.

Despite the peak of global imperial might, Edwardian Britain had retained the cultural insularity of a small island, most especially perhaps in the matter of the prevailing national diet. Bland rations owed nearly as much to limited horizons as low resources. Cave's Oriental Cafés, with an Asia-inspired decor and exotic aroma of coffee, set out to broaden public taste via a bold departure from traditional teashops.

The Stamps had also widened their horizons from the late Victorian era, moving to South London and fields of fresh endeavour. Josiah, third of the Kilburn shopkeepers' children, became a hugely successful polymath: industrialist, economist, civil servant, statistician, writer, banker, authority of church architecture and, eventually, a peer of the realm. The former boy clerk in the Inland Revenue Department went on to be a Bank of England director, chairman of the London, Midland and Scottish Railway and one of the richest people in Britain.

Josiah's youngest brother, L. Dudley Stamp, a professor in Rangoon and at the London School of Economics, became one of the best-known British geologists and geographers of the twentieth century. He directed the Land Utilisation Survey of Britain and contributed to many official enquiries in the use of land and planning; also an analysis of the Norfolk Broads, for which he was ultimately knighted. Having reputedly achieved a life-long ambition to

Chancel Window
Kedington
Watercolour 2008
16 x 12 ins | 40 x 30 cm

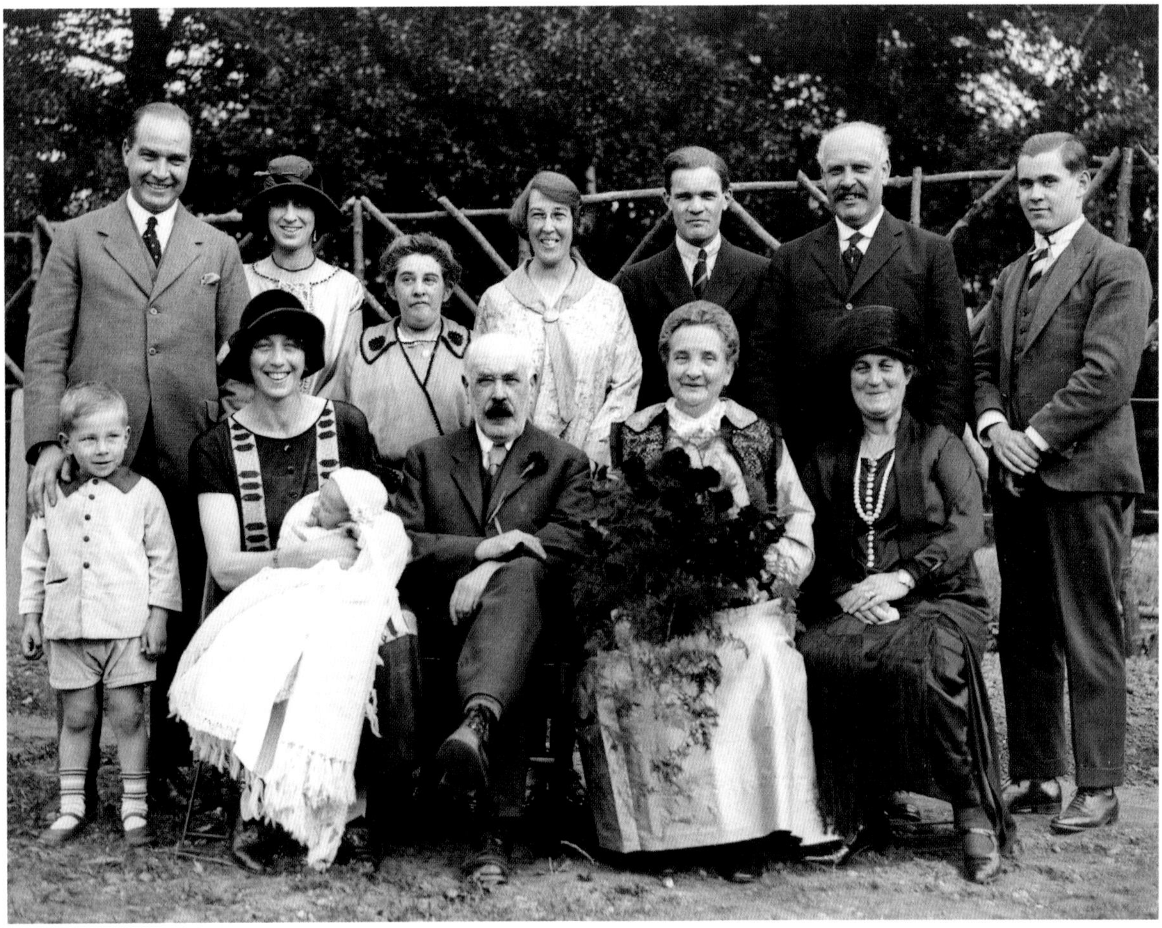

Charles and Clara Stamp's golden wedding, 1925

'Back row: Charles (my grandfather), Dudley's wife Elsa (he is not in the picture and was probably abroad), Addie, Bertha, Wilfred, Josiah and Trevor.

Front row: my father Barry, my grandmother Edith with Rosse on her lap, Charles, Clara, and Olive (Josiah's wife).' G.S.

visit every country in the world, he suffered a fatal heart attack at a conference in Mexico City.

The third brother, Charles Alfred, Gerard's grandfather, took over Cave Austin as the Second World War delivered fateful blows to the Stamp family. The company warehouse in Lewisham was bombed twice; cafés in Eastbourne, Hastings and St Leonards were destroyed. Close to the end of the conflict, a V2 rocket damaged the Blackheath grocery store.

Worst of all, the first Baron Stamp of Shortlands in the County of Kent had refused to leave his home in that district during the Blitz, despite its proximity to air bases and other targets. In April 1941 he and his wife and Wilfred, their eldest son, died in a direct hit on their air-raid shelter.

Wilfred Carlyle Stamp holds the record for the shortest tenure in the British peerage. The bomb blast killed his parents and himself, almost certainly simultaneously, but inheritance laws in England, as fixed in a special sitting of Parliament, made fact from fiction. For deaths in unclear order, the elder party was deemed to have died first.

This ruling, that Wilfred had been 2nd Baron Stamp for a split second, blitzed the estate with double death duties. It made for a bleakly ironic conclusion to the life and death of Britain's leading tax expert. Besieged Britain badly needed the income boost from this summary exercise in property confiscation. The 3rd Baron, Josiah's second son, inherited huge debts.

Barry Stamp, Gerard's father, had begun the war as a conscientious objector. He met and courted Norah Rich as a student in Bristol, to where King's College University London had been evacuated. But by the time they married, in the city's Redland Chapel in 1944, he had followed in a family line by joining the Royal Navy.

When demobbed he was enlisted in the clan company, and the couple moved closer to the centre of operations in south-east London. In the decade after the war Cave Austin added ten branches.

Gerard Stamp, the chairman's grandson, was born in 1955 in Bromley Hospital, between the launch of a new Lewisham warehouse (complete with offices, coffee roasters, ham cookers, cold store, wine and spirit cellar and sale room) and their first refrigerated mobile grocery shop taking to the road. The company was also busy developing its own-label lines.

A booklet of 1956 marked sixty years of trading for a business now running to more than 400 staff and twenty-four vans travelling nearly 200,000 miles a year. With over thirty tons of coffee roasted and 5,000 hams cooked per annum, 2,600 tons of food (100 tons of margarine, ninety-two tons of butter, fifty-four tons of tea) were delivered from warehouse to retail stores.

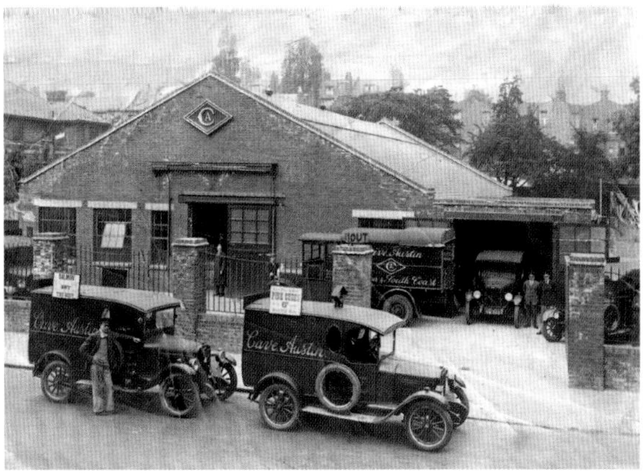

Head Office, Lewisham
This was the original warehouse which became inadequate, and in 1929 land was acquired to build a new warehouse in Eastdown Park

Branches now stocked a range of French wines and 'fancy' groceries including okra, lychees, Bombay duck, bamboo shoots and 'puppodums'. This at a time when food rationing had only just ended. Elizabeth David's Mediterranean cookery books remained fabulous reads since many of the ingredients were beyond the reach of most readers – though olive oil could be bought in small brown glass bottles from chemist shops for dislodging earwax. Five directors, three of them Stamps, were confident that six decades of progress would be 'followed by yet another period of similar development'. But when the chairmanship passed to Barry, Gerard's father, in 1963, the commercial writing was on the wall. Even a forty-store combine could not compete with the buying power of the big supermarkets. The company was sold, and the name disappeared three years later when the enterprise was sold again. Gerard rescued the CA roundel from the facade of the Lewisham warehouse when it was demolished in 2026, as a memorial feature for his Norfolk garden.

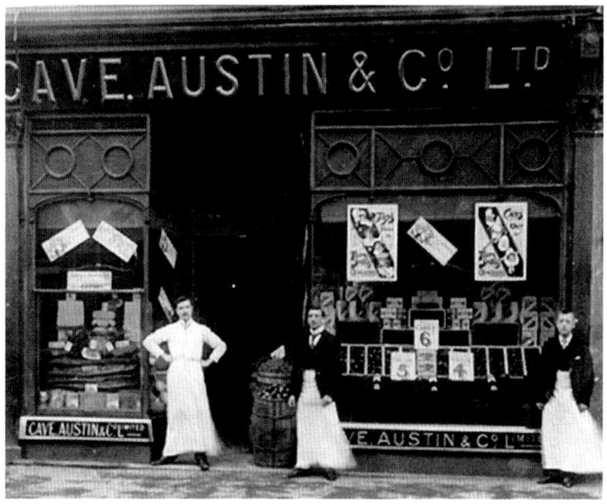

Cave Austin & Co Ltd
The Sidcup branch, typical of the stores at the turn of the last century

Norah's Bristol clan included Fabian Socialists and creative spirits bent on personal and societal improvement. Cousin Wally was a sculptor while his better-known brother, Eddie – Edward W. Sharland – was a cabinet-maker turned self-taught artist, who enjoyed considerable success in the etching revival of the early twentieth century.

His accomplished prints, depicting English cathedrals and architectural images from continental tours, hung on the walls of Gerard's childhood homes. Cousin Eddie profited from an etching boom bolstered by wealthy private collectors and the British Museum. Top prices for contemporary prints could beat those of Rembrandt – the Old Master they all revered and sought to emulate. With the Wall Street Crash of 1929, the etchings market on both sides of the Atlantic collapsed overnight and when finance recovered, artistic fashion had changed forever. Eddie latterly painted landscapes in Cornwall.

Early in the 1950s Barry and Norah Stamp moved to Hayes, which for 800 years had been a small and picturesque village in Kent. Given its proximity to the capital, stately Hayes Place, home to Georgian prime ministers William Pitt the Elder and Younger, also hosted Cabinet meetings. A nineteenth-century astronomer-vicar was the first to identify the planet of Neptune, while his neighbours were beginning to observe London, shooting towards them like a dazzling and devastating comet.

The final engulfment occurred between the world wars when the population increased ten-fold as Hayes Place and other landed properties were bought up and pulled down for suburban development. A resulting parade of shops would come to house Cave Austin's first self-service store.

The Stamps settled, albeit briefly, in Sandiland Crescent – one of several streets built on the site of Warren Wood by Durable Homes. The name of the builder was ironic given that the sturdier villa being demolished along with its wooded enclosure had risen and fallen in barely six decades.

Still, the couple had a detached Tudor Revival house with a gentle touch of Arts and Crafts – what cartoonist Osbert Lancaster would mock, with some affection, as 'By-Pass Variegated'. The poet and architectural historian John Betjeman lampooned

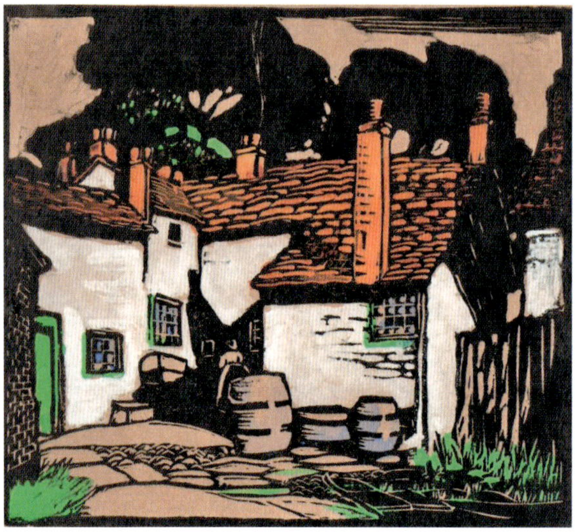

Old Rodney Inn, Prestbury

Woodcut by Bertha Stamp

'I remember visits to Tenterden to see Auntie Bertha. Down the garden was a shed she used as her studio, full of art equipment, all of which fascinated me.' G.S.

such lead-windowed and large-chimneyed castles for the middle-classes in his verses but loved them even more.

Barry Stamp believed more in progress than architectural purity, however. In the early 1960s he had the living room chimney ripped out and replaced with an unleaded plate-glass window stretching the width of the hipped roof. Out went the fireplace, in came central heating.

Gavin Stamp, born in 1948, was reborn at that moment as an architectural historian. 'I knew it was wrong at the time,' he said. 'They made what was quite a nice house into a complete sort of awful mongrel.' It was to be the making of a visual – and visceral – viewpoint for both Barry and Norah's sons.

Gavin, seven years older than Gerard, and with sister Jacqueline arriving at the mid-way point between them, was guide and mentor to the creed by which we not only look but think through our eyes. And, for these two brothers in arts, aesthetics

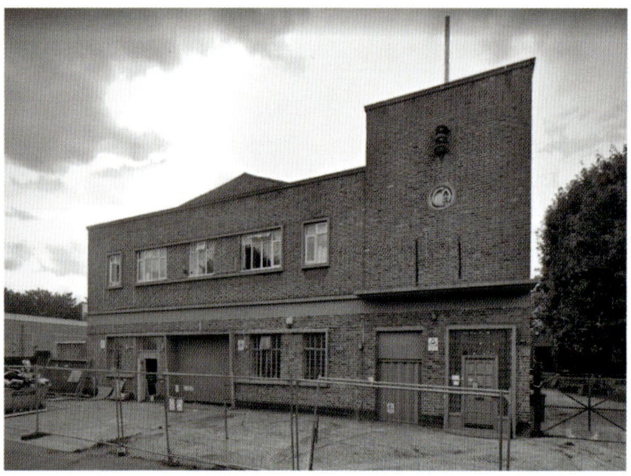

Head Office and warehouse, Eastdown Park, Lewisham

Built in 1955 on the site of the war-damaged premises, the building was demolished early in 2026

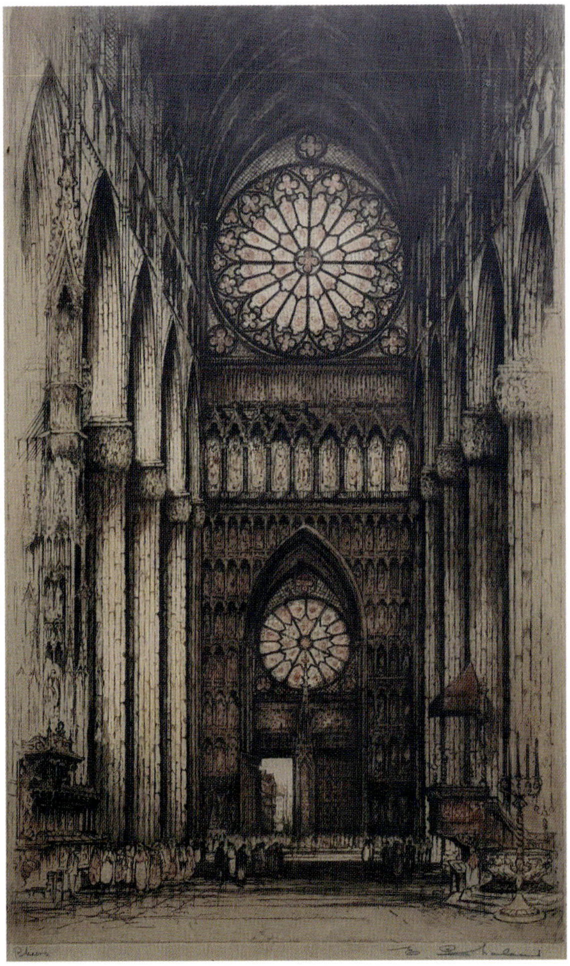

Reims Cathedral
Hand coloured etching
20 x 12 ins | 51 x 31 cm
by Eddie Sharland

would be close to everything. Gavin, an expert model maker from an early age, also steered the shared focus into three dimensions.

While religious faith would waver and be waived altogether for the youngest sibling – the house where Charles Darwin wrote *On the Origin of Species* loomed large beyond the remaining fields – they both came to worship beauty. Or, as the pithy and provocative Gavin preferred to put it, the prevailing belief was to be 'Anti Ugly'.

Hayes was soon to be swept up along with a cluster of similarly urbanised villages in the London Borough of Bromley. Former residents of the transformed district stand out as a strikingly creative escapist committee – from writers Enid Blyton, Richmal 'Just William' Crompton and W.E. 'Biggles' Johns to David Bowie and several punk-rock pioneers.

The sale of Cave Austin provided an early escape for Gerard Stamp since his father was required to move to Norwich in a managerial role for the buyers as part of the deal. While Gavin was already embarked on an academic trajectory which would take him from Dulwich College to Cambridge, Gerard was rescued aged eight from an 'appalling' prep school.

The parting shot of an antipathetic headmaster at Greenhayes School for Boys in West Wickham was a typical put-down. 'You will get on well in Norfolk,' he said. 'They're all backward there.'

Norfolk was to be just another staging post for Barry and Norah Stamp, who would move ten times during their married life. But Gerard, even with a few physical shifts still to come, was set for permanent emotional and spiritual settlement.

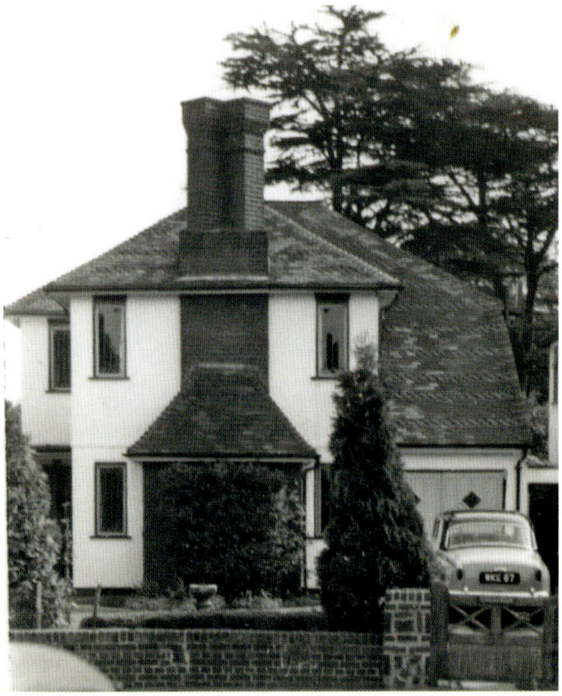

13 Sandiland Crescent
Hayes, Kent
'Photograph taken in 1956 before my father had the entire chimney removed, adding a room over the garage and a large plate glass window under the hipped roof.' G.S.

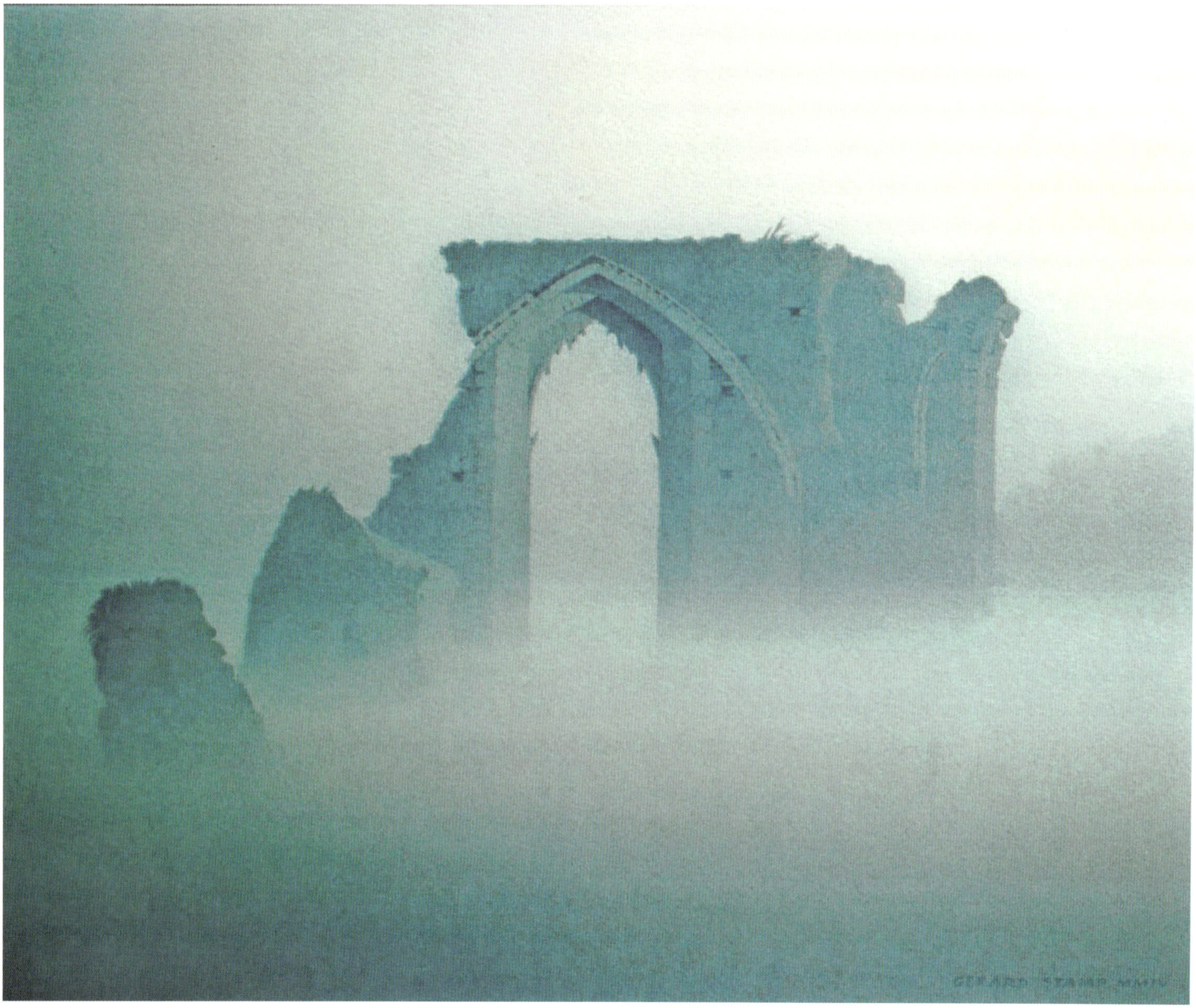

Coxford Priory

Watercolour 2004

14 x 17 ins | 36 x 43 cm

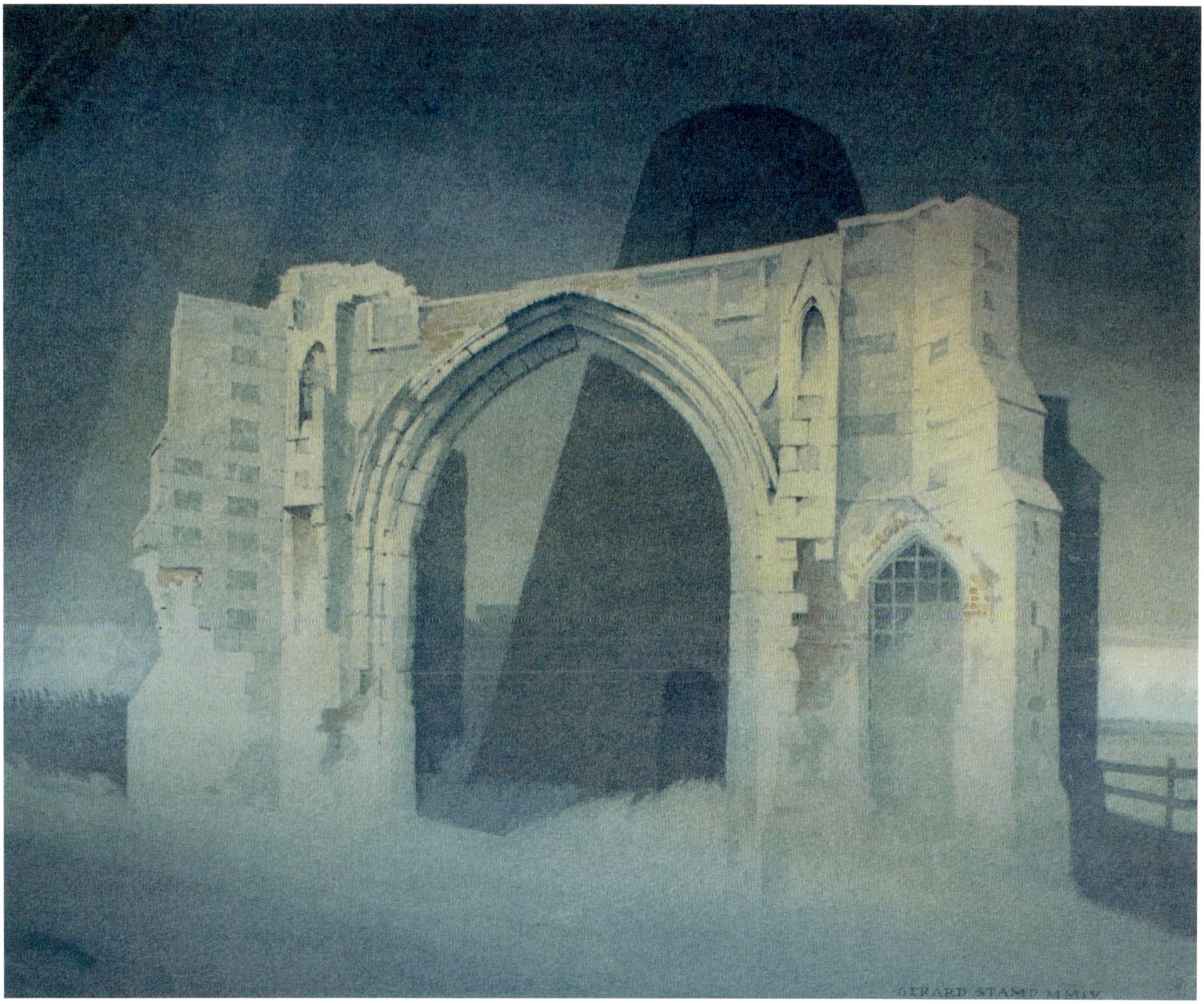

St Benet's Abbey Gateway

Watercolour 2004

14 x 17 ins | 36 x 43 cm

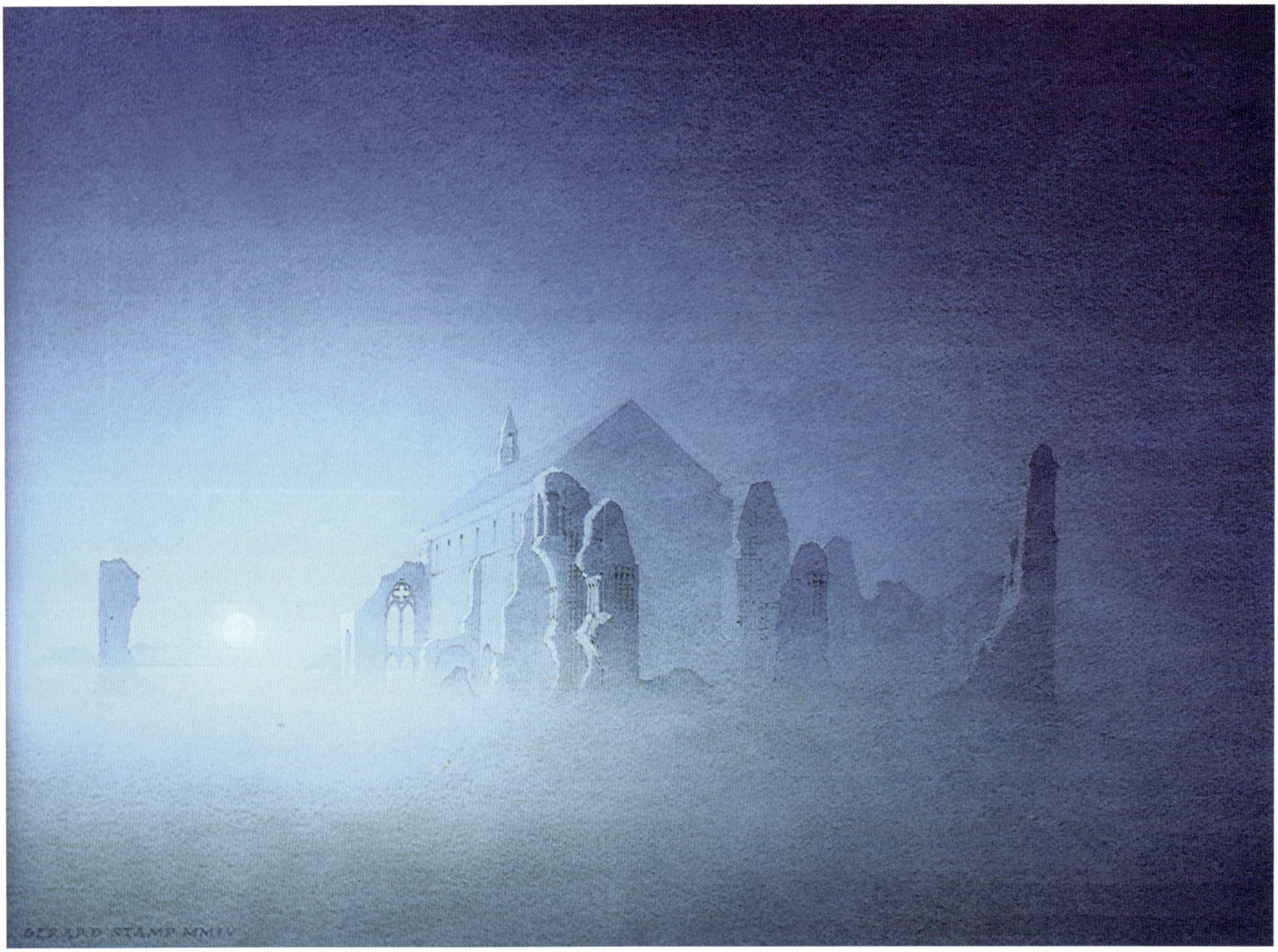

Binham Priory by Moonlight

Watercolour 2004

16 x 22 ins | 40 x 56 cm

Flushwork, Southwold

Watercolour 2013

23 x 18 ins | 59 x 46 cm

Norwich Castle Museum and Art Gallery

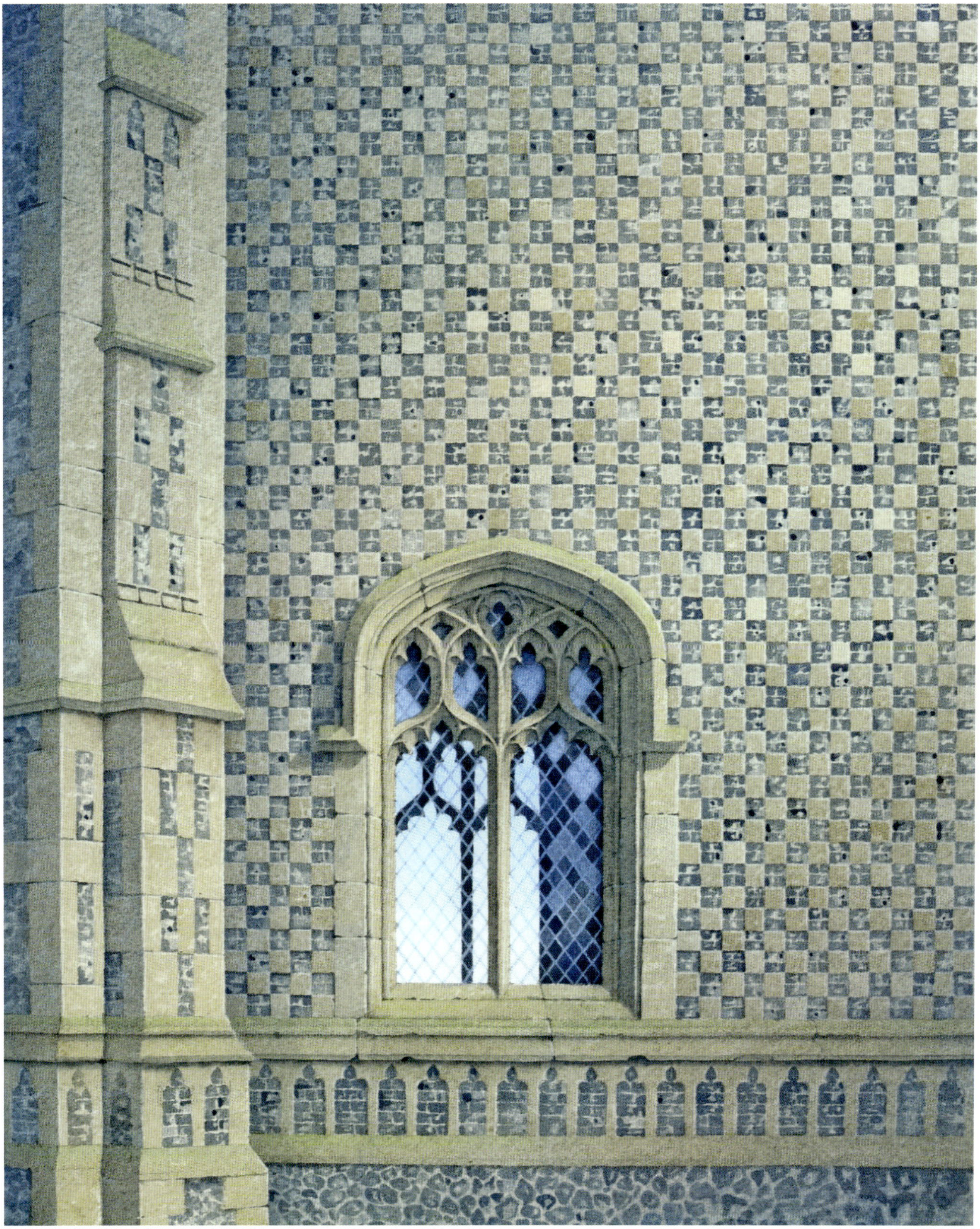

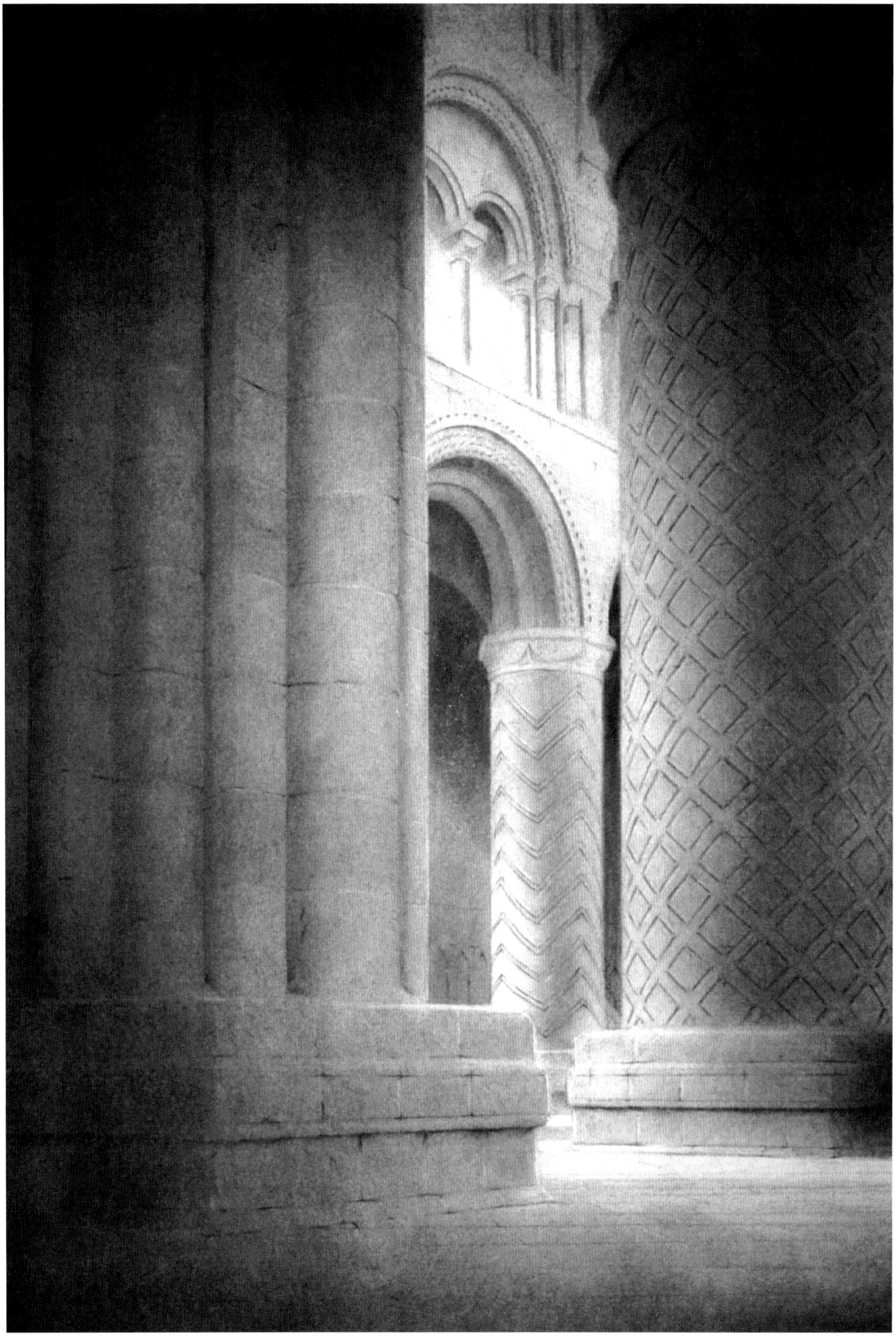

Durham Columns I

Charcoal 2007

36.5 x 25 ins | 93 x 64 cm

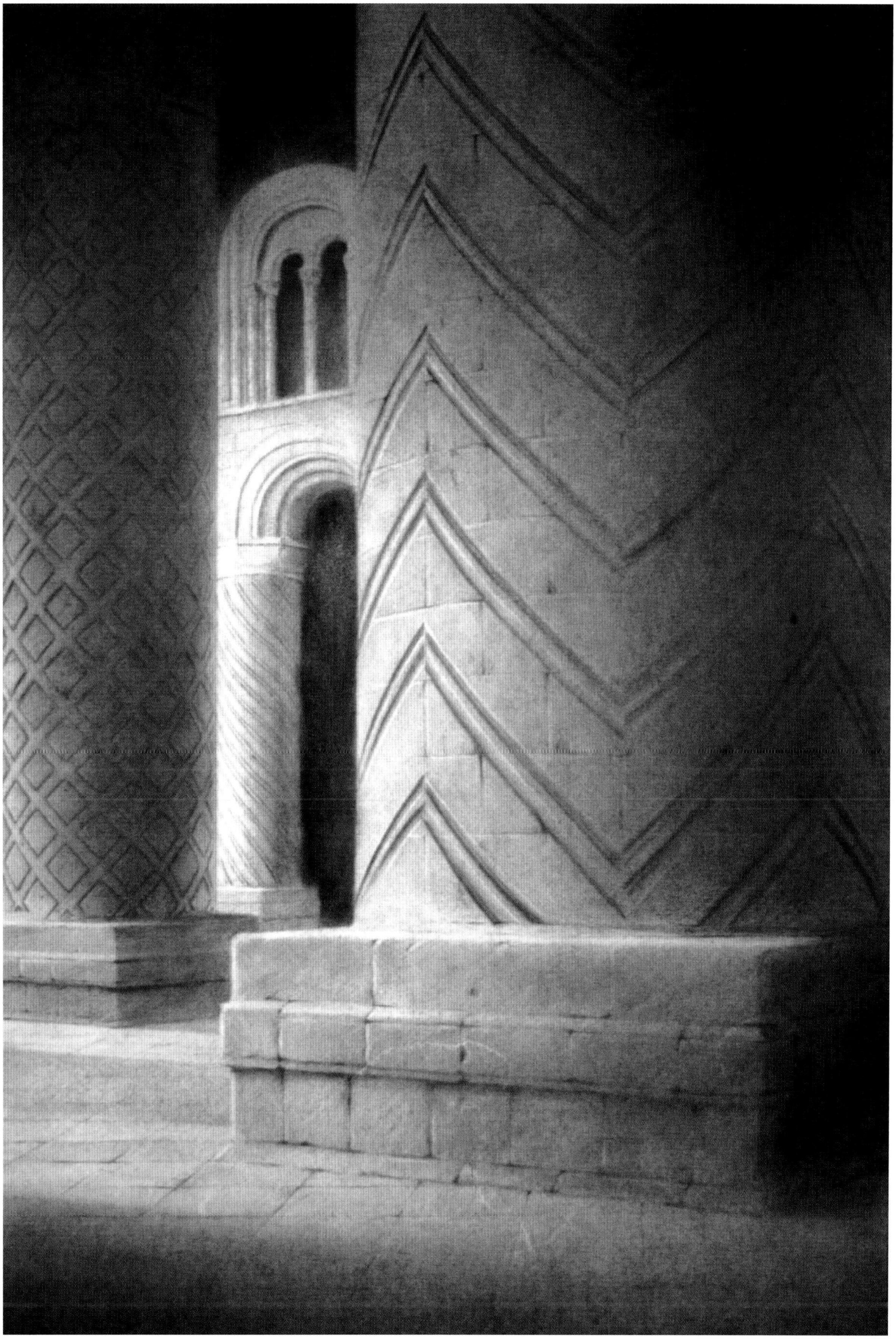

Durham Columns II

Charcoal 2007

36.5 x 25 ins | 93 x 64 cm

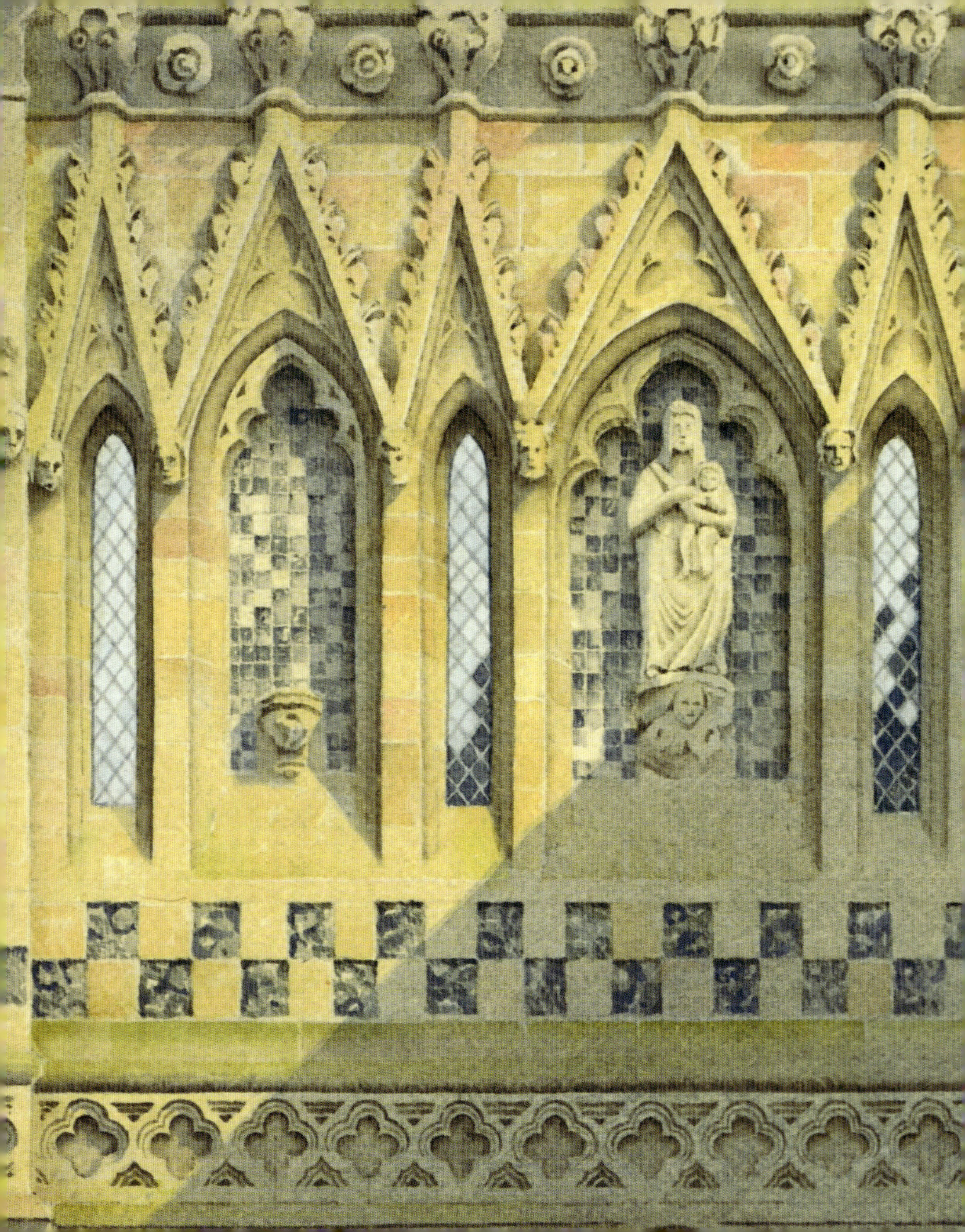

II Drawn to Art

Instantly and irrevocably, Gerard adored the ancient and modern city of Norwich. He loved the surrounding countryside in a watery county bordered by rivers and the North Sea, the far horizons and huge skies and the history of art. There were medieval churches everywhere.

Best of all, from his immediate point of view, he was enrolled in the Lower School of one of the oldest educational establishments in England. As his first art report summed up: 'A most depressing and inattentive beginning followed by a transformation.' A lightning bolt had struck when Gerard suddenly discovered, while drawing in an art class, that he could do something well. Now, when he chose, the nine-year-old had a laser-like attention.

'A most depressing and inattentive beginning followed by a transformation'

Norwich School had been founded as an episcopal grammar school by the first Bishop of Norwich in 1096. Relaunched by Royal Charter from Edward VI in 1547, it had occupied its present site beside the magnificent city cathedral – a building it actually pre-dated – since 1551.

Despite the lofty history of divines, scholars and warriors – with a rollcall of luminary Old Norvicensians headed by Admiral Lord Horatio Nelson and James I's Chief Justice Sir Edward Coke (whose death was greeted by his wife with the words 'Sir Edward is dead. We shall not see his like again – thank God') – Norwich School was also bang up to date.

For all the academic and athletic focus, and the grim persistence of corporal punishment, there was an ethos of fostering individual talent. For one very particular new boy that meant a broad and deep training in art.

This too was part of a long tradition. The name of the educational establishment was often confused with the Norwich School of painters – the first provincial art movement in England, flaring from the turn of the nineteenth century – for good reason. Founder John Crome served as a drawing master at the boys' school for many years, and his painter son John Berney Crome became head boy. Other artists associated with the pioneering art movement were pupils at the school beside the cathedral – James Stark, George Vincent, Edward Thomas Daniell and, most importantly, John Sell Cotman. The last was to leave the most lasting impression, not least on Gerard Stamp.

Norwich School artists were greatly influenced by Dutch painters of the preceding two centuries, but their chief inspiration came from studying local landscapes – switching from mythical, classical and academic idioms to the actual life and light of East Anglia. The true glory lay all around them.

Cotman displayed a revolutionary creativity as he set new standards in etching, painting and, most especially, watercolour – with dazzling washes which might seem to prefigure modern abstract art. For Gerard he was to be a rich source for investigation and emulation – even if the travails of a troubled life, during which a

Ethelbert Gateway
(Detail)
Watercolour 2023
'Some of my happiest times at school were spent behind these windows.
It was the art room, situated in the upper floor of Ethelbert Gateway, one of the two main entrances into Norwich Cathedral Close.' G.S.

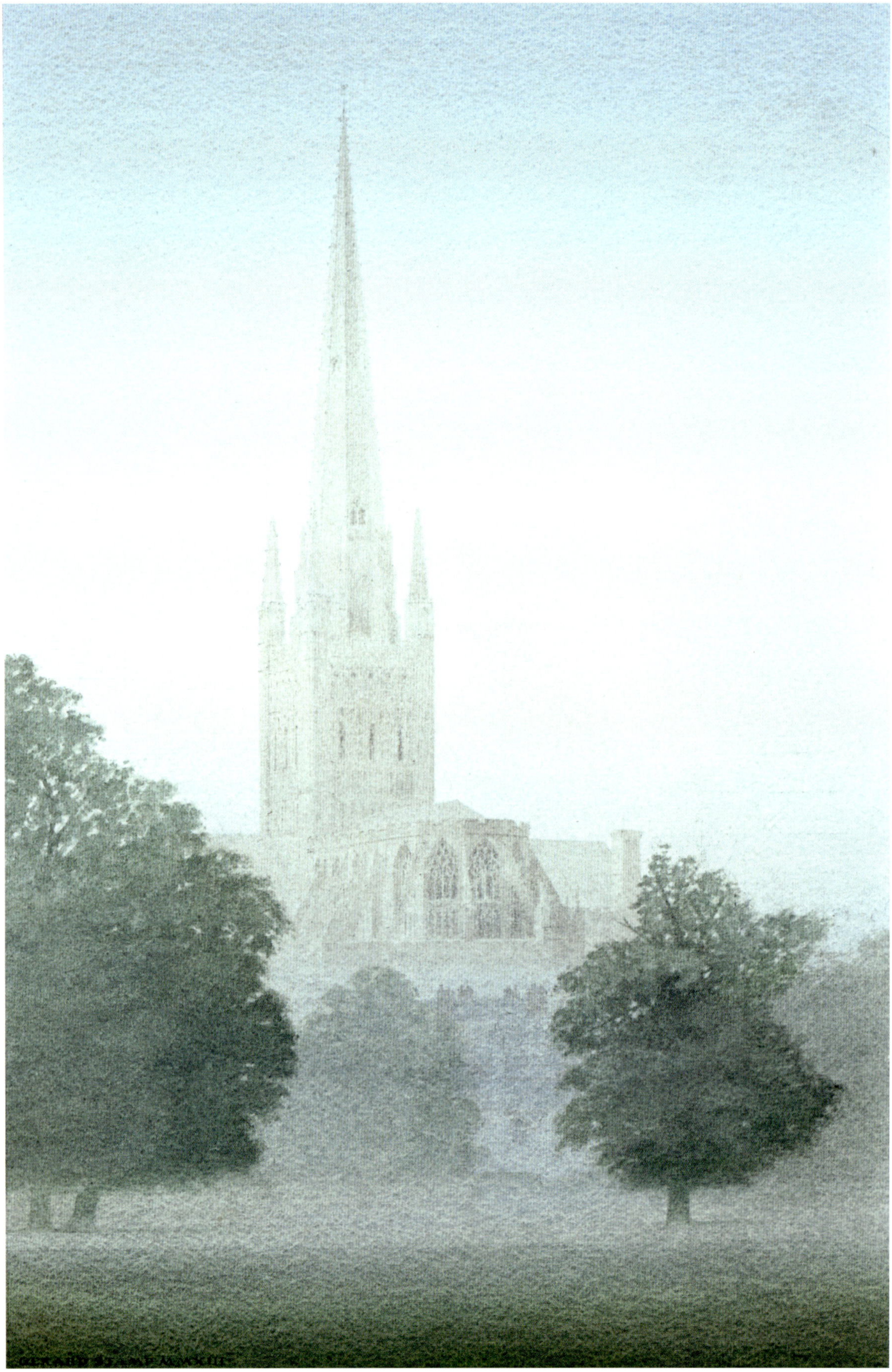

Norwich Cathedral from the School Playing Fields

Watercolour 2009

35 x 20.5 ins | 89 x 52cm

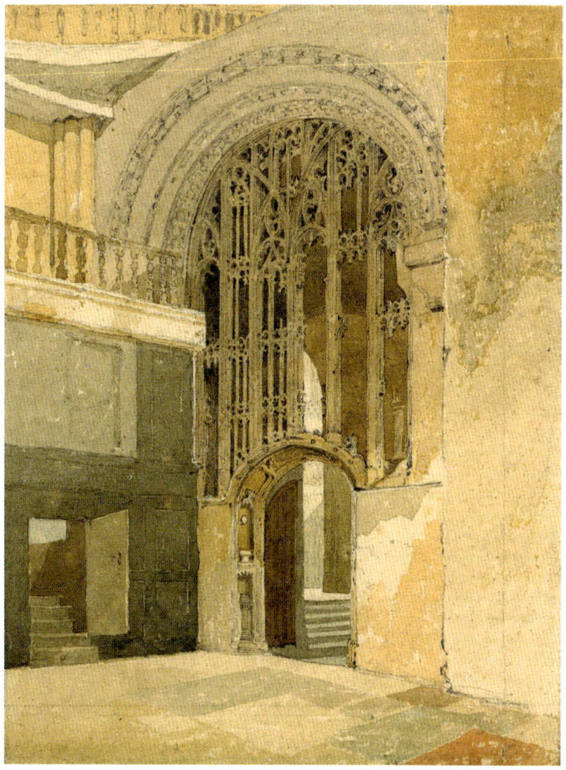

Interior of Norwich Cathedral Stone Screen

Watercolour by John Sell Cotman 1807

14 x 10.5 ins | 36 x 27 cm

pioneer was never able to live from picture sales, prompted a note of practical caution about the material cost of a life in meaningful art.

Other notably artistic Norwich School old boys included the Norfolk Pre-Raphaelite Frederick Sandys and the popular twentieth-century English impressionist Edward Seago – both of whose works, in all their variety, reveal a shared fascination for light.

While Yorkshire claims John Atkinson Grimshaw as the 'Leeds born master of moonlight', for a formative period from the age of six in the 1840s, the future painter attended Norwich School while his father worked locally. Gerard notes:

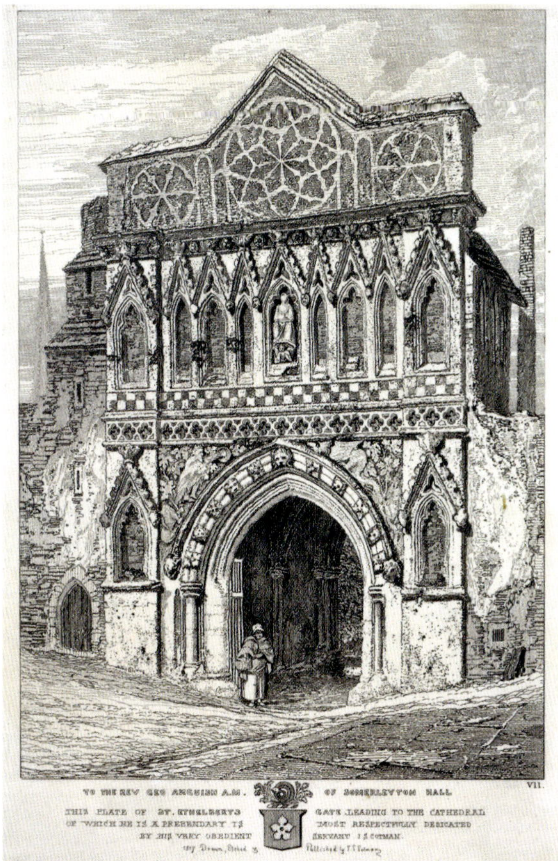

Ethelbert Gateway

Etching by John Sell Cotman 1817

13 x 9 ins | 33 x 23 cm

'Although Grimshaw is typically understood to be a self-taught painter, he will have received some form of art education during his six years at the school.

'It has been said that "What Turner did for sunlight, Atkinson Grimshaw did for moonlight". Of course we can't in all honesty steal him from the city of Leeds, but the emotional foundations of his artistic style, his moody, luminous depictions of Victorian urban life where he captured the industrial North with a kind of romantic melancholy, were surely influenced by his formative years as a young schoolboy walking through the Cathedral Close and the medieval streets of Norwich.'

Norwich School, staff and 600 boys, began each day with morning assembly in the great Norman cathedral. This deceptive study of permanence, with Gothic spire and the second largest cloister in England, soared above a graceful accumulation of historic buildings in the adjoining Close.

If the setting was sublime, the teaching was also inspirational thanks essentially to art tutor A.V. Humphris. He lived for the school and to nurture the spark of creativity in every child.

He took any failing in his charges as a personal disappointment so practically all pupils, however bad at art, took care not to let him down. 'When I drew something, his face shone,' Gerard says.

Such was Norwich School's belief in the arts that Gerard had a separate teacher for sculpture. A natural painter and draughtsman, he found he was also adept at modelling in three dimensions, but facility never lifted into passion.

After three years in Norfolk, the Stamps moved again, this time to Beaconsfield in Buckinghamshire. Gerard, aged eleven, was allowed to remain at Norwich School as a boarder. For nearly seven years the Cathedral Close became his main home. Although distanced from his mother, he admired her decency and morality, and always knew he had her support.

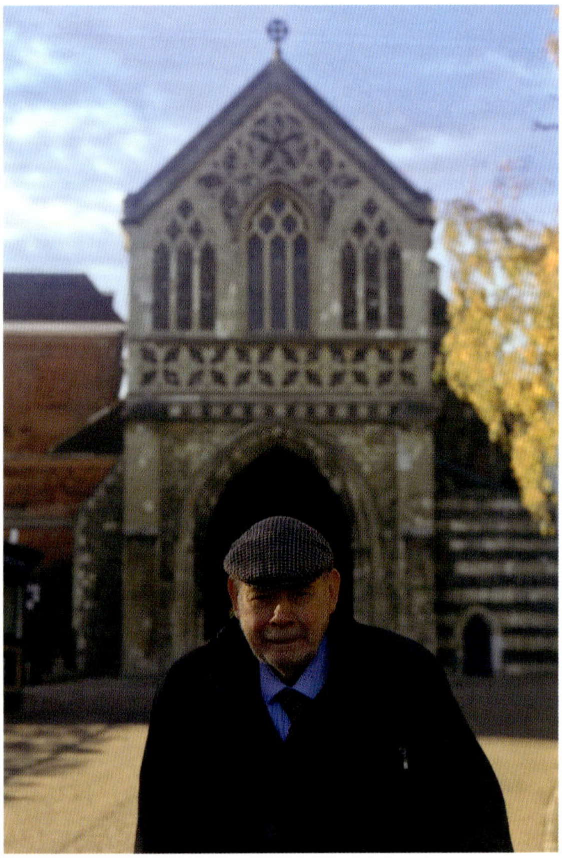

'The Close was like a city within a city; its own little world,' he says. 'I ended up boarding in the Old Bishop's Palace whose core is older than the cathedral. It was cold and dark and allegedly haunted. I still had problems paying attention in most subjects save for art but enjoyed being there more and more. No school in England has a better environment.'

It was a lesson in art and awe just to gaze out of the window.

The art room itself occupied a Gothic former chapel above the Ethelbert Gate – a grand cathedral gateway completed around 1325. Externally the building boasted some of the best surviving flint flushwork of the Middle Ages; internally things remained pretty basic. According to Gerard, 'When Alex Humphris joined the school in 1952 he had to fill buckets of water from the cattle trough in Tombland, often breaking the ice in winter, to mix the powder paints.'

It could be ice-cold inside too. 'By the time I got there we had a butler's sink, and gas heaters so high up they seemed to make no difference. I remember the excitement of getting the first paints in squeezy bottles – which turned out to be horrible muddy stuff.'

Reacting against the ready-made, Gerard turned to calligraphy and drawing – brilliantly tutored in the building blocks of perspective and scale. 'That led to an appreciation of the great illustrators such as Aubrey Beardsley and William Heath Robinson in his work for Hans Christian Andersen. Not just the technical skill; the graphic

A.V. Humphris, Art Tutor
Norwich School
1952–1988
Photographed in front of Ethelbert Gateway in 2018
'Some of us are lucky enough to have had a truly inspirational teacher who influenced the rest of our lives. I had Alex. This is what another Old Norvicensian said of him: "He gave me a means of expression, an appreciation for the visual landscape, and an understanding of the architecture that surrounds us. In short, he gave me a sense of place, wherever I happen to go. I'll remember his warmth, generosity and patience."' G.S.

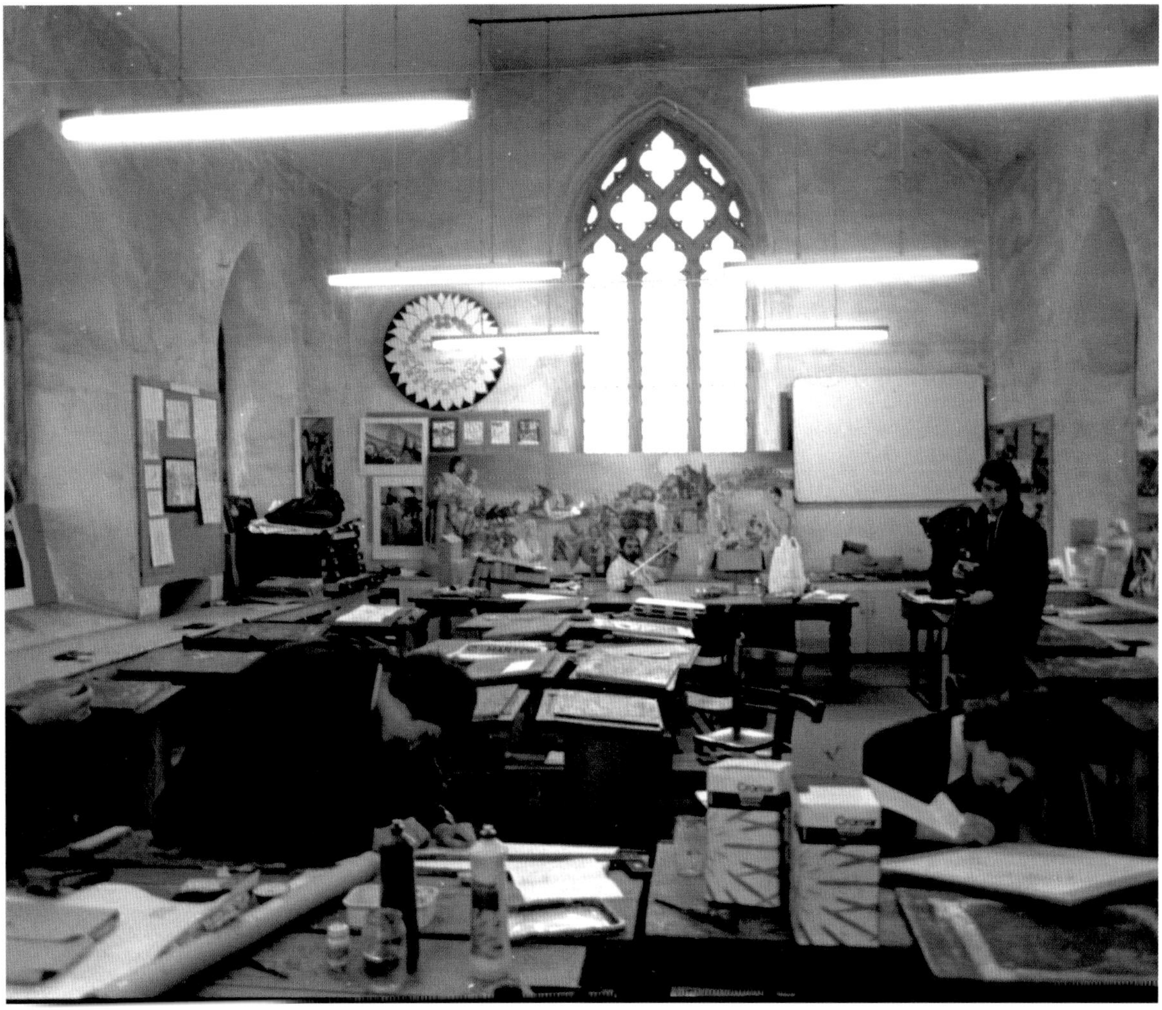

Inside the art room

Ethelbert Gateway, 1971

'Alex can be seen sitting behind his desk, wielding a classroom pointer. He taught in this room from 1952 -1975 before moving to a brand new, state-of-the-art arts centre. He confessed to me he much preferred teaching back here.'

G.S.

design was a revelation: it was so considered. I've always liked books, but picture books especially.'

The only appeal of the science block was the presence of a dark room as he developed an interest in photography. A large part of the appeal lay in atmospheric monochrome plates by Edwin Smith illustrating the 1950s book *English Parish Churches*. Together with Pevsner's *Buildings of England*, it formed a twin bible for the young Gerard Stamp.

Exploration with a camera also forged a link to his brilliant uncle Rosse Stamp. The naval scientist developed underwater television and used it to locate the wreck of HMS *Affray*, the new submarine which mysteriously sank with all hands off the Channel Islands in 1951.

As a boy Rosse had built his own cameras, even grinding his own lenses. He listed his hobbies as 'scientific instrument making, domestic engineering and taking anything to pieces to find what makes it tick'. Gerard loved to visit him in his Herefordshire house of books and clocks. There was a lathe in the dining room and a multitude of Rosse-made gadgets – including fly zappers which left some human visitors in fear of electrocution.

Gerard, a lover of classic cars, was to inherit Uncle Rosse's beloved 1964 MG sports car. If the dismantler had ever taken it to bits, he had taken care to put it back together again.

Although on a very different educational and career path, given his formidable intellect and campaigning zeal, brother Gavin remained the key influence even from a distance. A mutual adoration of architecture would unite them always, together with a shared gift for drawing. But Gerard felt rather less cause for rebellion.

'During the school holidays my parents would take me to visit churches, cathedrals and

National Trust houses. In the summer we paused in marvellous places – Chartres, Rouen, Reims, Amiens, Avignon – while on drives to the South of France.'

His mother applauded prowess in art but his father poured doubt on a fourteen-year-old's expressed wish of pursuing its practical application in architecture. 'You need to be good at maths and physics to be an architect,' he said.

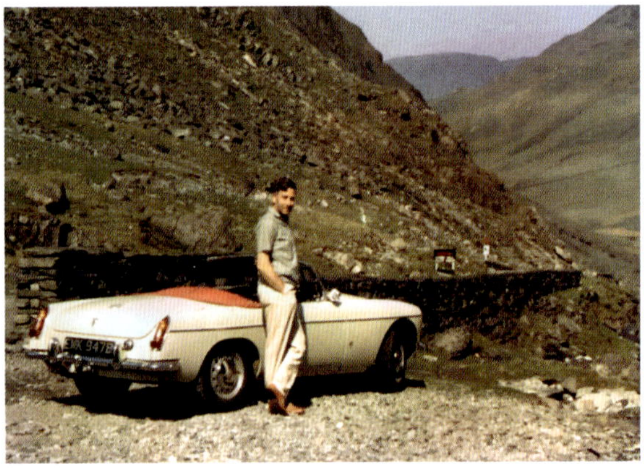

Later – too late in career terms – Gerard realised that an architectural draughtsman could employ an engineer to produce a successful practice.

But there was always a piano at home – both his parents played, and the children were pressed to follow suit. 'Unfortunately, my lessons were with an old lady in a bungalow smelling of mothballs. She used to get really angry because I didn't practise my scales and had no desire to play Chopin so I didn't keep it up.' A life-long keyboard player who could play by ear, his lasting regret was that he had not learned to read music.

Barry Stamp was addicted to jazz while Gavin favoured the blues. Gerard tried to spin more popular music on the disputed turntable – Yes, Pink Floyd, Emerson, Lake and Palmer. 'Take it off!' Barry cried. 'It's ruining Bang & Olufsen.'

In fact, jazz was to be the one paternal passion which the younger son inherited. The late great American jazz pianist Art Tatum would remain one of his fantasy dinner party guests. And in the meantime the strong musical traditions of Norwich School – providing generations of choristers for the cathedral choir – passed him by entirely. All he did was play jazz compositions on school pianos when no one else was in the room.

Gerard was rescued by his exemplary art teacher: 'Alex Humphris imparted everything from the history of art, calligraphy, print-making, stage design and graphics, to composition, perspective, colour theory and tonal values. He taught all the stages of medieval architecture: Anglo-Saxon, Norman, Early English, Decorated, Perpendicular – all the way through, via church and cathedral elevations.'

There was also a foray into sailing, which would prove invaluable since East Anglia can never be fully appreciated without a vantage point from water. It was no coincidence that Mr Humphris served as president of Horning Sailing Club.

By the age of sixteen the visual arts nut was besotted with cinema. While staying with his parents in Buckinghamshire he cycled to Iver Heath for the Pinewood Studios where James Bond films were made. He peered through railings at the vast set recreating Victorian London for Carol Reed's *Oliver!* Wandering along the back lot he pondered the pond where Jack Hawkins had floundered in *The Cruel Sea*.

At Denham he climbed over a fence and thought of Alexander Korda's production centre

Rosse Stamp pictured in Wales with his brand new MGB Roadster in 1964

'This was the last car he ever bought, and he kept it until he died in 2017. He and his wife, Alice, took it all over the country towing a caravan. Rosse did all the servicing on the car himself, rebuilding the engine to his satisfaction. When I treated the car to a bare metal respray by the MG Owners Club Workshop in 2023 they said "Whatever you do, don't touch the engine. It's the best we've ever had in here!"' G.S.

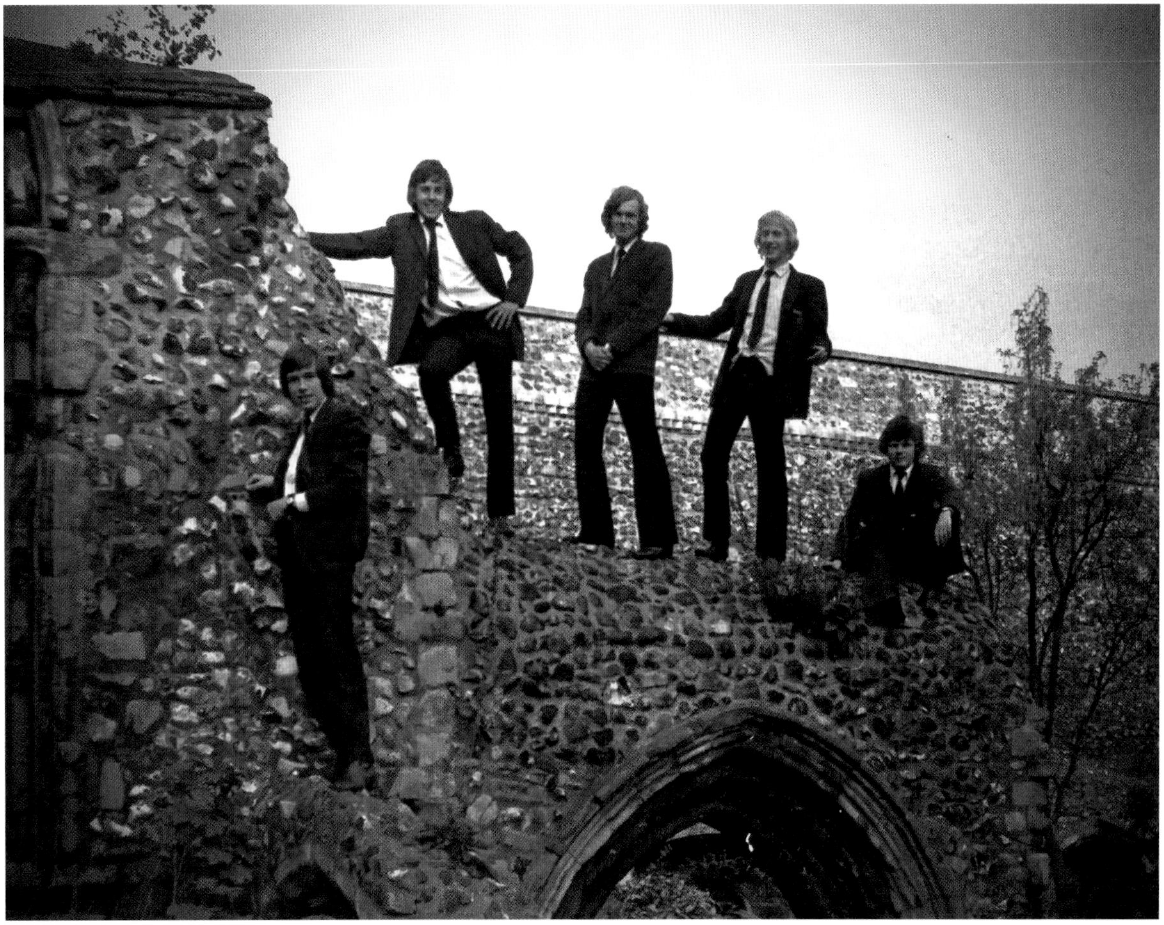

Schoolfriends standing on medieval ruined monastic doorway

'In 1972, our last year at school, I photographed school friends in various locations around the Cathedral. This 13th-century doorway is now the main visitors' entrance (see page 82). From left to right: Gerard Stamp, Mike Etherington-Smith, Richard Flaye, Chris Curwen, Adam Lotinga.' G.S.

in its mid-century heyday. A now deserted building designed by Walter Gropius and Maxwell Fry had brought to screen life classic movies from *Brief Encounter* to *Great Expectations*, and all was now silent abandonment and ruin.

Gerard wrote script synopses and set up the school film club, where he was allowed to screen the movie *If* – Lindsay Anderson's murderous satire on an English public school which ends in insurrection – to a sixth-form audience only. Now he was going to be a famous film director.

That ambition did not last but a love of cinema would be life-long. 'My absolute favourite film is *The Third Man*, directed by Carol Reed and written by Graham Greene. Shot in black and white, every frame is designed and fabulous. It's all light, of course.'

Scraping his O-levels, he learned later that he made the sixth form only because the headmaster was away. The wife of the missing master, checking the applications, had determined that the school's star artist should not be rejected.

As Gerard would remember: 'The cathedral was used as a short cut through to the lower close (not allowed), or through the bishop's garden past the north transept (definitely not allowed). Later that hallowed garden also became a handy route under cover of darkness to the pub on Palace Plain next to John Sell Cotman's house (definitely, definitely not allowed).'

And now he posed on a ruined wall in what might have been a group photo for a teenage rock band. More secretly, he and fellow daredevils had already made the most of an extensive programme of cathedral repairs and cleaning: 'Scaffolding to an adventurous schoolboy was too much of a temptation, and in those days it was easy to climb past the rudimentary obstacles designed to deter such activities.

'I went everywhere: round the tower and up the spire, up and down all the Norman spiral stairs, on the roof under the flying buttresses,

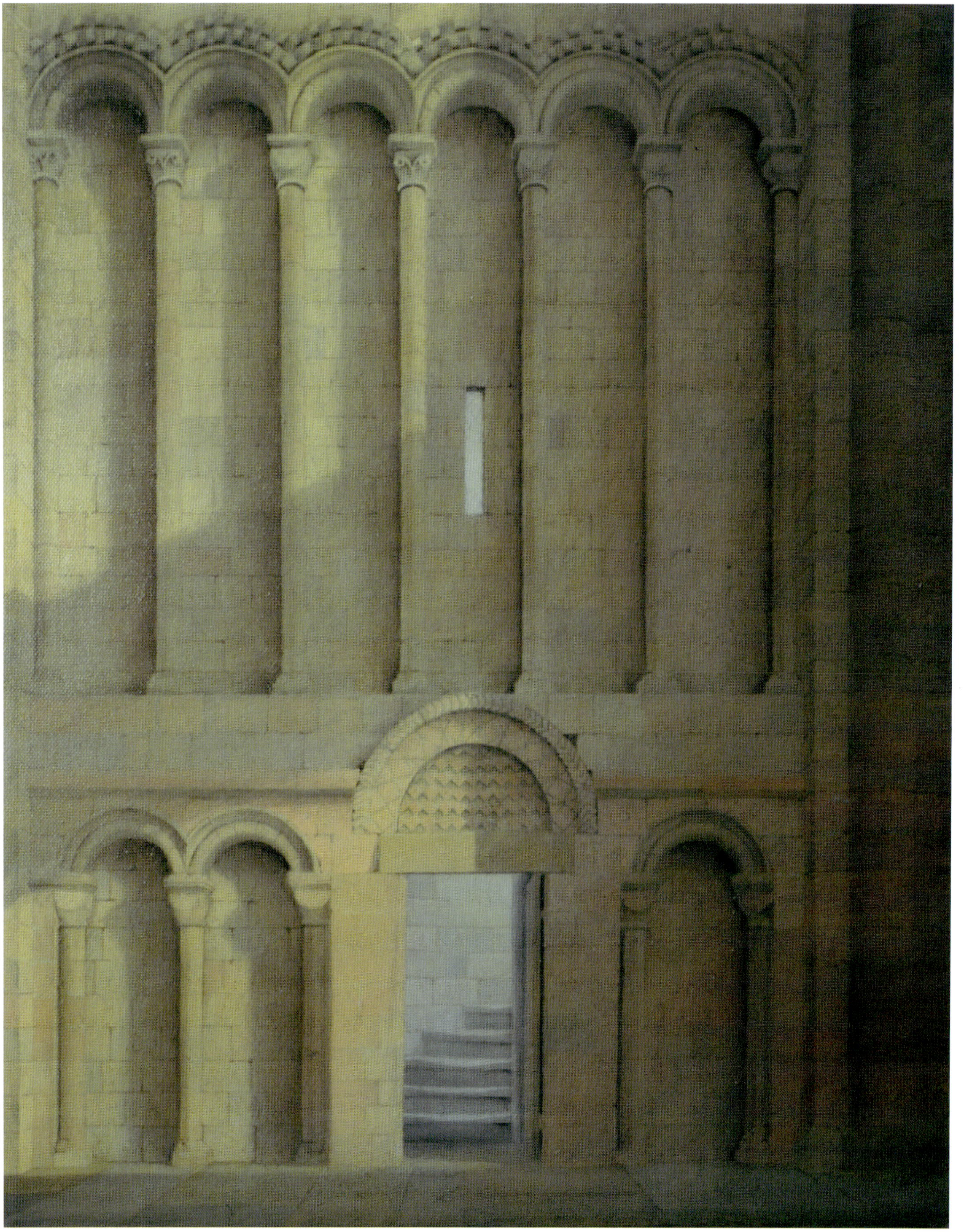

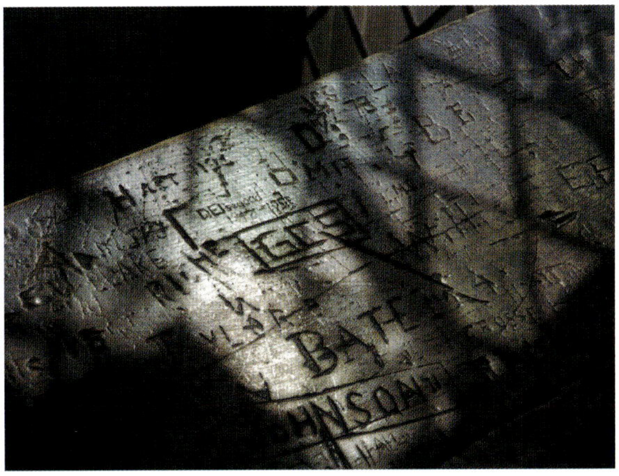

Initials in the school chapel organ loft

'My initials GCS (my unused middle name is Christopher) are also at the top of the Cathedral Spire. But now you'll never get me up there to prove it.' G.C.S.

over the nave between the vaulting and the roof, round the triforium and the clerestory.'

Ending his ascent via three rickety ladders, he signed off on the wall behind the spire's highest window.

'All is now heavily padlocked but back then a friendly steward let me into the one door that opened up a world of medieval adventure.' This hallowed entrance would feature in the later Stamp painting *Steps to the Triforium*.

More conventional school sport could now be jettisoned for the joys of the Local History Club. 'That meant I was left free to walk around Norwich and cycle into the countryside to draw and write about architecture. Bliss!' Gerard visited every church in Norwich to draw the fonts.

He also joined other Norwich residents in a failed campaign to prevent the destruction of medieval Magdalen Street for the Inner Link Road. They marched to save Timber Hill – and stop modern blocks stretching from the medieval city walls to the Castle Mound – and won.

Aged seventeen, he completed a thesis on the then obscure Norfolk Victorian architect Thomas Jeckyll – maker of Aesthetic Movement houses and churches and of metalwork and furniture influenced by Japanese design. The homage won the school's Local History Prize. He chose to receive a book called *Ruins*, featuring several sites he would subsequently paint.

One stressful Monday (3 July 1972), wrongly thinking he had ruined his A-level History exam, he spent a consolatory afternoon drawing the cloisters. The sketch remains with him to this day.

Norwich School – later doubling in size as a co-ed day school – was adding an impressive arts block as Gerard was leaving. But what he would remember always was the potency of the ancient setting and the power of one inspirational teacher.

Given his father's insistence that he would never make an architect, Gerard decided that the next best course was graphic design at art school. 'It encompassed all the things I liked – drawing, calligraphy, typography, illustration.

'I knew also that I wanted to eat as well as paint. How do you get a job as an artist? You get a job as a designer.'

Steps to the Triforium
Norwich Cathedral
Oil on canvas 2017
20 x 16 ins | 51 x 41 cm

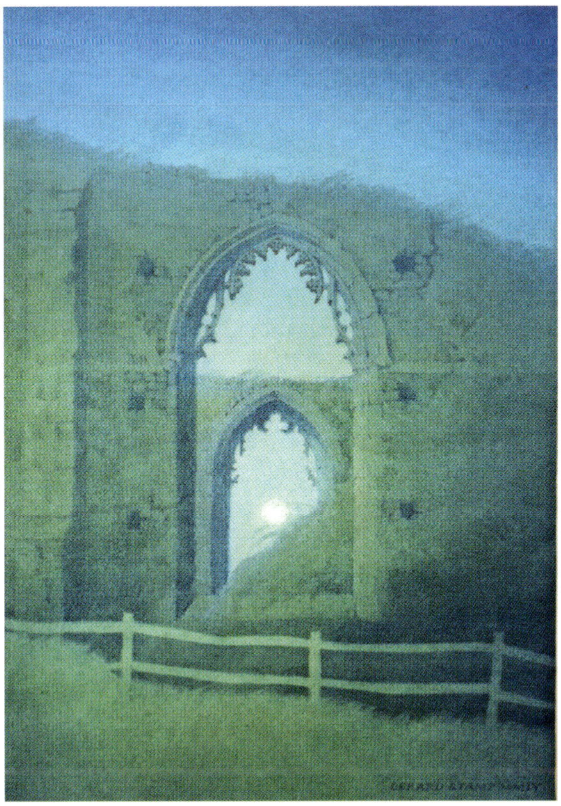

Billockby at Full Moon
Watercolour 2004
14.5 x 10 ins | 37 x 25 cm

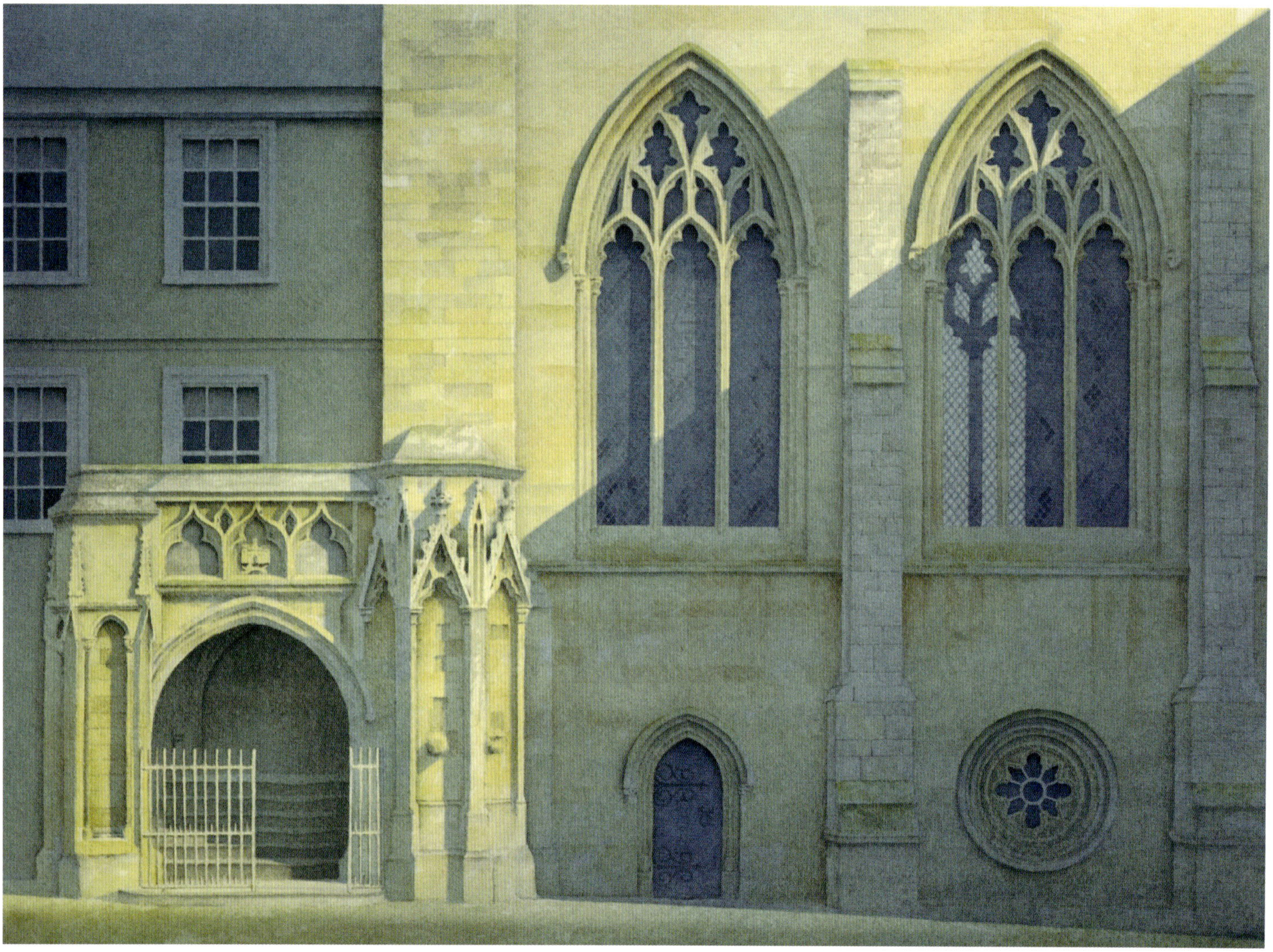

School Chapel Shadows

Watercolour 2021

26 x 18.5 ins | 65.5 x 47 cm

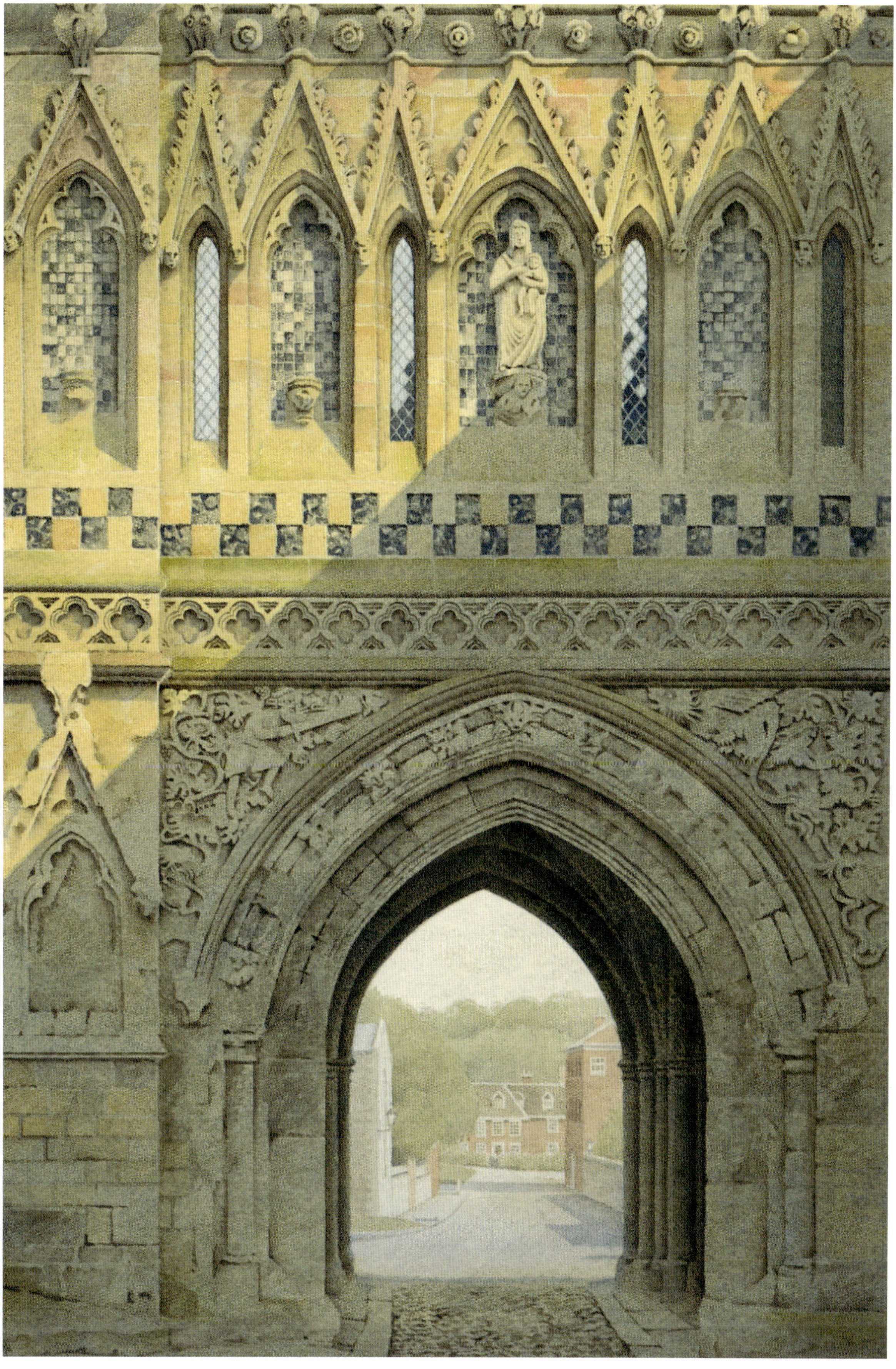

Ethelbert Gateway

Watercolour 2023

21.5 x 14 ins | 55 x 36 cm

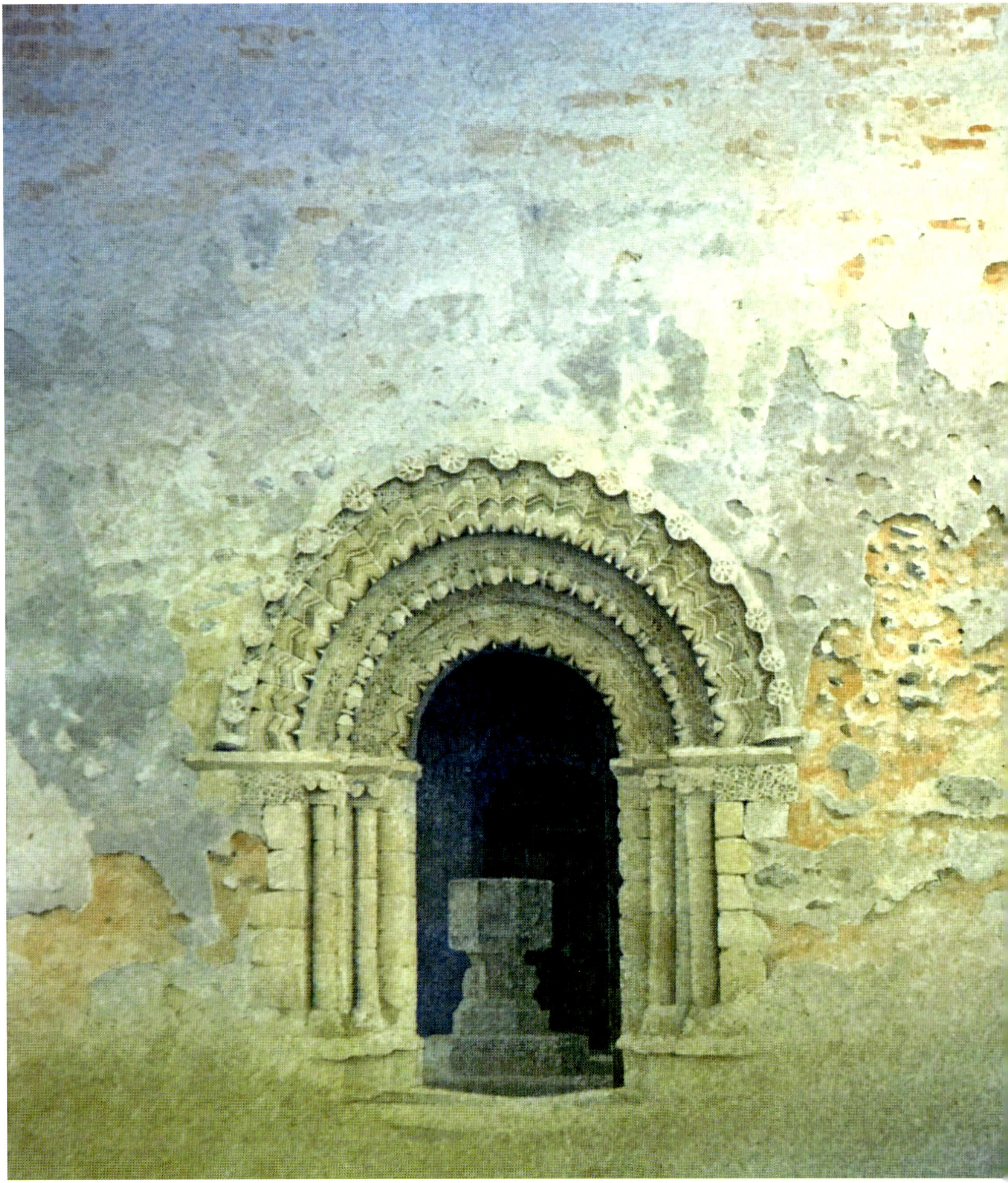

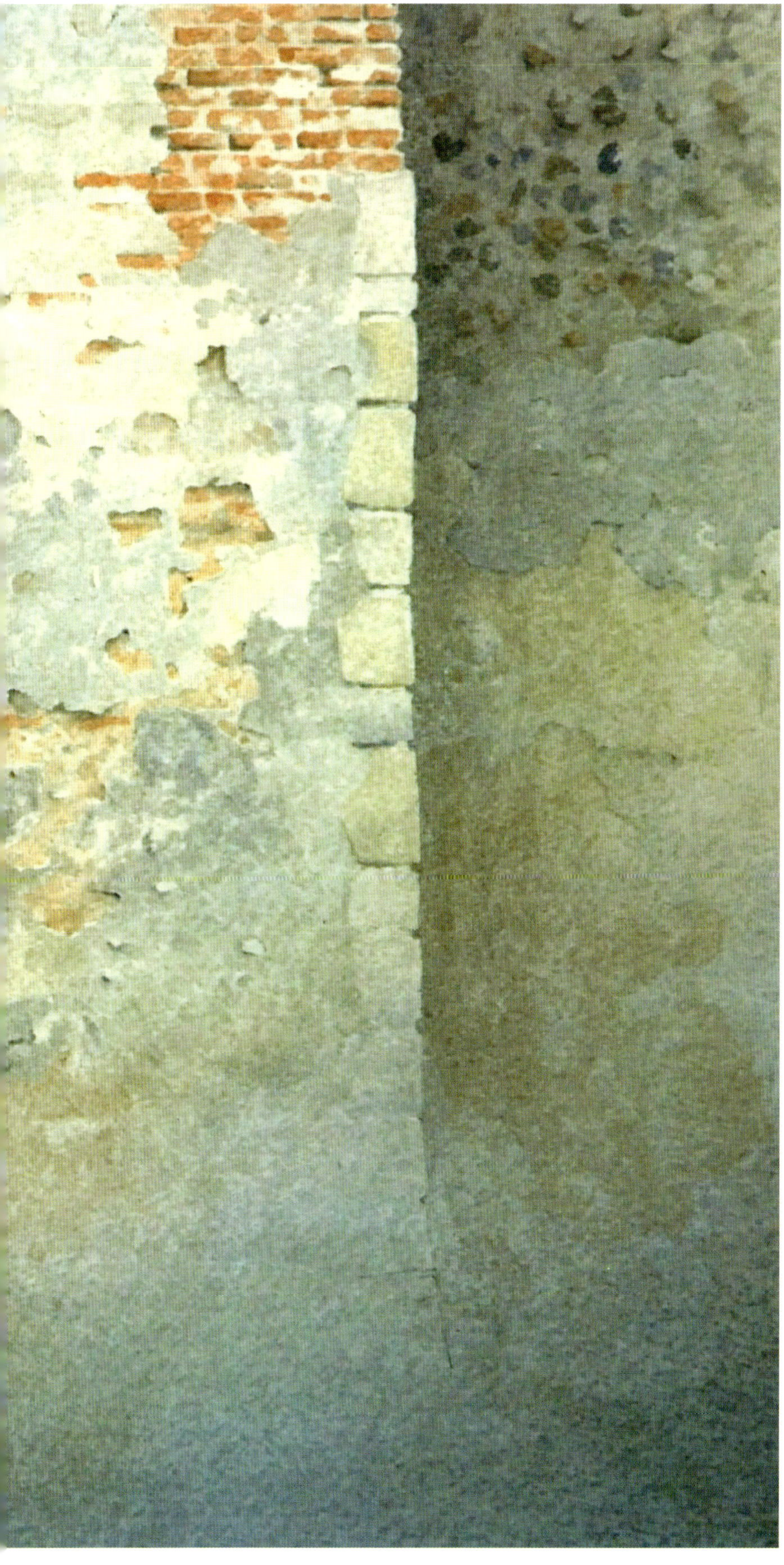

Hales North Door III

Watercolour 2012

16.5 x 23 ins | 42 x 58 cm

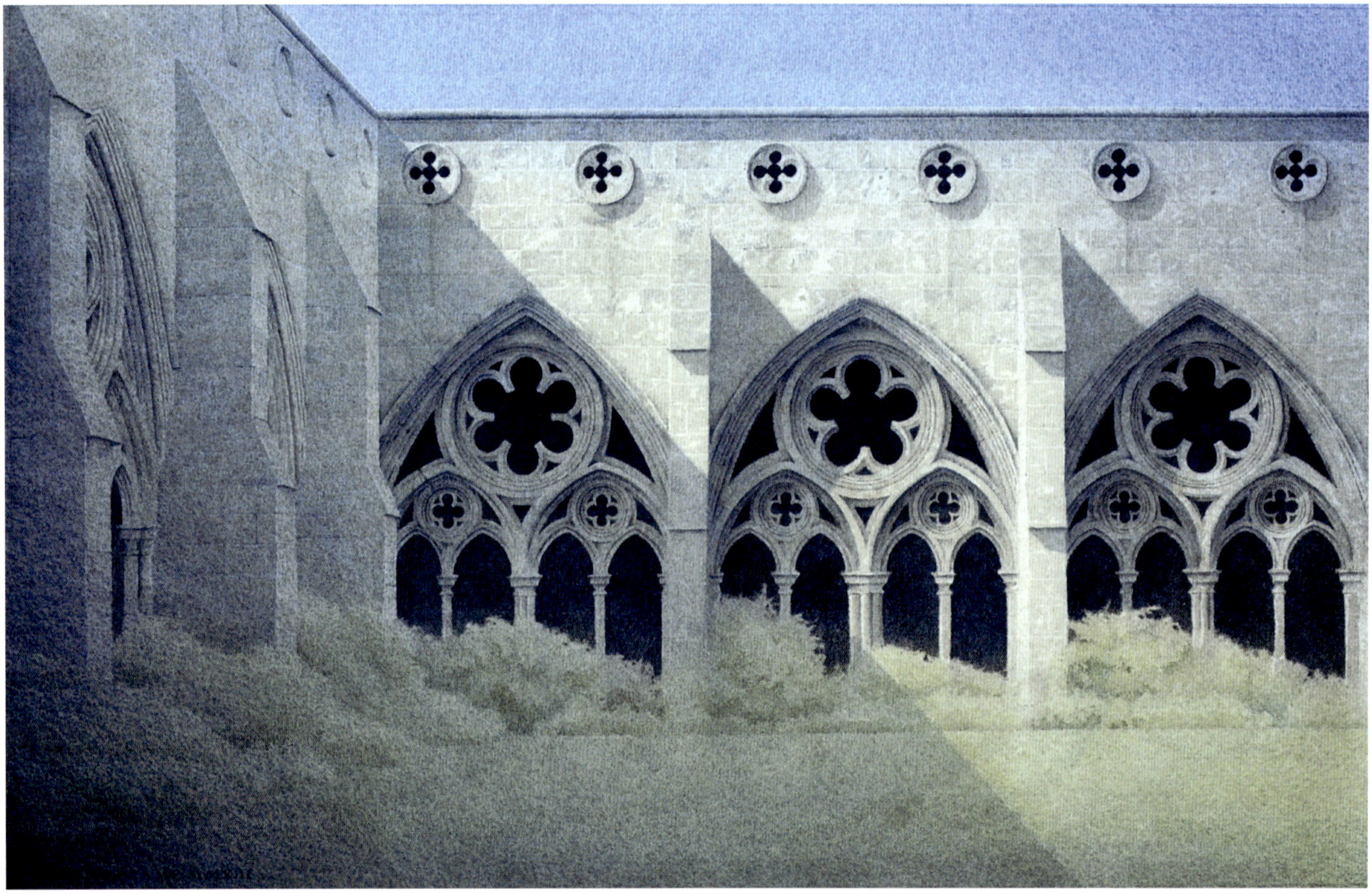

Salisbury Cathedral

Cloister

Watercolour 2013

17 x 25 ins | 43 x 63 cm

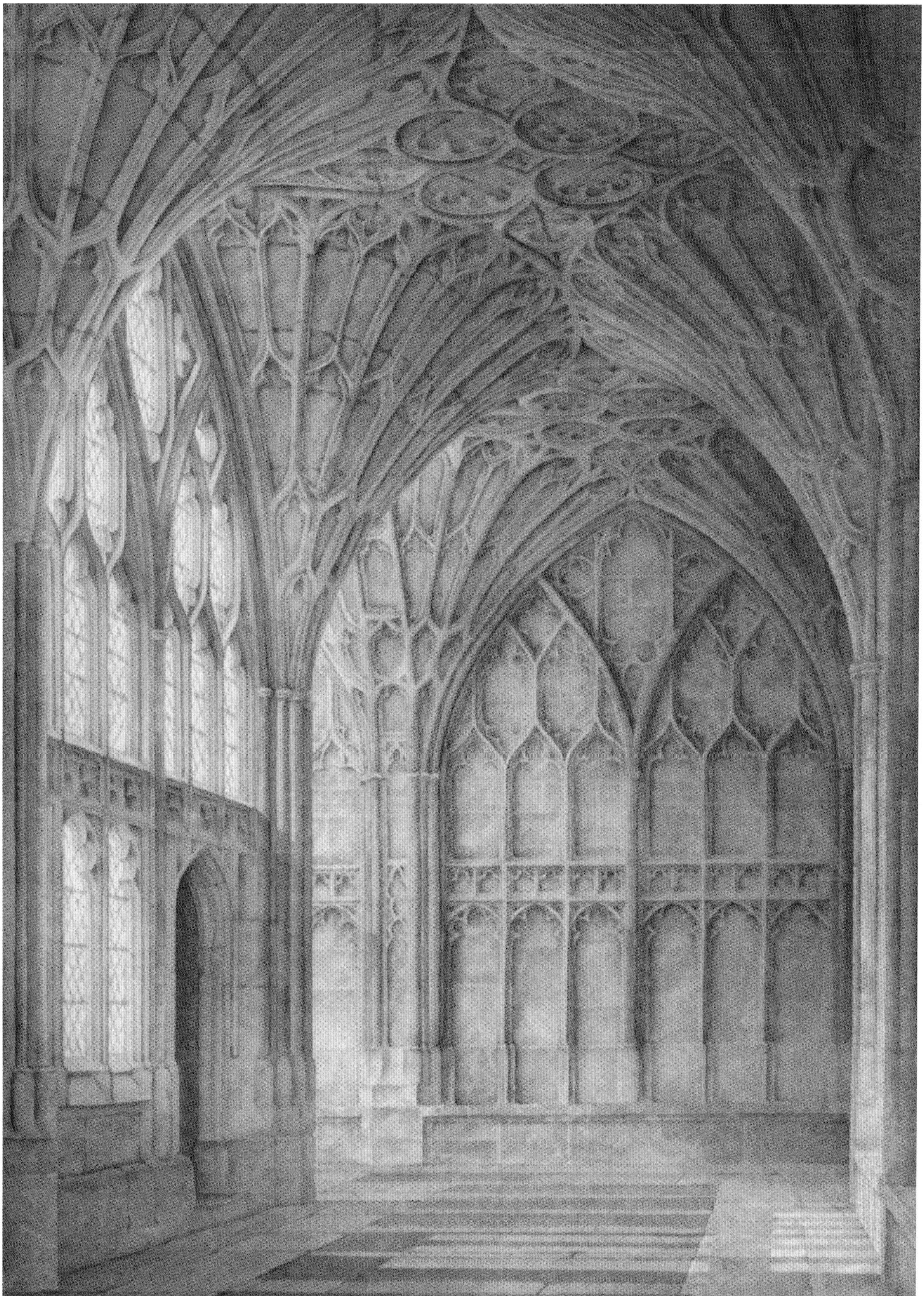

Cloister Corner

Gloucester Cathedral

Watercolour 2019

23.5 x 16.5 ins | 60 x 42 cm

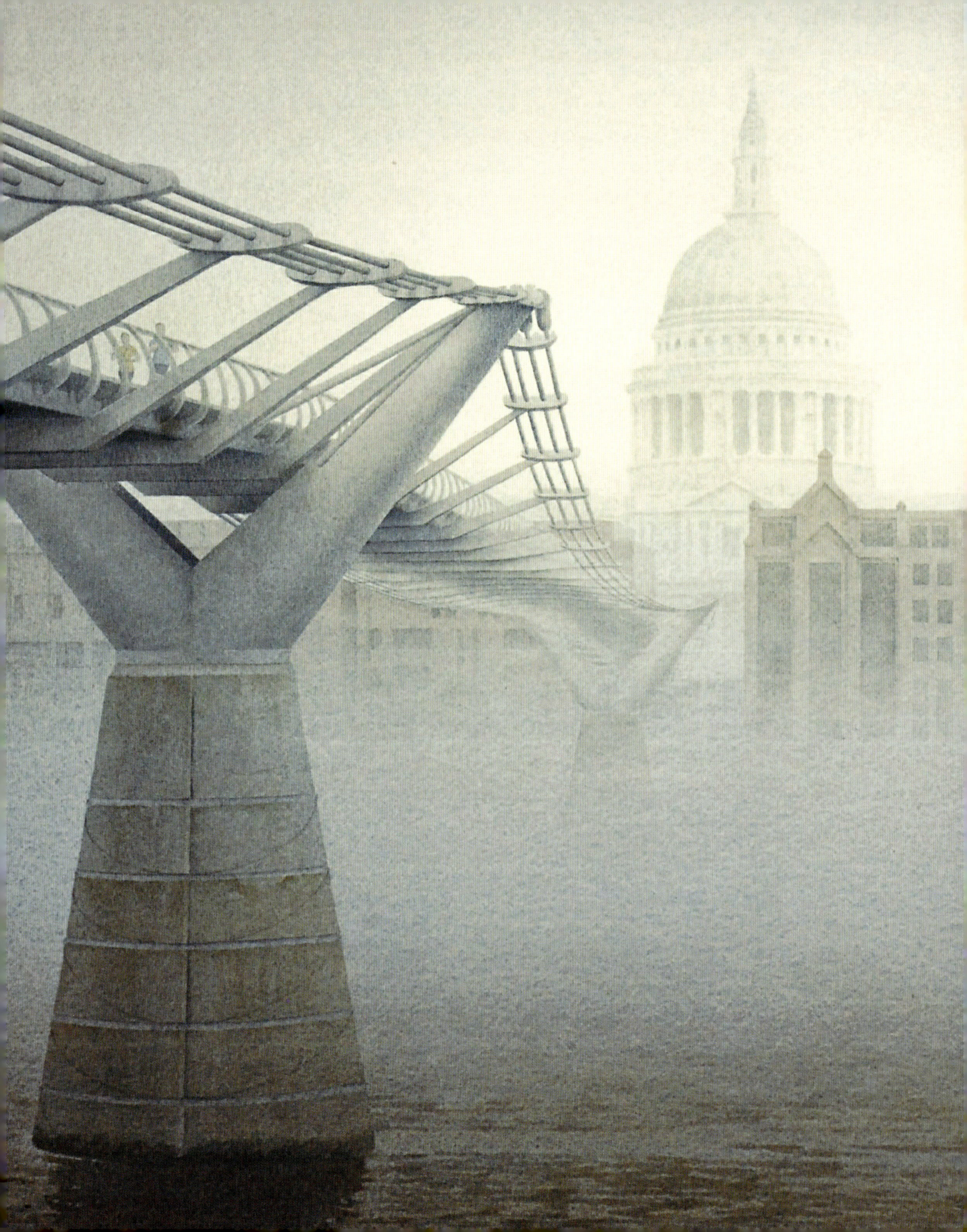

III Design for Living

Alarmed by the prospect of London since still only seventeen, Gerard was accepted for a foundation course at Bath Academy of Art. But Buckinghamshire gave county wide grants only, so he was compelled to attend High Wycombe College of Art and Technology and to live with his parents.

It made for a miserable year. 'As well as a creative freedom, I wanted to get out and meet the opposite sex. At eighteen, I was an involuntary celibate. A foundation year is about trying anything and I was stuck at home. I knew also that I absolutely wanted to study graphic design.'

One consolation was fondly remembered: overnight trips with his father in a beloved river cruiser. They visited the many pubs beside the beautiful upper reaches of the Thames.

'But you were so good at art'

Now he secured a place at Bristol Polytechnic's Faculty of Art and Design (formerly the West of England Academy of Art) in the familiar territory of his mother's native city. Although badly Blitzed, the historic centre had the atmosphere of a rather bigger Norwich – with similarly wonderful countryside beyond.

Bristol, a student city, was enormous fun and a great relief. Absorbing studies in 'visual communication' ran between weekend parties. Such students of design and illustration relished a mutual hostility with the fine-art department. It wasn't just that the painters had abandoned representation; their big abstract canvases had discarded drawing too.

Millennium Dawn

Watercolour 2010

45 x 34.5 ins | 115 x 88 cm

Now he made several friends for life including David Sprague, a fellow design student who had been a chorister at Bristol Cathedral School. Both felt a strong connection to sacred spaces. 'Gerard was quite a modest and reserved character, not at all a Billy Big Boots,' David remembers. 'And for all his sensitivity, there was also a strong streak of determination.

'Nobody worked harder than he did – he had this concentration and application coupled with an unusual approach to things and he was the only one in our year to get a first. He was the first to get a job and of course at a good salary. There was a sense that he knew what he was about while the rest of us were still finding ourselves. There was also some serious fun. He led us to the Old Duke – with a portrait of Duke Ellington on the pub sign – where he was absolutely absorbed in live jazz,' David continues. 'I was the first to get a car and would drive everyone into the countryside, aiming for pubs with pianos so Gerard could play and we could get free beer. That made him even more popular.'

In retrospect, David could recognise his friend as a master of reinvention but always with a deep grounding in art. Gerard would take him to visit an elderly cousin in Portishead – the surviving sister of sculptor Wally and etcher Eddie Sharland. 'Eddie's huge old printing press was still in the garage – holding up the roof.'

Gerard was developing an interest in advertising, coming to admire the creativity of a commercial tradition in which great artists such as John Constable had also worked as sign-painters and sign-writers. He especially liked posters by the Brothers Beggarstaff – aka artists William

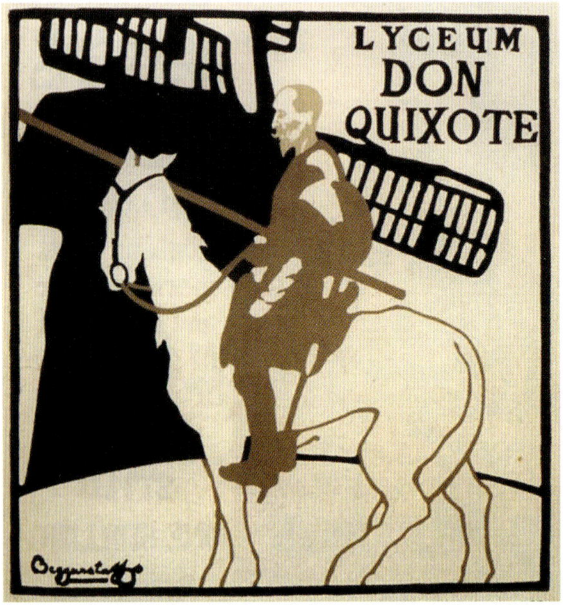

Poster for the Lyceum Theatre

By the Beggarstaffs
Two-colour stencil and hand painting on wrapping paper 1895

Nicholson and James Pryde. Even then, there was the vague thought of making enough money early in life to set himself up as a painter.

The exhilarating art-school experience culminated in the sweltering summer of 1976 – in which Gerard Stamp graduated with both a first-class BA degree and a job. His final-year show featured an intricate internal signage system for his father's cash and carry business complete with model aisles and overhead banners. A London design company executive saw it and signed him up on the spot.

The thrill of a career in the making was rather countered by ongoing alarm over looming life in the capital. 'London seemed too big,' he says. 'I had yet to learn that it was just a large number of villages locked together.'

By way of consolation, his mother, having affronted his father by striking out for financial independence with a secretarial post in which she excelled, saved enough money to buy the family a cottage in the Broadland village of Reedham. So, Norfolk explorations had resumed. That was and would remain a lifeline.

The director who had enlisted him promptly left the design company, and two lucrative but creatively unsatisfying years followed in which he changed his mind about London. It teemed with art and architectural wonders, as well as the opposite sex. Ironically, he began to see the light and the life when he and brother Gavin rented rooms for £4 a week in a Waterloo nunnery. Gavin's roof-top parties were legendary. 'To this day I am astonished nobody fell off,' Gerard says. That billet gave way to rental flats around Clapham.

An elder brother was more than ever a guide and hero. His many campaigns during the destructive 1970s included making drawings for John Betjeman and the Victorian Society of a bomb-damaged Chelsea church which developers wanted to bulldoze. Holy Trinity Sloane Square – described by Betjeman, the Poet Laureate, as 'the Cathedral of the Arts and Crafts Movement' – is now rescued and Grade I listed.

For Gerard the appeal of Britain's capital only grew when American clients pressed a move

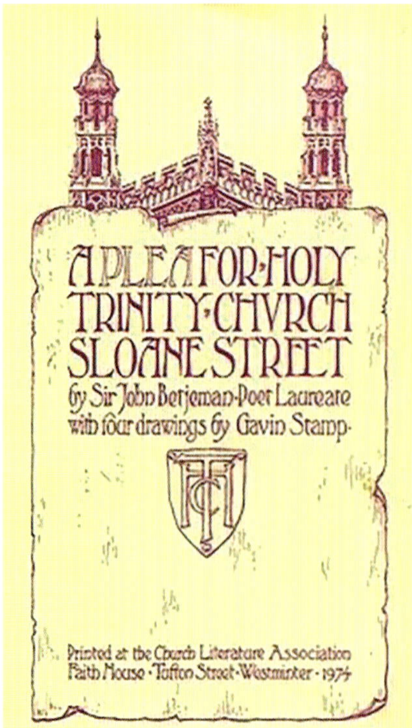

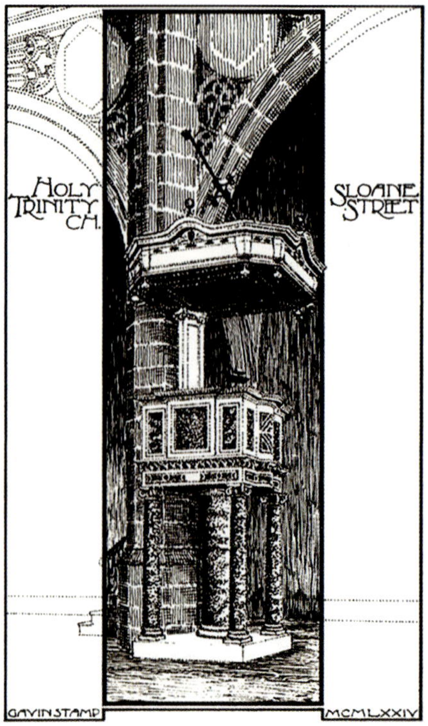

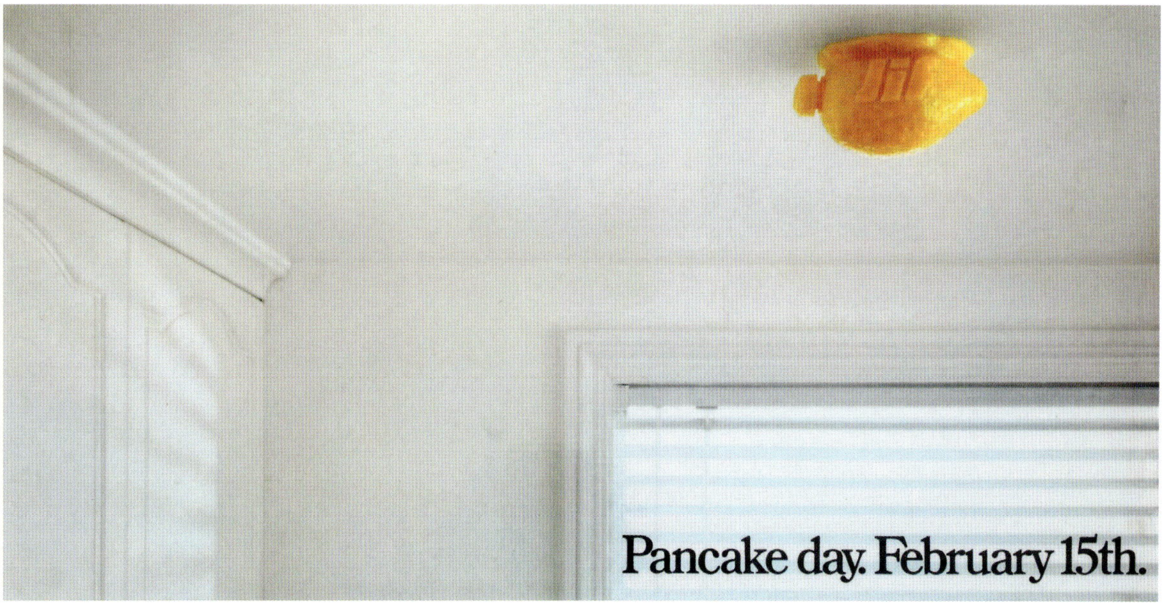

Jif Lemon poster
48 sheet 1983
Art Director: Gerard Stamp
Copywriter: Loz Simpson
Photographer: Stak
Client: Colmans of Norwich

to Pennsylvania. That helped to persuade him to abandon a large income for the pittance offered on the lowest creative rung of a London advertising agency ladder.

The way for a junior art director to get ahead was by winning awards – chiefly a salary-doubling Design and Art Direction Pencil. Gerard Stamp won three in the heyday of a creative industry awash in cash and artful talent. When he showed his mum a prized commercial she said, wanly: 'But you were so good at art.'

'But advertising was a fantastic business to be in back then,' Gerard says. 'People were very positive, enjoying entertaining commercials, good posters, intelligent ads. Future film directors were working in clever agencies.'

During the 1980s and early 1990s Gerard rose through well-regarded agencies from Boase Massimi Pollitt to KMP, and then to FCB and Bates Dorland. Then he was appointed UK executive creative director at expanding Leo Burnett.

A love of carefully applied detail would be displayed in a series of award-winning promotions. The first was a poster campaign, a pancake-day project for Jif Lemon. He particularly delighted in the happy coincidence that the client was Colman's of Norwich. Another big hit was a huge production for Halifax Building Society as Britain's leading mortgage lender. Scores of athletic Brits and a pair of Ancient Greek caryatids formed themselves into living walls, portico and roof as the *'Our House'* song by Crosby, Stills, Nash and Young played. They followed the cast of *Alien* in a shoot at Shepperton Studios.

To Gerard's delight, two of the following commercials were shot at Pinewood, on the 007 stage. 'You always made sure you were on set early for those.'

Talent-spotter Andrew Cracknell hired him twice, commenting after the second occasion: 'He is one of the best art directors I have ever known. He is always calm. He eschews gimmickry and has a reason for everything he does.'

As it turned out the best reason for joining the Cracknell ship was an introduction to art director Jacqui Newman. This led to both Gerard and Jacqui's most successful creative collaboration of all since it culminated in their marriage.

Jacqui, born in Barnet and raised in Berkshire, had been plucked from Reading College of Art to work for the legendary advertising agency Collett Dickenson Pearce. The glamour group was responsible for Hovis commercials directed by Ridley Scott and Cinzano ads by Alan Parker.

Other CDP campaigns were being led by future Oscar winners David Puttnam and Hugh Hudson. But, as she advanced through several agencies, Jacqui became a high-flier longing to migrate back

A Plea for Holy Trinity Church, Sloane Street
Design, lettering
and illustrations by
Gavin Stamp 1974

to the countryside – and, in her case, to the world of horses. Youthful gallops in Windsor Great Park had left an indelible mark.

In 1985, the year they married, the couple had bought a small flint and brick cottage in the picturesque North Norfolk village of Binham, beside grand priory ruins. Six-hour and nearly 300-mile round trips did not make for the most restful weekends, but the purchase bought a breathing space, a holiday base and a tantalising glimpse of a happier future.

At Binham Priory Gerard revered 'a sense of timelessness, an almost biblical scene'. Since drawn to 'places where you have no sense of the present', he also loved nearby coastal saltmarshes. And across North Norfolk he savoured the sensation of being on the edge.

'There is also a feeling of quiet poignancy, which I love. The buildings are the survivors from the past, the nearest you can get to touching history. It's a foot in another world.'

In London, Gerard had long moved north of the river where most of his friends congregated and Norfolk was an easier journey. A Highgate flat had now been left for an unmodernised Edwardian terrace house in East Finchley, which became the Stamps' main marital home.

Jacqui says: 'I knew from the start that he wanted to give it a go as an artist. For some years he got up at 5am to paint in the spare bedroom before he went to work. But then promotions kept coming and he realised he couldn't do both things really well. And advertising certainly paid the bills.'

Heady times for the British advertising industry – with budgets for single commercials topping £1 million – also produced stresses and

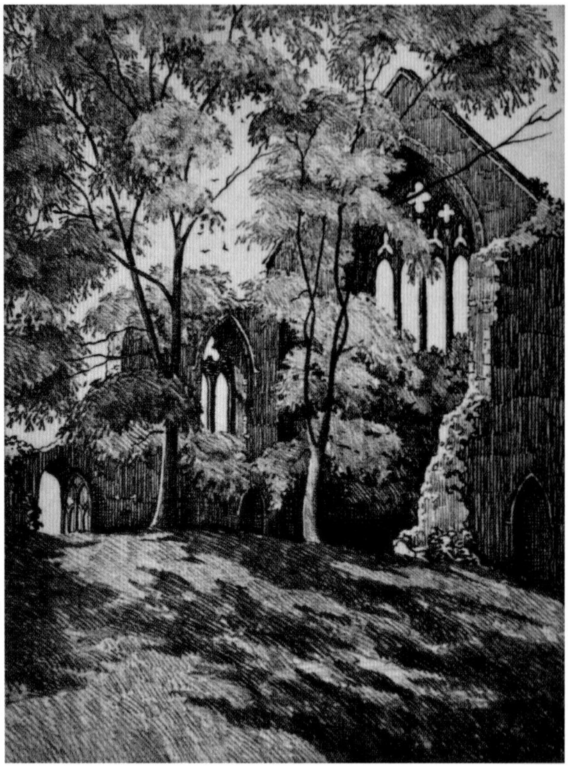

Walsingham Refectory

Soft ground etching 1991

8 x 6 ins | 20 x 15 cm

clashes. As Gerard amassed a pride of four Cannes Gold Lion awards – advertising industry Oscars – he often thought of packing it all in for a life as a painter. And he also took a series of exploratory steps beyond maintaining copious and meticulous sketchbooks.

After initial guidance from the inherited works of Cousin Eddie, Gerard had developed a deeper interest in etching. He had studied and collected the prints of his beloved John Sell Cotman who, in a marathon mission from 1811, had set out to etch 'all the ornamented antiquities in Norfolk'. The monumental *Architectural Antiquities of Norfolk* volume published in 1818, with sixty etchings, became a manual for excellence in draughtsmanship.

Like Cotman himself, Gerard then fell under the spell of the Venetian-born eighteenth-century architect, archaeologist and artist Giovanni Battista Piranesi. He had attempted to etch all the ancient buildings of Rome and achieved a fresh breakthrough in Italian art.

Now, in evening classes at London's Slade School of Fine Art from 1991, Gerard tested the very exacting medium for himself – scratching delicate Norfolk designs into hard wax grounds on metal plates, or impressing pencil drawings on paper into softer surfaces. In both cases the plates were then dipped in an acid bath so that exposed metal was etched away.

It was part of the appeal that soft-ground etching had been pioneered by Norwich School artists. Gerard's images in either form were more than competent, but mostly a means to an end. It was another part of an exhaustive process of trying to understand artistic materials and methods as he worked towards an individual vision.

He attended several Royal Watercolour Society summer schools and took a stand at the 1991 Holkham Country Fair, offering Cotmanesque watercolours of Norfolk churches and a charming catalogue. An economic downturn, and an artistic talent still to develop, stopped him from snapping golden chains.

Inching forward towards a different existence, the Stamps sold East Finchley and rented in Hampstead Garden Suburb so they could move more readily. Jacqui says: 'I may have helped to instigate things a little by saying things like "What the hell are we doing worrying about Tetley teabags over the weekend, or whether there are enough chocolate chips in the photograph I arranged on Friday?" But that was very discouraging because Gerard did work on some good accounts. He was always a perfectionist with an excellent work ethic.'

Aggressive aspects of the advertising industry had always repelled him. 'I do not like the type of creative director whose style is to bully,' he says. 'It is something that simply does not come naturally to me and I would not want it to.'

He preferred collaboration, not least in a long-term working partnership with copywriter Loz Simpson. His 1994 *Campaign* magazine profile

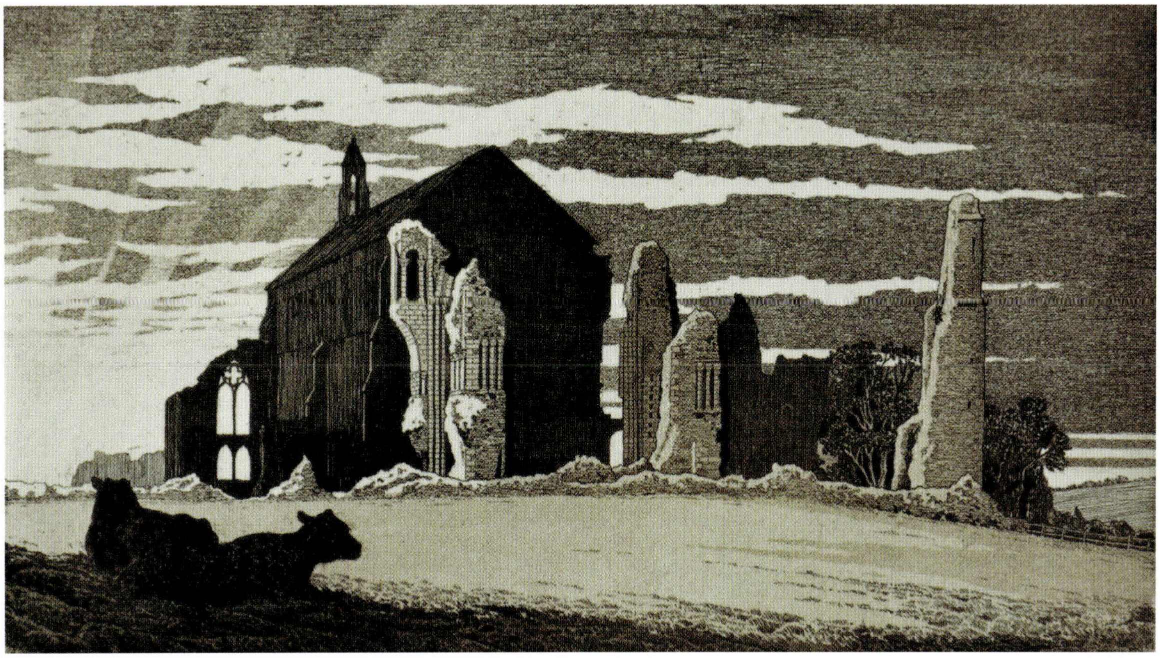

Binham Priory

Etching 1992

5 x 9 ins | 12.5 x 23 cm

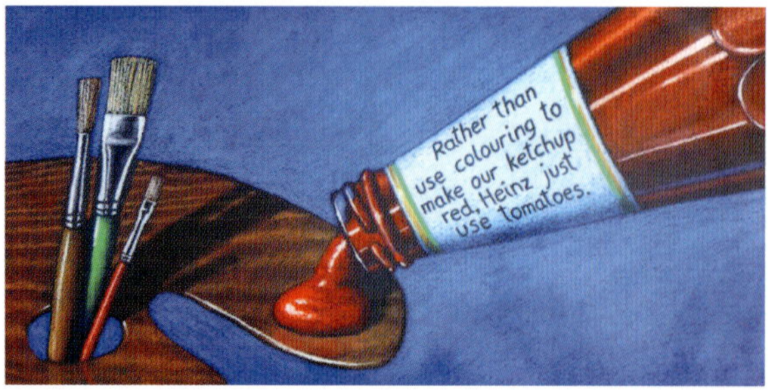

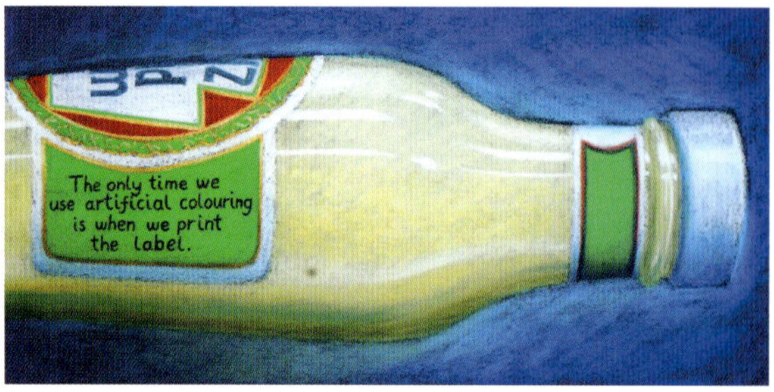

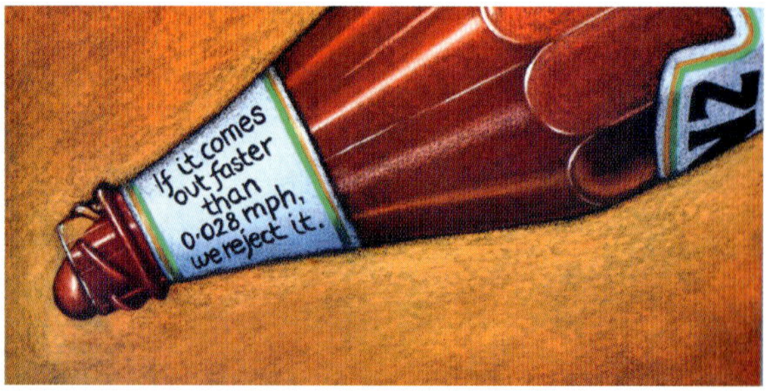

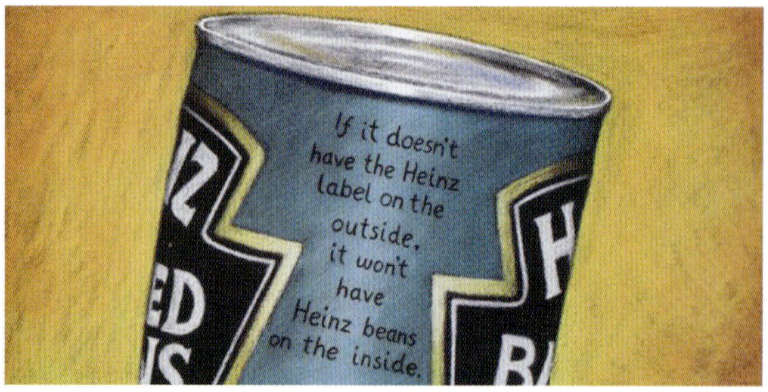

Heinz Posters

48 sheet 1992

Art Director: Gerard Stamp

Copywriter: Loz Simpson

Illustrator: Robin Heighway -Bury

Client: H.J. Heinz Co Ltd

ended thus: 'Stamp's uncannily mild manner and obvious unease with his own authority may prove to be a grave disadvantage when it comes to cracking the whip over the troops. He may have to spend some time in front of a mirror practising looking stern and giving terse orders. On the other hand, his undoubted creative talent may provide exactly the kind of inspiration that Burnett needs.'

Leo Burnett had a mediocre reputation for creativity at that point. During Gerard's eight-year tenure at the top it won multiple awards, including the Cannes Grands Prix, and *Campaign* magazine named two of its clients (McDonald's and Heinz) Advertiser of the Year.

In 2001, under the Stamp chairmanship, it became the second most awarded advertising office in the world. Looking back a quarter of a century later Gerard says: 'My uncannily mild manner and obvious unease with authority didn't prove to be a disadvantage after all.'

The angel was in the detail. Having spent long hours in Victoria and Albert Museum vaults, examining John Sell Cotman watercolours in a bid to crack their code, Gerard applied the same level of research and precision in his advertising style. Scores of illustrators' portfolios were scoured before he identified and commissioned the perfect crayon drawing style for Heinz posters.

Roger Nokes, a copywriter colleague, described him as 'a country gentleman aesthete'. While wishing to celebrate a great many historic buildings, he was critical of a lot of modern architecture.

In fact, he fully, if rather more quietly, endorsed the excoriating views of the *'Piloti'* architectural correspondent of *Private Eye* magazine. That caustic critic, named after a column of steel or concrete, was widely known to be brother Gavin.

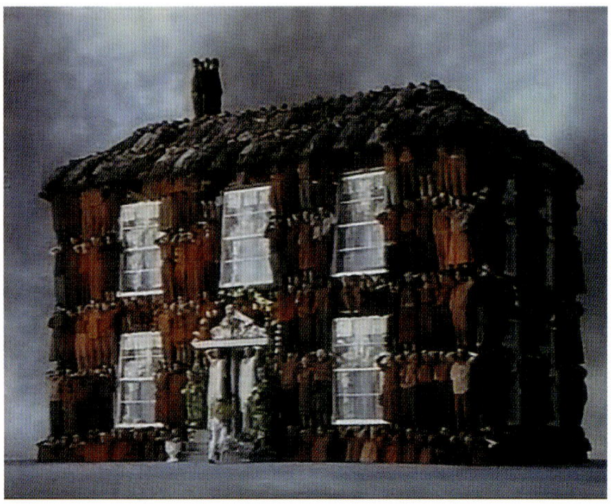

Halifax Building Society 'House'

60 second commercial 1991

Art Director: Gerard Stamp

Copywriter: Loz Simpson

Director: John Amiel

'This cost a small fortune, filmed without C.G.I. Everyone was strapped to scaffolding. The walls and roof were shot separately and fitted together in post production.' G.S.

Gavin Stamp was having a ball, writing, lecturing, broadcasting and poking fun via very serious jokes such as an annual Hugh Casson Award for Britain's worst new building. At the same time he built up The Twentieth Century Society by successfully campaigning to save every recent and modern good thing from Bankside and Battersea power stations to red telephone boxes. As ever, the brotherly creed was Anti Ugly.

But, for the time being, Gerard tried to content himself by confining picture making to leisure hours: he practised drawing and watercolour painting; his Christmas cards were beautifully crafted works of art. The lures of profitable professional life became golden snares as the Stamps started a family – with Eleanor-Rose born in 1990. Rupert followed in 1994.

Jacqui, the higher earner in the partnership when they met, had intended to return to work after Eleanor-Rose's birth, but never did. Following the marital vow for richer and poorer, it was also a case of better and worse when, in 1994, they found what turned out to be the perfect home in Norfolk. That piled on pressure, too.

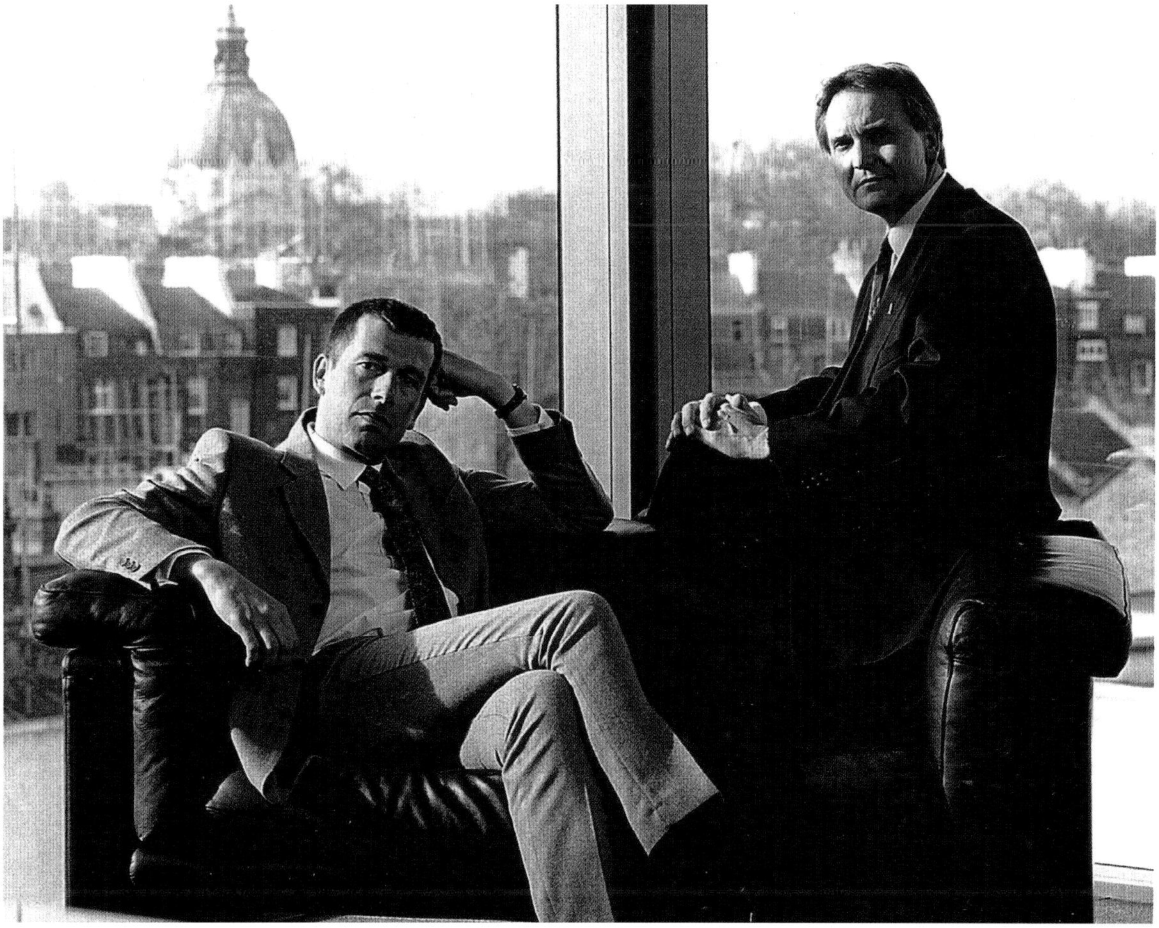

Mad Men

Gerard Stamp with advertising colleague Goff Moore, photographed in 1997 for a *New Yorker* magazine article on European advertising

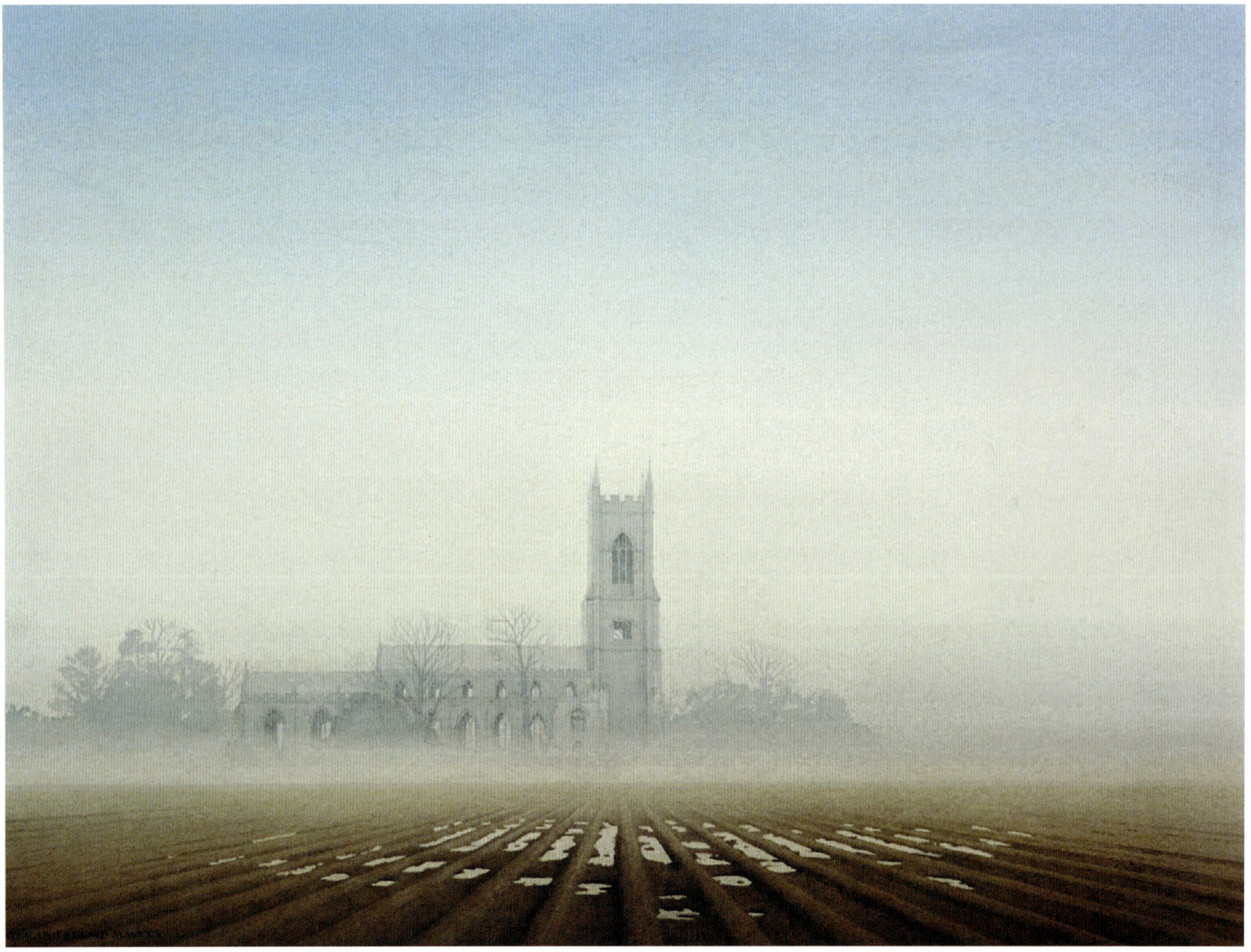

Norfolk Winter

Watercolour 2025

23.5 x 32 ins | 60 x 81 cm

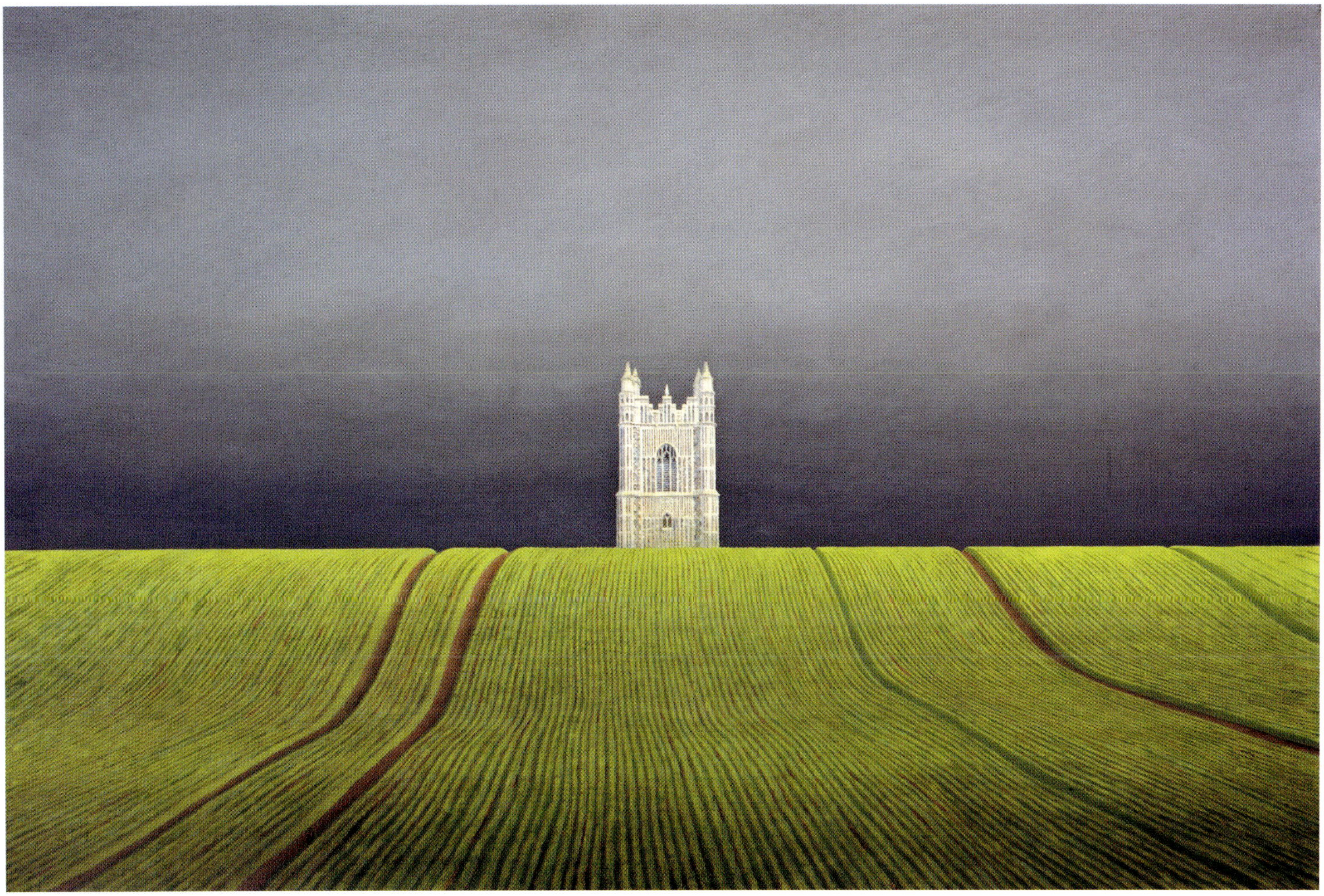

Redenhall

Oil on canvas 2017

24 x 35 ins | 61 x 89 cm

(Overleaf)

Norfolk Harvest

Watercolour 2025

23 x 32 ins | 58 x 81 cm

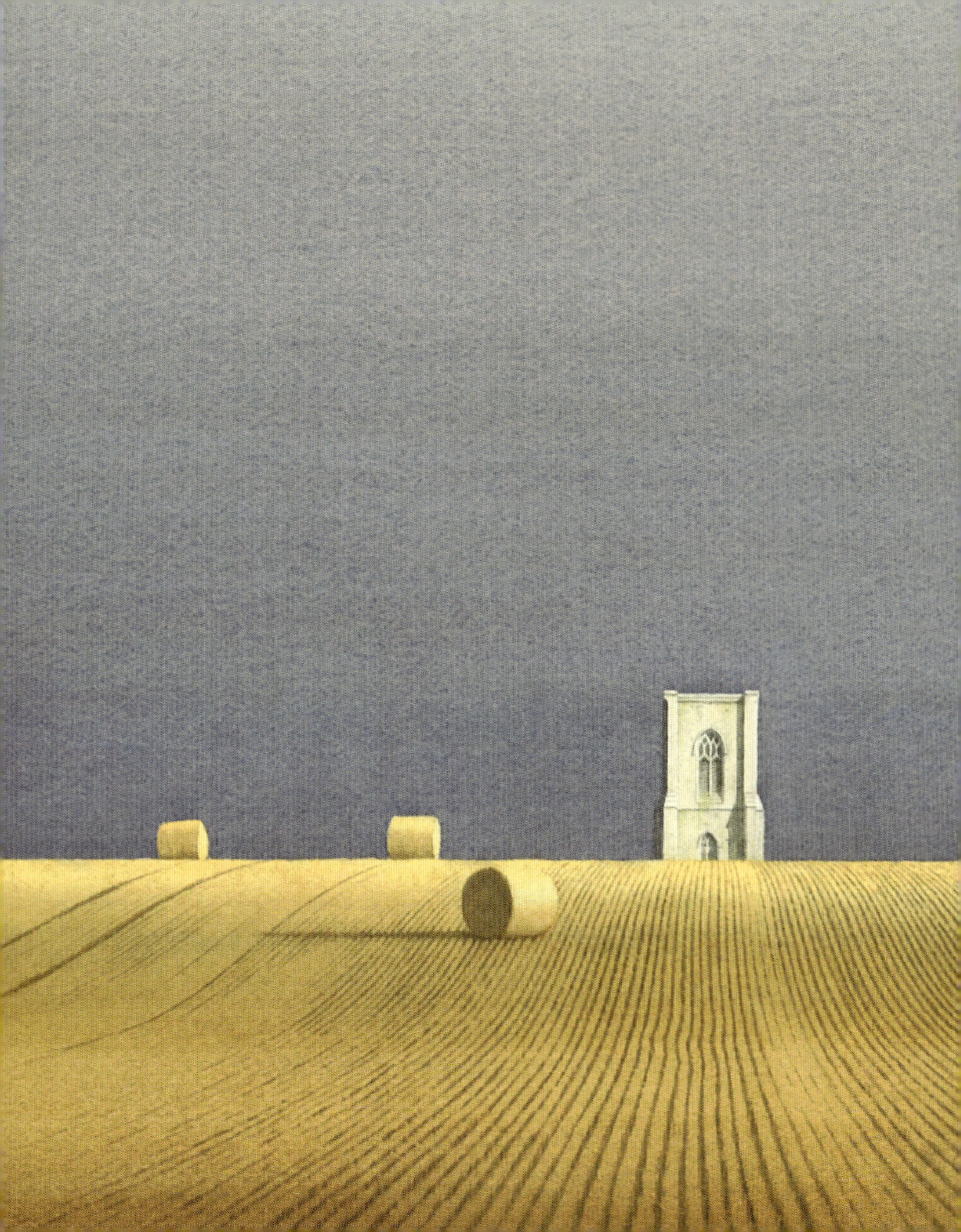

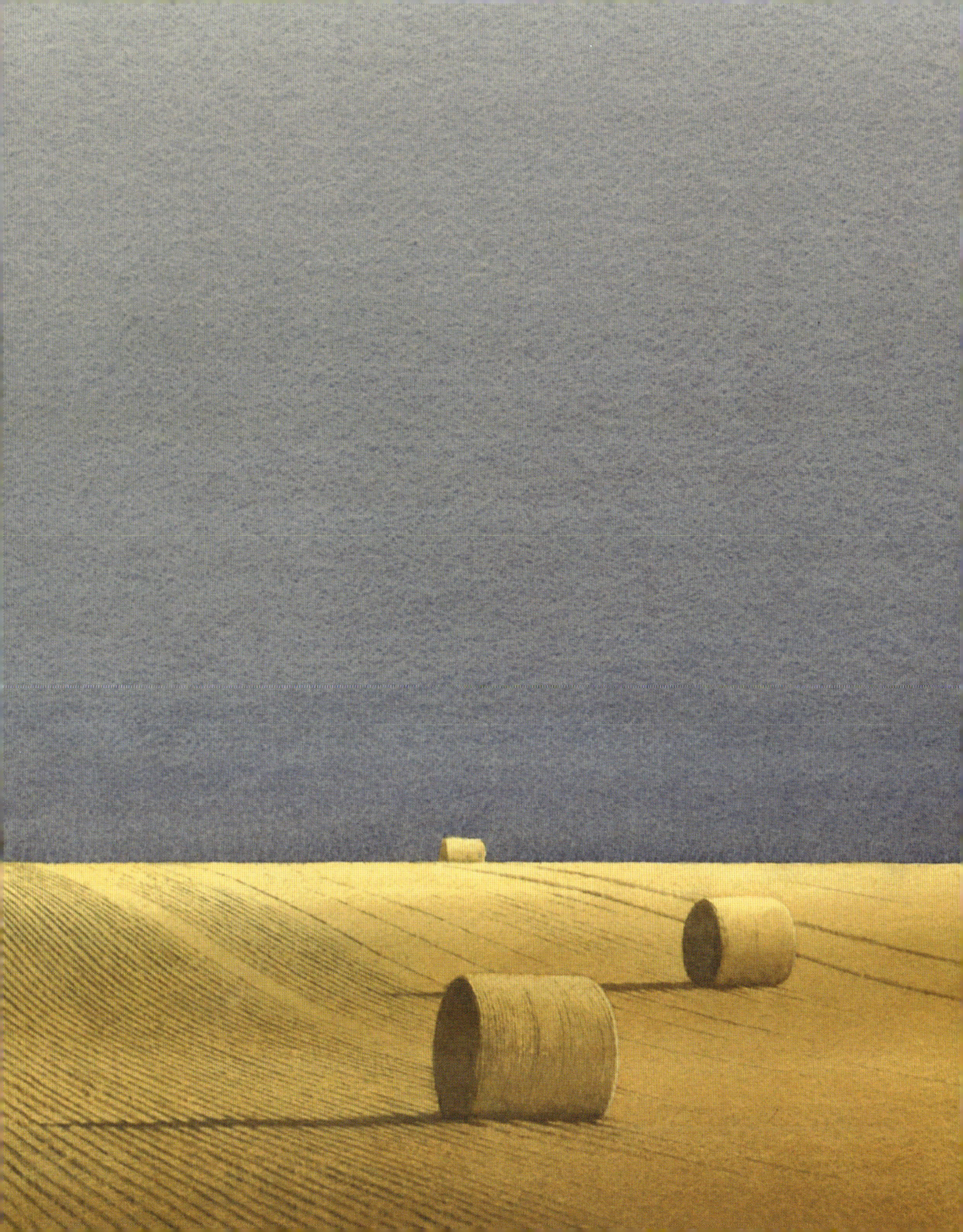

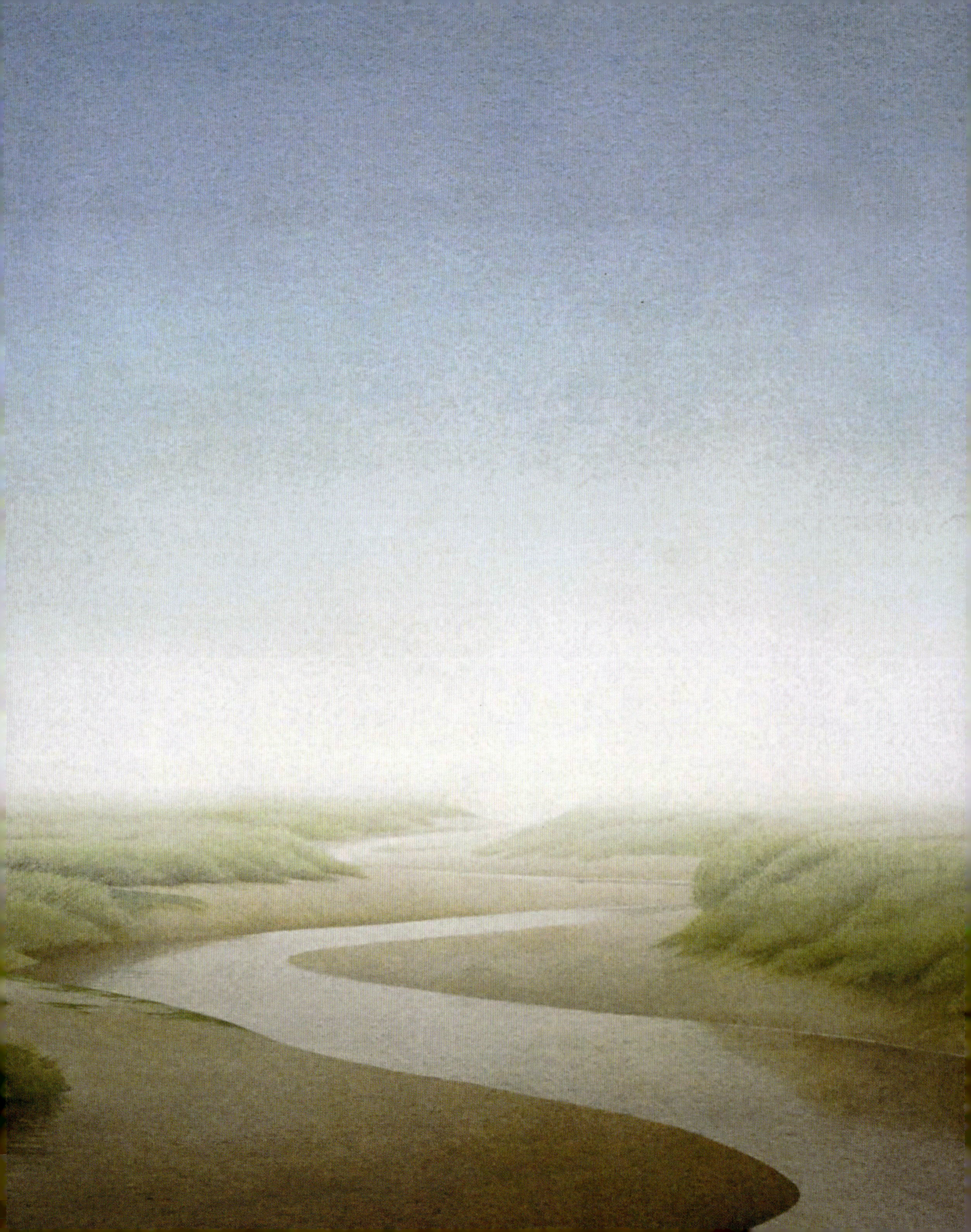

IV Norfolk for Ever

While they were still looking for a permanent Norfolk base, Gerard's mother died. His parents had moved on all their lives and never really settled. His father, Barry, would eventually marry again and remain in transit. He found late happiness but openly regretted much of his life and work choices. It was a spur to his children not to follow suit.

Now Gerard and Jacqui, given the pressing challenge of education for children of their own, hit upon Gunton Park, in the hope of a lasting home. Various rectories and farmhouses had been rejected – too expensive, too remote. 'As I was going to be on my own most of the week, I needed to be part of a community,' Jacqui says.

'A Georgian terrace in the middle of the country'

With its own stop on the railway line between Norwich and Cromer, the Gunton estate had centred on a hall built to a Palladian design for the Harbord family by architect Matthew Brettingham in 1745 after an earlier property burned down. A Robert Adam church and stately house additions by Samuel Wyatt followed soon afterwards.

A Harbord was raised to the peerage and it was the 5th Baron Suffield who achieved the family's greatest – and, as it turned out, most ruinous – social prominence. His prime shooting estate delighted Bertie, playboy Prince of Wales (the future Edward VII) who came for extended stays while Sandringham was being rebuilt.

Royal mistress Lillie Langtry might be readily concealed in a lodge, but the overall expense of extravagant hospitality could not be overlooked. In 1882, Lord Suffield, in fear of looming penury, resorted to a desperate remedy when another princely visitation was proposed. According to a story handed down through generations of Gunton tenants he instructed a maid to arrange a small fire in a guest room. It was meant to produce minimal damage and the smokescreen of a perfect excuse for Bertie and entourage not being accommodated. But the blaze took hold, and much of Gunton Hall was gutted. As, no doubt, was Lord Suffield.

A century of decline ensued before architect and entrepreneur Kit Martin bought the romantic remnant in 1,000 acres of neglected parkland, to create a cluster of interesting dwellings and, it was hoped, a community of like-minded people. In partnership with the art dealer Ivor Braka and Charles Harbord, the 13th Lord Suffield, a deer- and sheep-grazed park was to be recreated and 500,000 trees planted.

The Stamps fell for the cellared and galleried house in the rather noble service wing containing Georgian state-of-the-art kitchens by Samuel Wyatt. This was also too expensive, but Jacqui put in a 'ridiculous' offer which was accepted. Unknowingly they were in a contract race with the then Prince Andrew's former girlfriend, Koo Stark. They found out once they had won.

'It was still a gamble,' Jacqui says. 'I was concerned that we would feel like a commune, but since the divisions have been made vertically rather than horizontally, the hall has become a Georgian terrace in the middle of the country.'

In 1997 the couple quit North London in order to commit to the countryside for themselves and

Norfolk Estuary
(detail)
Watercolour 2013
34 x 55 ins | 86 x 140 cm

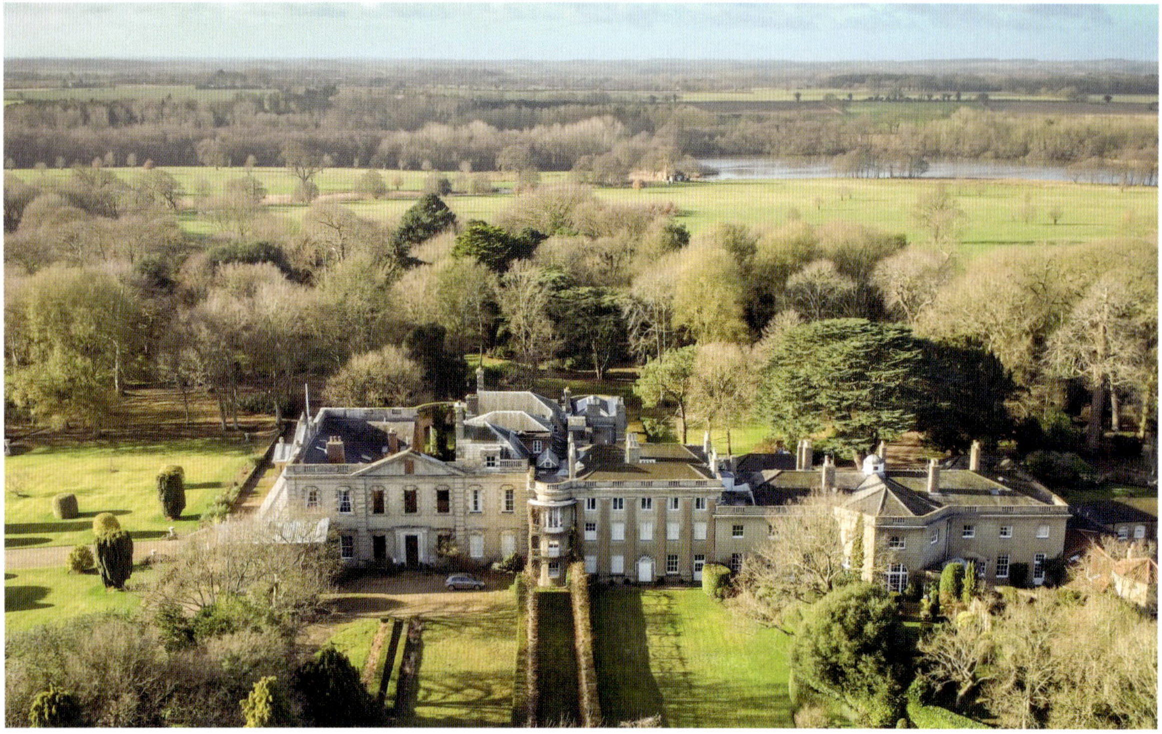

Gunton Hall and Park

The Old Kitchens are on the right, octagonal with a white bell turret. The Boathouse studio is in the distance beside the lake.

their two small children. Jacqui could acquire not only horses for riding and eventing but also a pony and trap (as well as a Land Rover and bicycles).

In another move in preparation for a different future, Gerard commissioned the total restoration of a beautiful but neglected 1932 Broads sailing cruiser. It was built by Jack Powles of Wroxham, in the yard next to that of Ernest Collins and Sons.

Jacqui had always had dogs, and now she had an ideal base for Humphry (Repton), a Norfolk terrier – and Samuel (Wyatt), a labradoodle in need of a home. When they eventually passed on to canine heaven, Viktor, a rough-haired pointer and Jackson, a multi-mix terrier, arrived.

Meanwhile the advertising executive still lived in London during the week and saw his family and his real life only at weekends. But not always even then, since work had a way of spilling over.

Gerard bought a tiny flat in Chelsea close to the agency to save time. 'Basically, I was mortgaging my life for a better future.' He continued sketching – practically as essential as breathing – but no longer had the heart to paint.

'I felt increasingly estranged from the children. They might be sitting with me doing their homework, but if they needed anything they would run and find their mother from another room. I hated returning to London and became increasingly determined that my life must change.'

He finally made the leap of faith in January 2002, when in his late forties. Ironically, the jump was determined by a bid to make him the Leo Burnett agency's global creative director, with a base in Chicago and a life on planes. Faced with blank incomprehension from colleagues, he said:

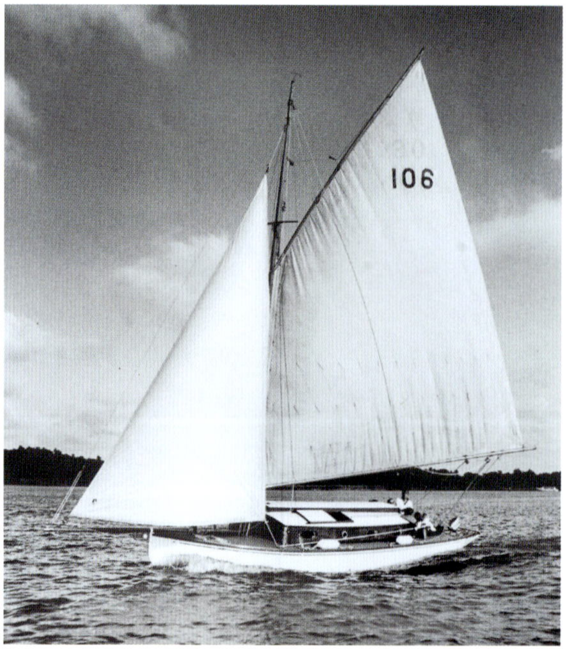

Westward V

Photographed on Barton Broad, 2001. Built by Jack Powles in 1932 for their hire fleet and restored by South River Marine, Norfolk 1997–8

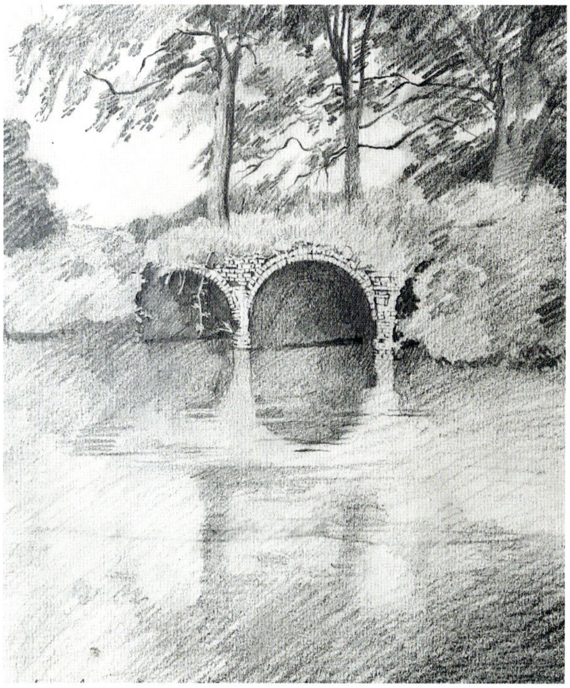

The Old Boathouse

Graphite on paper (1994)

'I sketched the ruined boathouse beside Great Water the month we moved into Gunton Park having no idea that one day we would own and restore it.' G.S.

'We all have to follow our bliss. I have to paint. No other option.'

Far from idling in a rural idyll in the painterly equivalent of a picnic, the result of this particular mid-life crisis was a creative impasse. It ran for three incomeless years.

Gerard strove to produce watercolour pictures in the great Romantic tradition from Thomas Girtin, John Sell Cotman and J.M.W. Turner to John Piper, also introducing an individual and highly personal style. For all his forensic studies of Cotman, the magic would not rub off. Deftly drawn studies refused to spring to life. A lot of experimental pieces were burned.

An easel in a corner of the bedroom only added to the problem, so a veteran commuter plotted a new work journey. Barns and Cromer flats were viewed and rejected. Then Jacqui had a brainwave which resulted in a half-mile cycle ride to a waterside studio. The sale of the Chelsea flat helped to pay for it.

'We had seen the remains of a nineteenth-century boathouse beside a thirty-acre lake,' Gerard says. 'We bought it from Kit Martin, together with a building plan – and had to take the lake as well.'

On that 1820s footprint the architect had already won planning consent for an oak- and brick-framed pavilion roofed in Norfolk thatch. Gerard extended windows overlooking the lake and

The Boathouse studio

Built 2002–2004

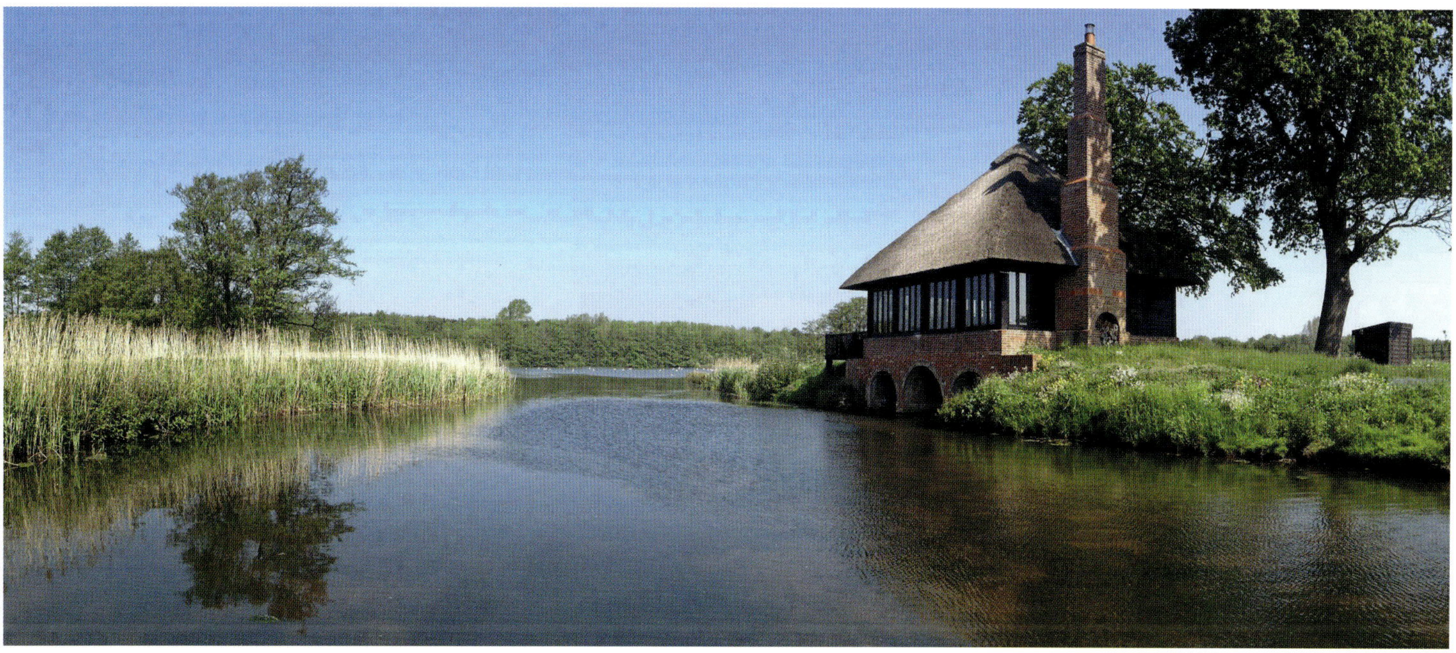

added a large fireplace and chimney to finesse a structure gently in the Arts and Crafts style and apparently growing out of the landscape.

Actually, for an initial spell it sat rather ill with the setting of a sugar beet field. Then Ivor Braka stepped in to recreate the tranquillity of eighteenth-century parkland. The lake became a nature reserve for ospreys, otters and kingfishers.

Installed since 2004, so that every picture of his professional career has been created there, Gerard Stamp has one of the loveliest workspaces of any artist currently working. It won several prizes, including the Royal Institute of British Architects Heritage Award, for a new building in a historic context.

'In reality it is not very practical as a studio,' he counters. 'It's hard to heat. And being south and west facing, the blinds have to be pulled down half the time, but that's a small price to pay for the stunning location. I sit facing the lake. Some people wonder how I ever get any work done, but to look out onto a Site of Special Scientific Interest is a wonderful relief from the intensity of painting.' It is also a social hub – and one of the key reasons why an artist of frequent and widespread travels is always happy when heading home. Once asked to describe his perfect day, he said: 'Wake up without a hangover, finish a painting that turns out much better than I ever dreamt it would. Sit in late afternoon sun overlooking the water, with my family and close friends.

'We will drink champagne, eat fresh asparagus, local leg of lamb – barbecued – and sticky toffee pudding. I will play some blues on the piano and get to bed fully expecting to wake with a hangover!'

While the studio was being built, and he was still in creative limbo, Gerard attended some adult life-drawing classes in Norwich. He tried lots of rapid – one- to ten-minute – sketches in pure watercolour to train his hand and eye. These exercises were another part of the casting around before he could cast off as an artist.

It was in the boathouse that he had his eureka moment. After one especially frustrating session, a mediocre image was dumped in a sink. That act of rejection turned out to be the best thing he ever did. The following morning water had erased most of the pencil and colour marks but a ghostly

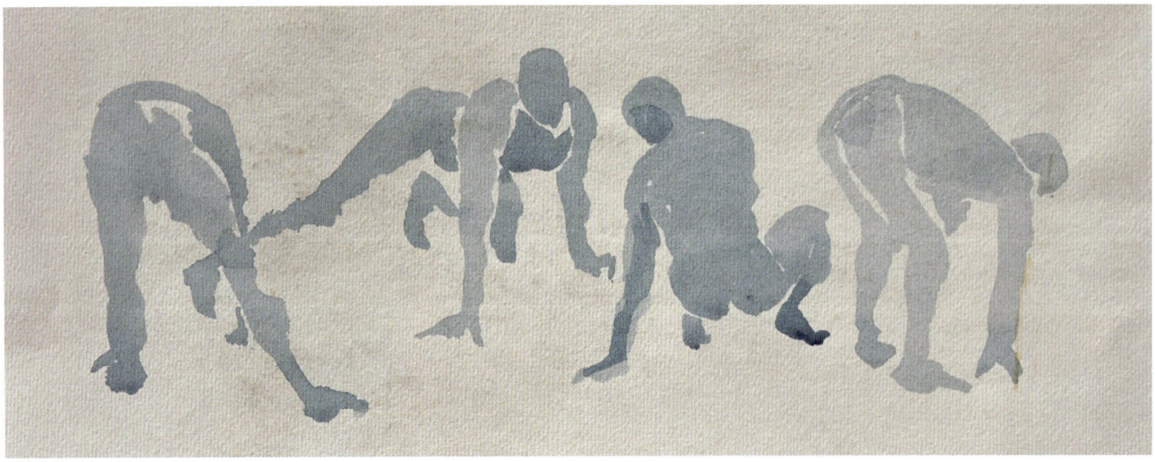

One-minute life drawing sketches

Watercolour 2003

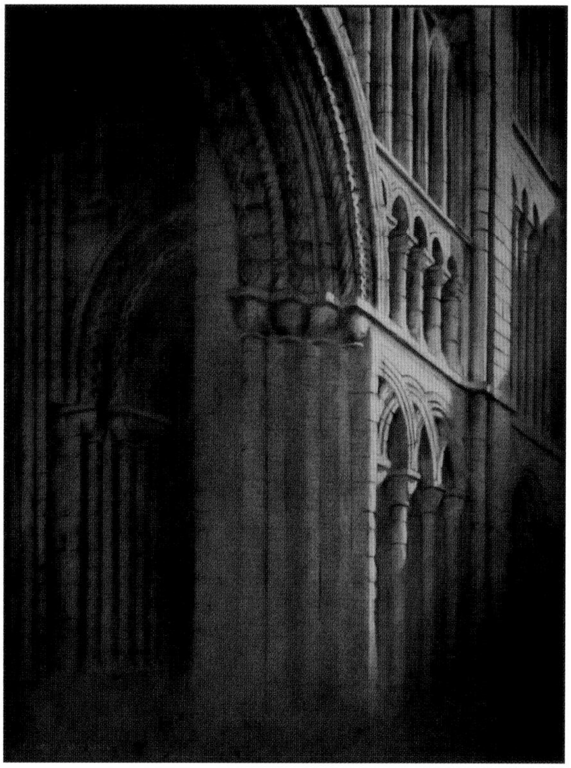

Castle Acre Priory

Charcoal 2005

42 x 33 ins | 107 x 84 cm

vestige remained as the foundation for a haunting picture. He had found a new way of working. 'It's not one that I would recommend,' he says, laughing. 'But it is exciting.'

The artist discusses his unorthodox technique in an afterword to this monograph. Suffice to say here that his exquisite compositions require sturdy materials to weather an exceptionally rigorous production process.

Using rough Arches paper and natural gelatin size, he slowly builds up an image of immense depth and detail before attacking it with a sponge. Then the building and sponging all over again: on, off; on, off; on and on and on.

Evoking atmosphere – breathing life and spirit into the picture through an impression of layered centuries – is a long and painstaking process. Gerard will be forever grateful to Jacqui, first viewer and best critic of his evolving work. 'Her response is more natural, less emotional than mine,' he says.

Having always seen herself as a designer, Jacqui had no desire to paint. But Eleanor-Rose was out sketching with her dad from an early age, and it was soon clear that she had the flair as well as the drive. She was also a gymkhana child – wanting to jump back on a horse as soon as she was thrown.

Rupert was rather to alarm his parents when an inveterate teenage gamer. In fact, both daughter and son were picking up future careers with their own take on fascination and dedication. Just like Dad...

By a process of observation, selection and obsessive effort, Gerard was now elevating telling detail in watercolours of daunting scale. It was all about the quality of light and shadow and tone and colour playing on weathered stone, brick, tile and wood.

Then huge charcoal drawings further emphasised the elemental and monumental – after the drawing medium was treated every bit as rigorously as watercolour. A massive early view

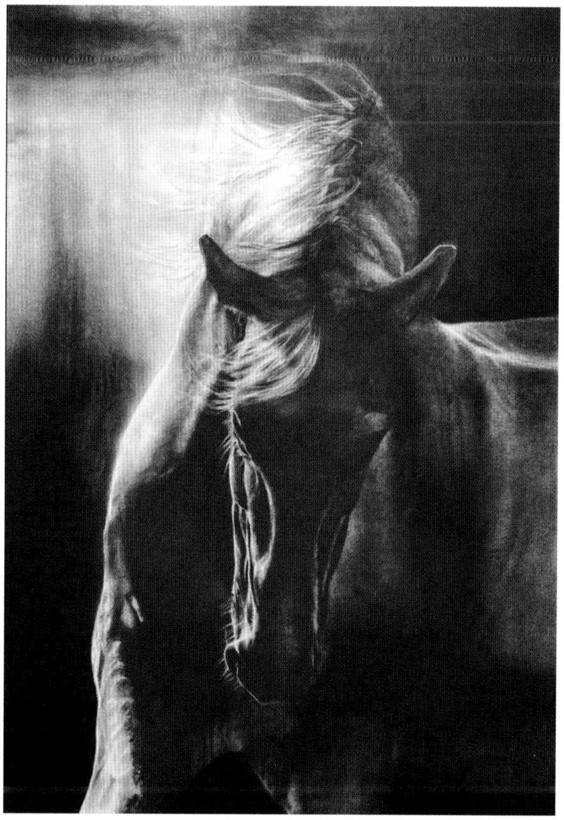

Shoulder In

by Eleanor-Rose Stamp

Charcoal 2025

29.5 x 25.5 in | 75 x 65 cm

of Castle Acre Priory was a masterly exercise in perspective. The artist would always choose his vantage point with care.

And whether achieved in pigment or monochrome, the sensation being recorded was the intensity of a particular moment of calm – in misty dawn, noon blaze, golden afternoon, shaded dusk and blue moonlight – within the immensity of time.

Now he was up and running, steadily creating a body of work through responses to Norfolk churches and priories, and also to the great building he knew best of all: Norwich Cathedral. And his focus spilled into Suffolk, where he followed Cotman and Piper and many others to the ship-like ruined church at Covehithe, above the cliffs north of Southwold. It became a favourite composition.

For all the remaining beauty, he was well aware that the region's great fifteenth-century burst of church building owed as much to ostentation as piety. He knew, too, that Taliban iconoclasm English-style – the stripping of the altars and the smashing of devotional art – was especially acute in sixteenth- and seventeenth-century East Anglia.

Between the bouts of vandalism these historic buildings have waged epic battle not with sin but nature. The strength of medieval masons may be pitted manfully against wind and ice and rain. But in the end, for masonry too near the edge, it is no match for marauding waves.

With rising seas and retreating shores, the church at Covehithe could topple over the cliff within decades – like the dozen churches, chapels and religious houses of Suffolk's great medieval port of Dunwich, whose wrecks now lie miles out to sea. This tension of physical survival and oblivion – of permanent peril – is somehow evoked alongside spiritual peace in a Gerard Stamp picture, and as much or more so when the buildings were removed.

For now, in eerie charcoal panoramas and watercolours, again often of dazzling size, he set

Steppe

by Arkhip Kuindzhi c1895

Oil on canvas

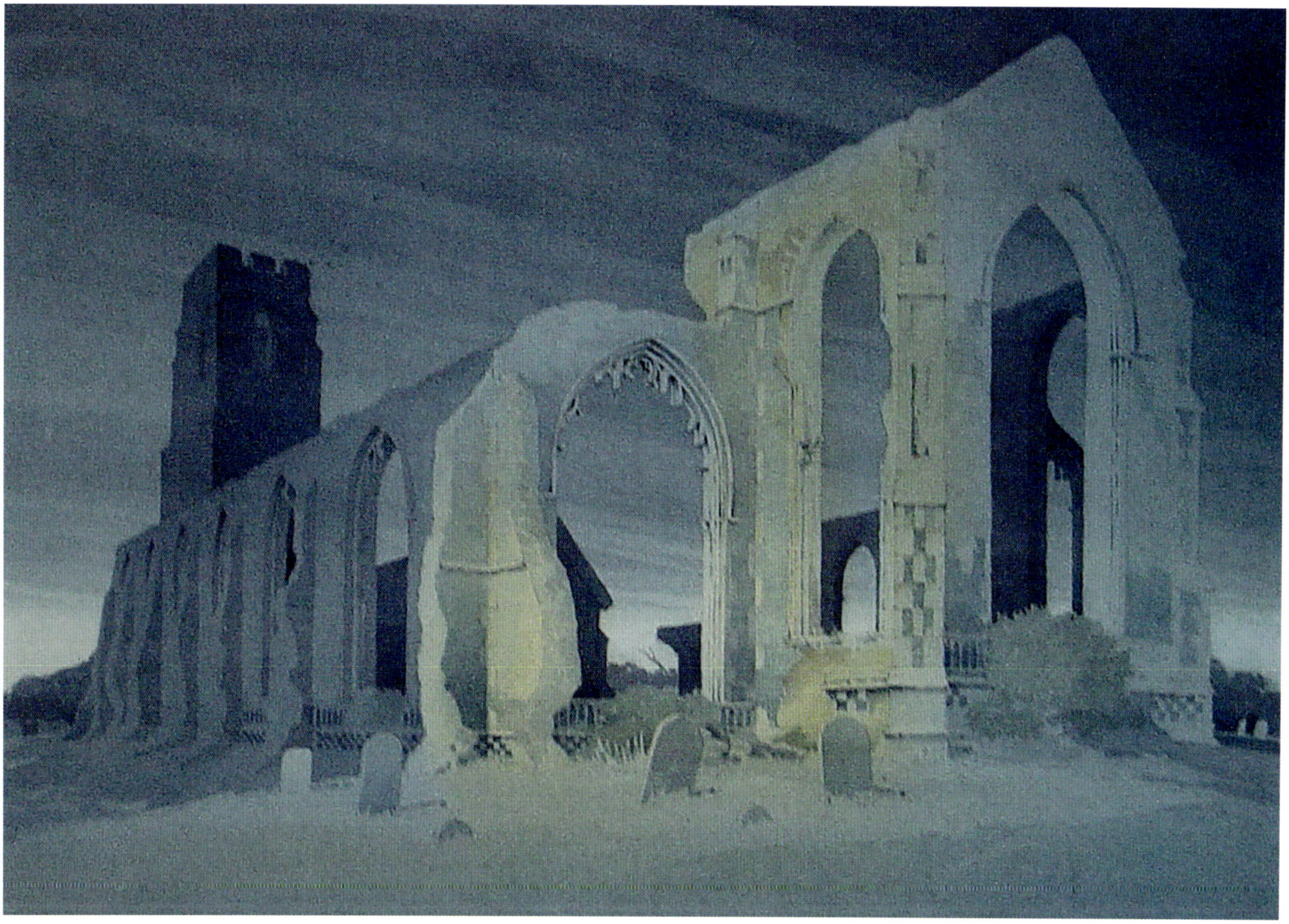

Covehithe

Watercolour 2002

17 x 24 ins | 43 x 61 cm

about evoking ethereal and monumental Norfolk saltmarshes. The method of their making, via repeated accretion and erosion, echoed the action of wind and wave daily and millennially.

An extraordinary *Russian Landscape in the Age of Tolstoy* exhibition, at the National Gallery over the summer of 2004, had been a ravishing revelation. The nineteenth-century painter Arkhip Kuindzhi stood out with panoramic pictures of the Russian steppes in luminous colour which seemed to be without precedent. Now, far from home, such superb and sublime simplicity lit a spark in one inspired viewer.

(Overleaf)

Stiffkey Freshes

Watercolour 2009

21 x 37 ins | 53 x 94 cm

On the unstable and undefended coast between Thornham and Morston, via Brancaster and Stiffkey, Gerard drew out an epic drama in depictions of terrain like miniature Amazonian river basins and oceanic archipelagos. Marsh gullies loomed as large in Stamp imagery as Grand Canyons wrought in rock.

Sea lavender forests seemed suspended in sea fret. Poised at low tide as if for a returning tsunami, mudded margins – neither landscape nor seascape – appeared to be dissolving into light. All these vast impressions amid the stark fact that a now unrepaired shingle bank protecting saltmarshes at Cley-next-the-Sea was being pushed back on average by a metre a year.

Great art should never reveal the manner of its making – just as a masterpiece must retain an element of enigma, a core of mystery which cannot be explained away. It's that strange alchemy by which laborious effort is suddenly recast as magician's work.

But an image of creative certainty rests on humility and hidden struggle. As Gerard has said:

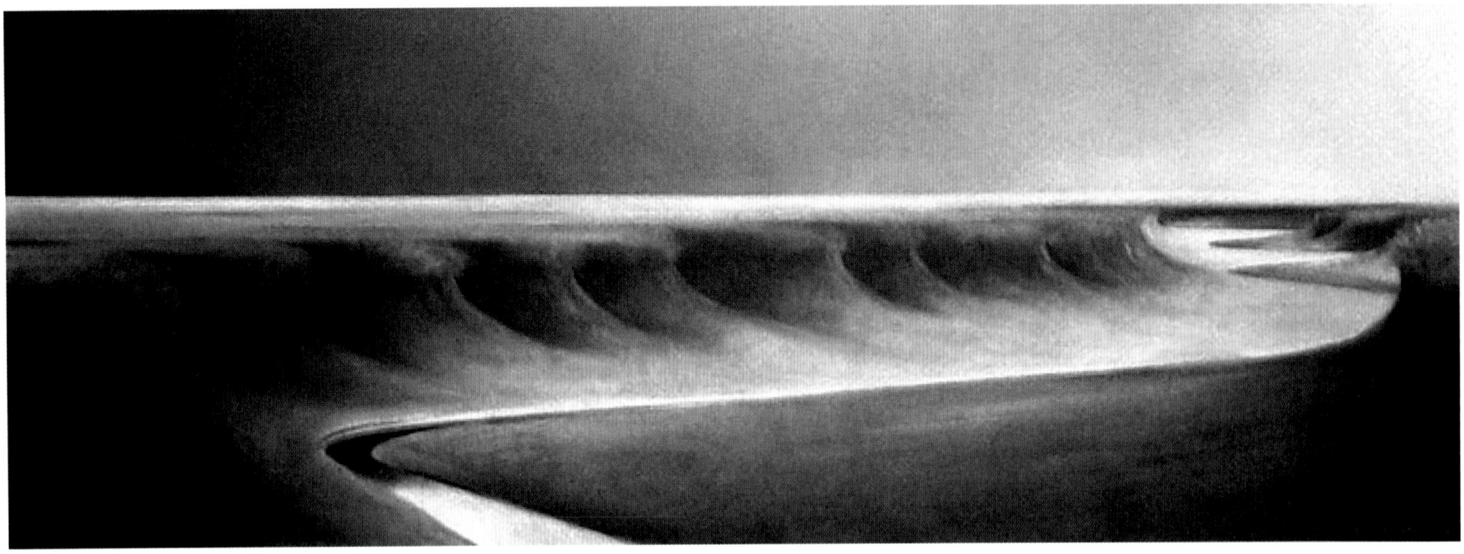

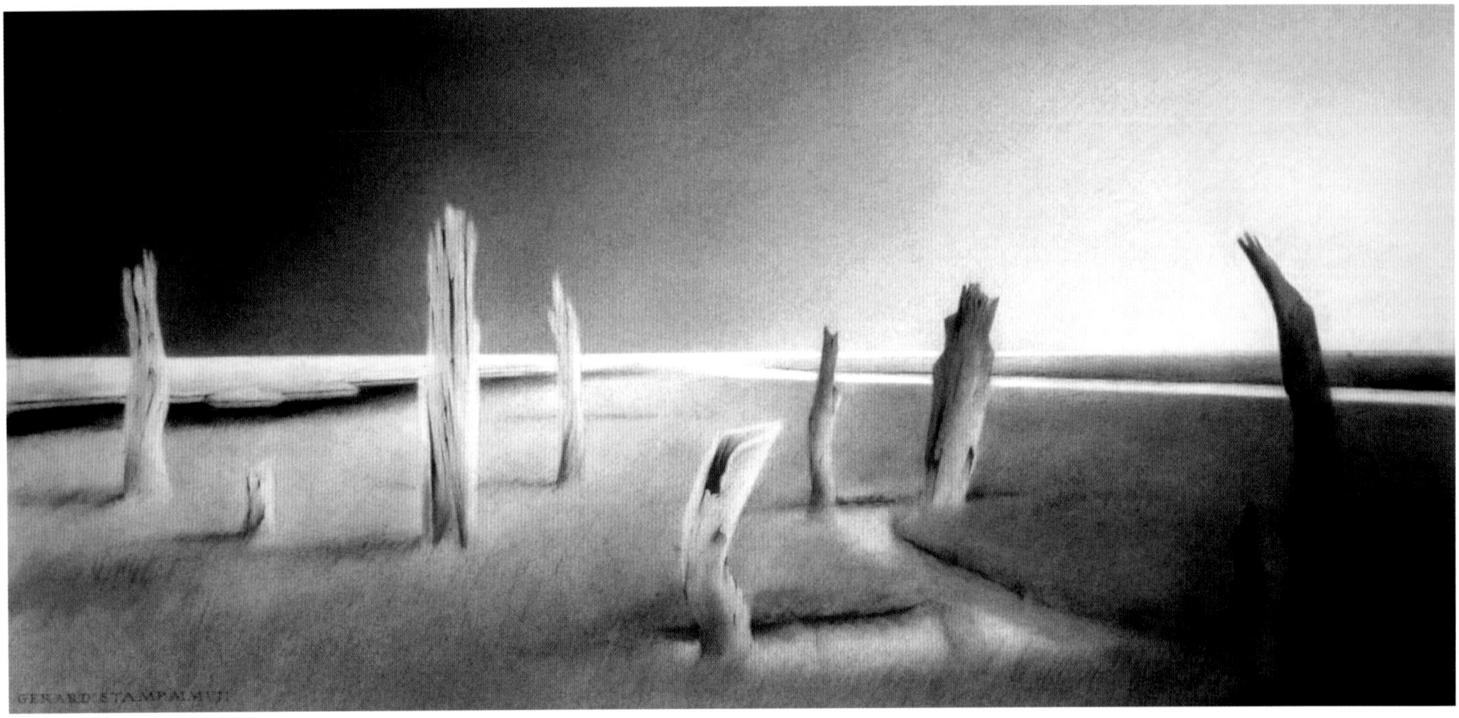

Morston Panorama

Charcoal, winner of the inaugural Norwich Castle

Open Art Show 2005 24 x 72 ins | 61 x 183 cm

Thornham Old Harbour

Charcoal 2007

18 x 38 ins | 46 x 96 cm

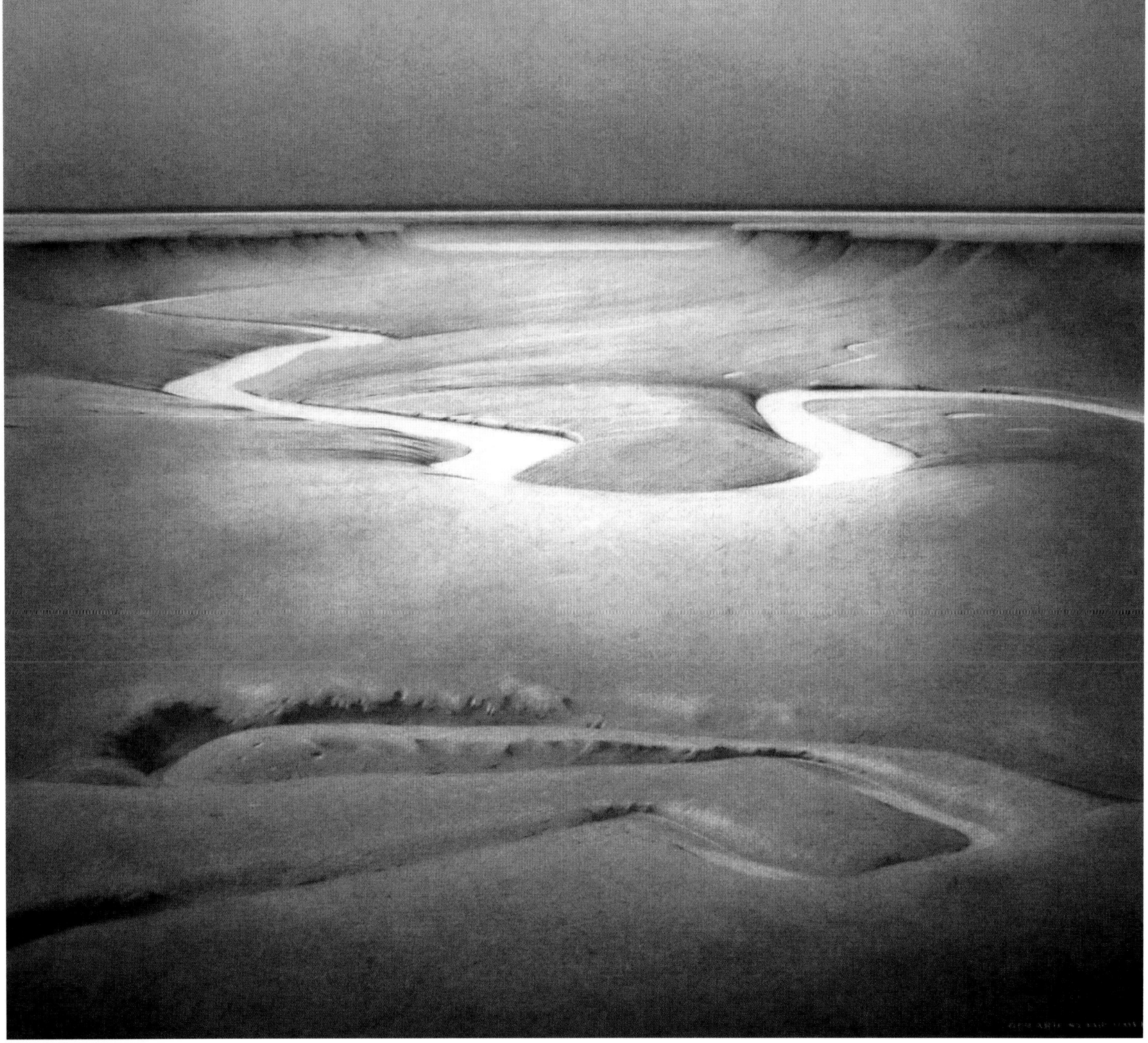

Follow Me Follow

Charcoal 2007

35 x 42 ins | 89 x 107 cm

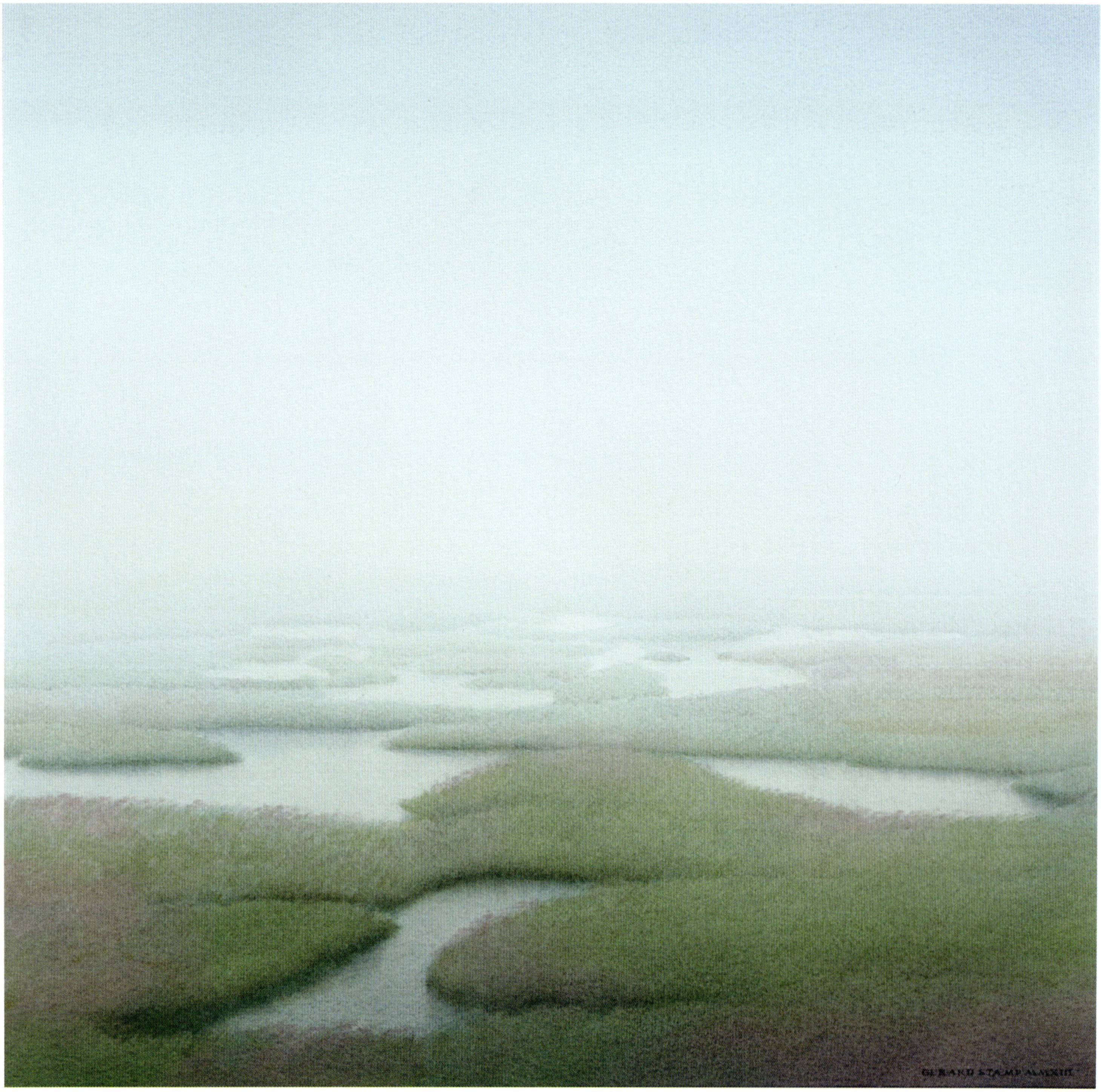

Saltmarsh Fret

Watercolour 2013

36 x 37 ins | 91 x 94 cm

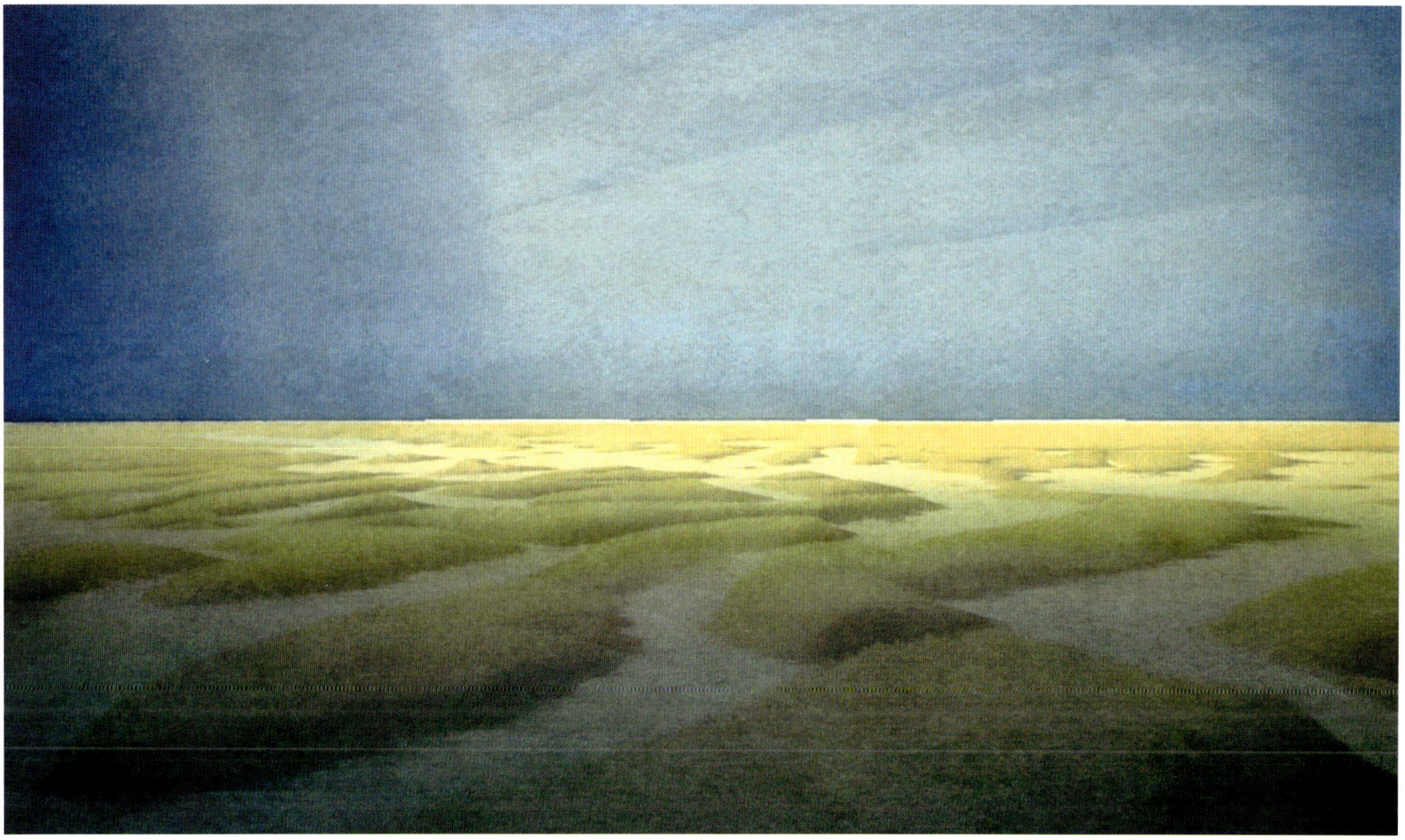

Samphire Beds

Morston

Watercolour 2007

21.5 x 37 ins | 54 x 94 cm

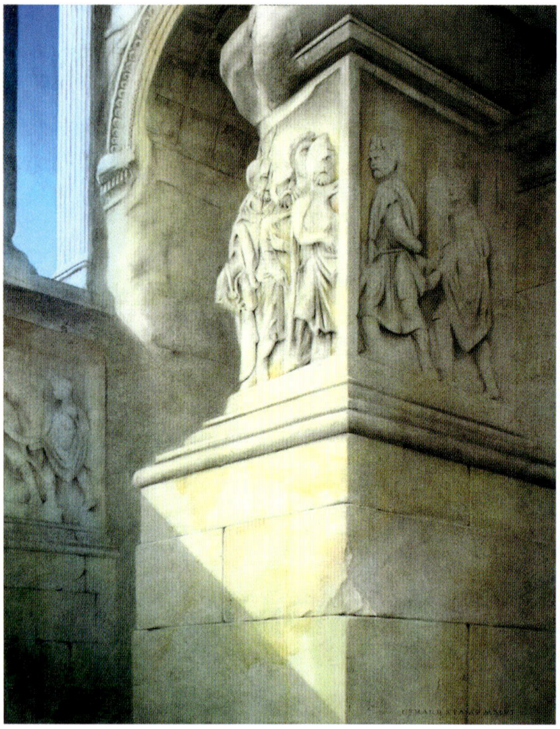

Arch of Severus, Rome

Watercolour and charcoal 2006

42 x 30 ins | 107 x 76 cm

'I am never satisfied with what I paint. I doubt my abilities all the time. Throwing away many pictures has taught me how to rescue things that I thought unrescuable. It's amazing how much you can abuse watercolour and charcoal.'

Teaming up with his neighbour Peter Low, who co-founded the Grapevine gallery with his wife, Alison, Gerard Stamp had a first solo exhibition in Norwich in 2005. He asked Peter to drop him off at his old school so that he could walk to the private view, where Alex Humphris was among the throng, as if to erase the intervening decades.

It was a masterly debut delivered at the age of fifty – and a sellout just for starters. Gerard was astounded. 'I had thought "Whoever is going to buy a picture of some obscure old church?"'

Eleven years and nearly as many exhibitions into their partnership, Peter Low summed everything up when he wrote: 'Over the years I have watched and listened, and yet to me – more familiar with his work than many – it remains a mystery and a wondrous mystery. Yes, his technique is painstaking and his skill consummate but it is that ineffable and inexplicable ability to turn the intangible into the tangible that is fundamental. One might reasonably expect to have become conditioned to this – to no longer be surprised – but this is not the case. With each painting, I still experience that thrill first felt some twelve years ago when he made that leap from competence to miraculous, the same thrill that others tell me they feel when they first see his work.'

Meanwhile, in October 2006, there was a second successful launch via Peter Low in London's Cork Street. The subject range now extended to Lincolnshire churches and abbeys, York and Ely cathedrals, and ancient relics (Arch of Severus, Forum fragments, Pyramid of Cestius, Temple of Hadrian) in Rome.

The campaigning nature of the brothers Stamp was also demonstrated in the 10 per cent tithe from sales of York Minster pictures donated to the development appeal – a vital fund since the lightning strike and fire of 1984. The suite of pictures was also exhibited

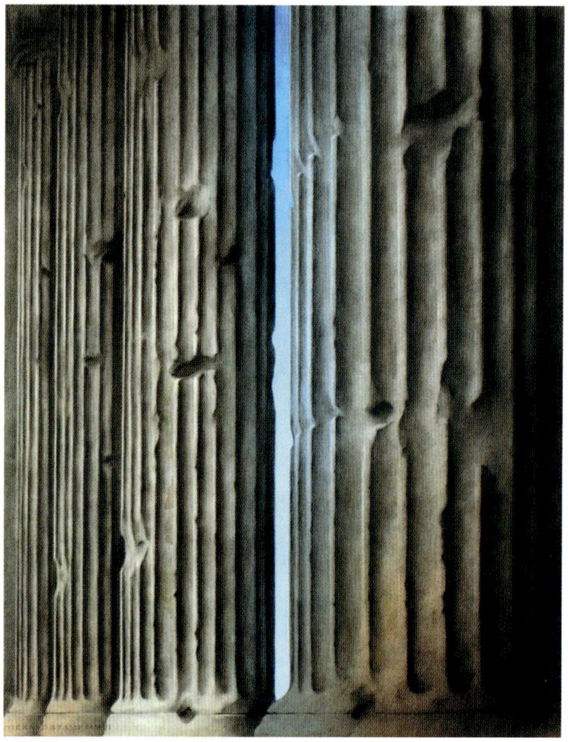

Temple of Hadrian, Rome

Watercolour and charcoal 2006

43 x 32 ins | 109 x 81 cm

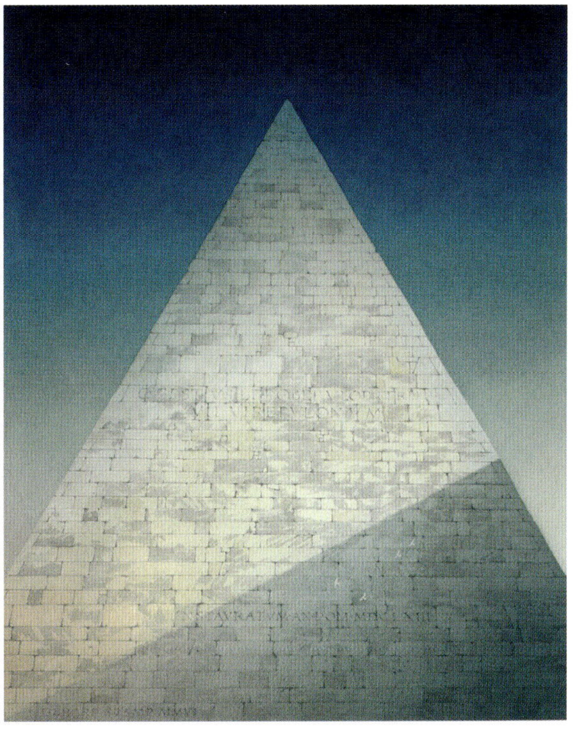

Pyramid of Cestius
Rome
Watercolour 2006
32 x 24 ins | 81 x 61 cm

in the Minster's undercroft. That set a pattern as Gerard would further assist specific buildings and the Norfolk Churches Trust, East Anglian Air Ambulance and the East Anglian Children's Hospice. National bodies such as the Churches Conservation Trust and SAVE Britain's Heritage were also aided.

A catalogue foreword had been sought from the architectural historian Dan Cruickshank – friend and brother in arms of Gavin, whom the artist had known by association many years earlier. The might-be writer was intrigued by small photos but unsure whether the original works would possess 'artistic power and presence, the force to overwhelm and capture the imagination, or were no more than competent illustrations'.

So Gerard was invited to take sample pictures to the Cruickshank house in Spitalfields, the London district of seventeenth-century silk weavers' houses behind Liverpool Street station lately saved from bulldozers. As Dan Cruickshank went on to write: 'It was instantly clear that in a miraculous and magical way Gerard had – through a process of hard work, and critical observation – achieved something wonderful. He had, while toiling alone in Norfolk, blossomed, come of age as an artist of skill, power and originality… What was obvious immediately is that Stamp is a man with a mission, on a quest to capture, express and communicate his feelings for the architecture and the places he loves, that move him. Clearly he is obsessed with the quality of light and muted colour, the sense of space and the architecture of Norfolk – it inspires and fascinates him…

'The great thing is that these watercolours give you the eye to see familiar things in an exciting, inspiring, new and strangely unfamiliar way. They are haunting, challenging and reveal the beauty around us that we so often take for granted and are blind to. They make you think and yearn. They make you want to rush out and look at buildings. What more could any artist do?'

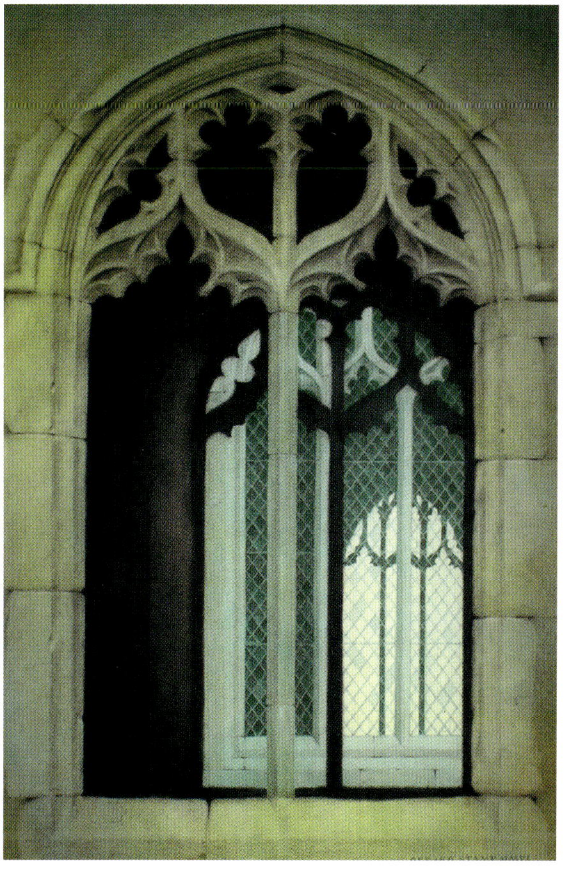

Porch Windows, Salle
Watercolour and charcoal 2006
27 x 17 ins | 68 x 43 cm

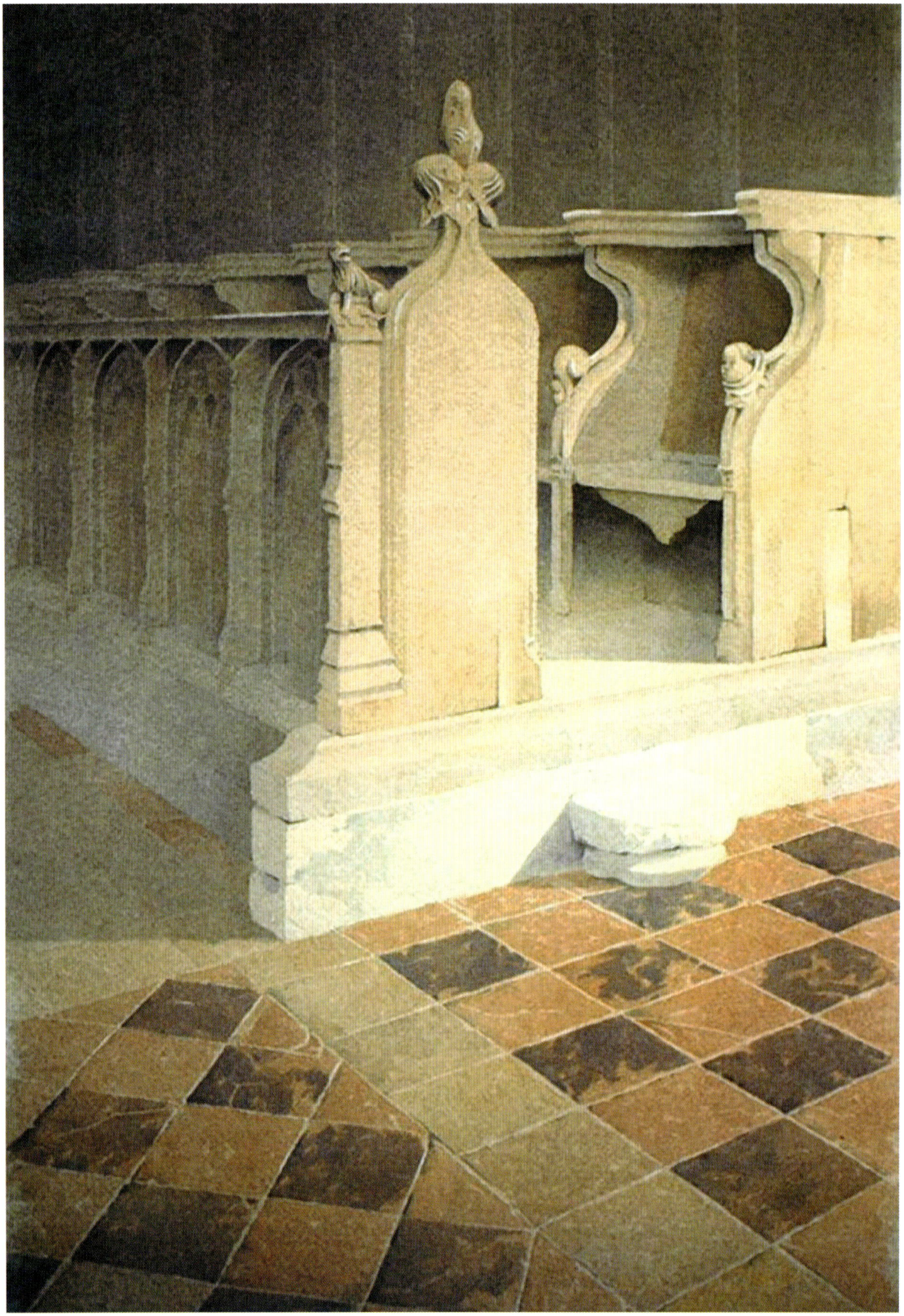

Salle Church Stalls

Watercolour 2006

21 x 15 ins | 53 x 38 cm

'Sir John Betjeman once said "Lovers of Norfolk churches can never agree which is the best and I think one is either a Salle or a Cawston man." Between the two I'll go for Salle, but in truth I'm a Binham man.' G.S.

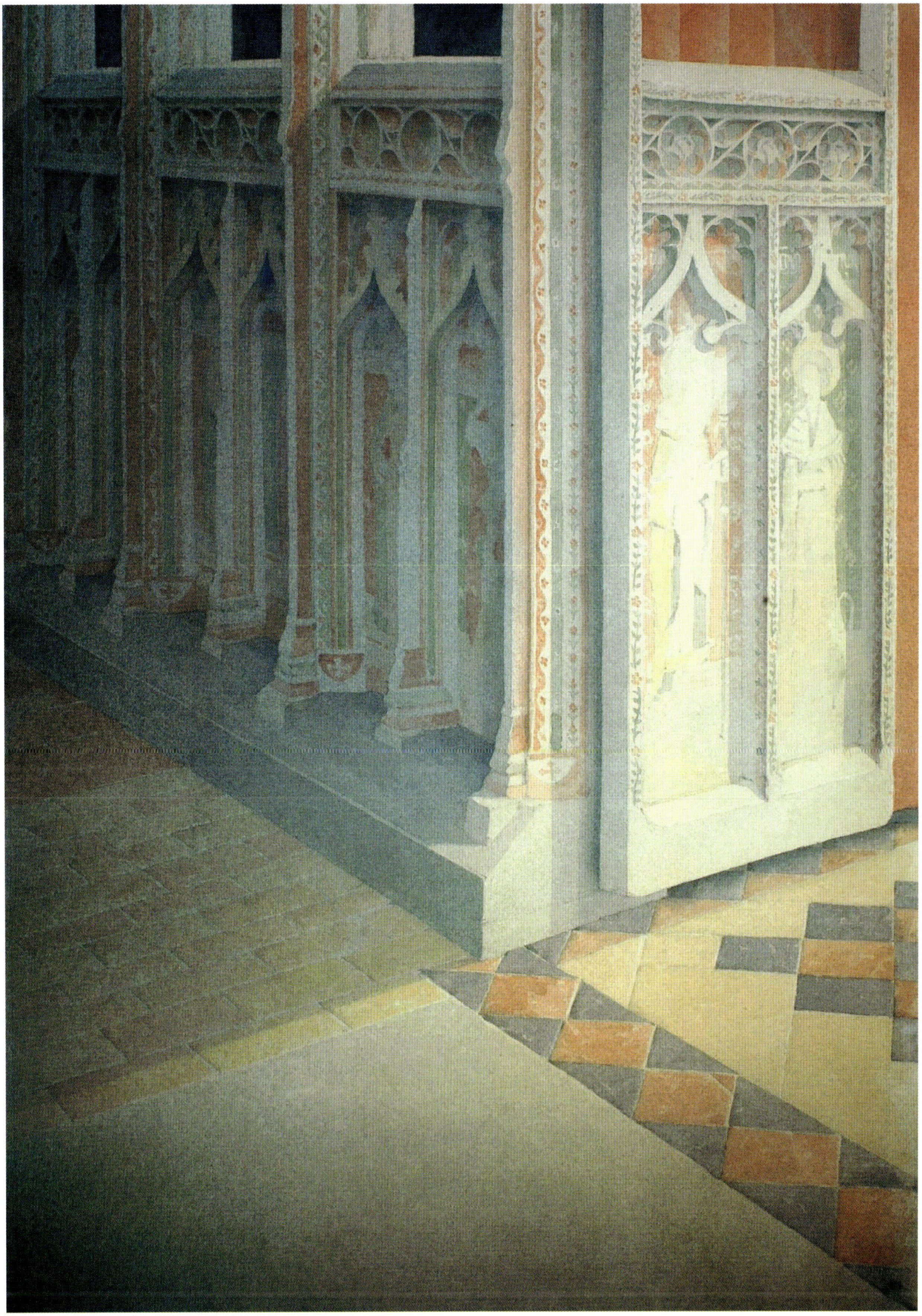

Cawston Screen

Watercolour 2006

21 x 16 ins | 53 x 41 cm

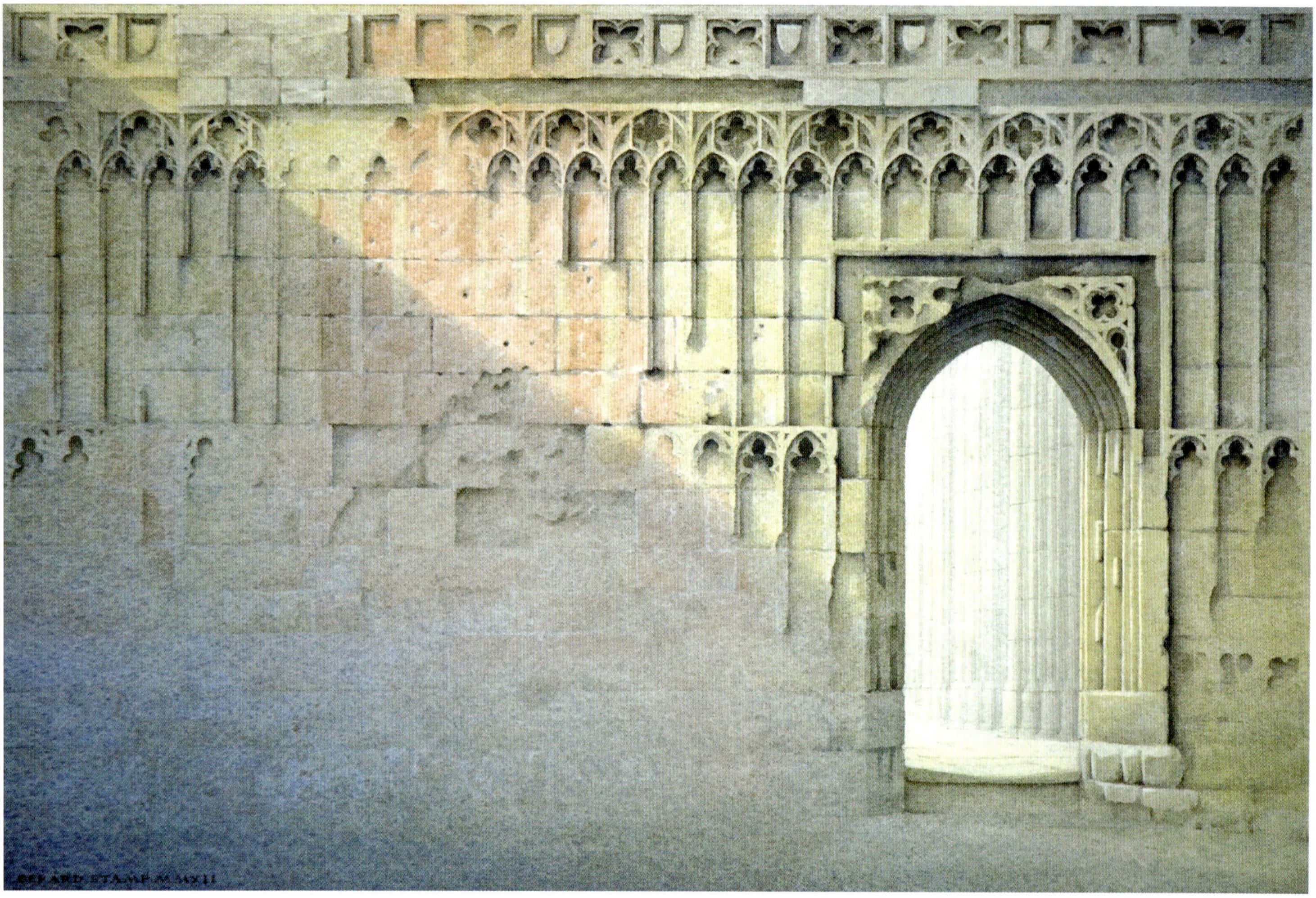

Pulpitum Screen II

Crowland Abbey

Watercolour 2012

17 x 25 ins | 43 x 63 cm

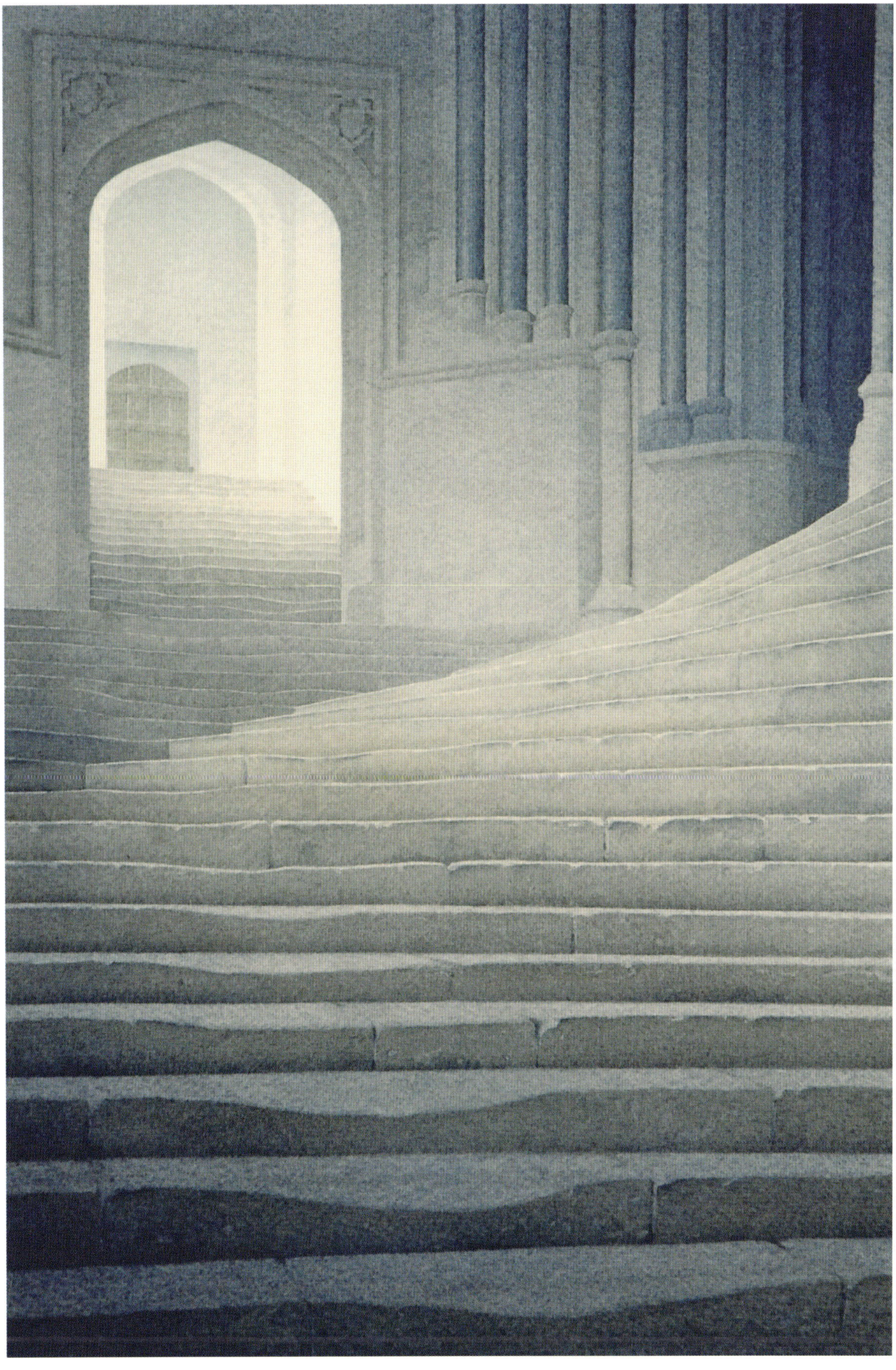

Chapter House Steps

Wells Cathedral

Watercolour 2012

24 x 16.5 ins | 61 x 42 cm

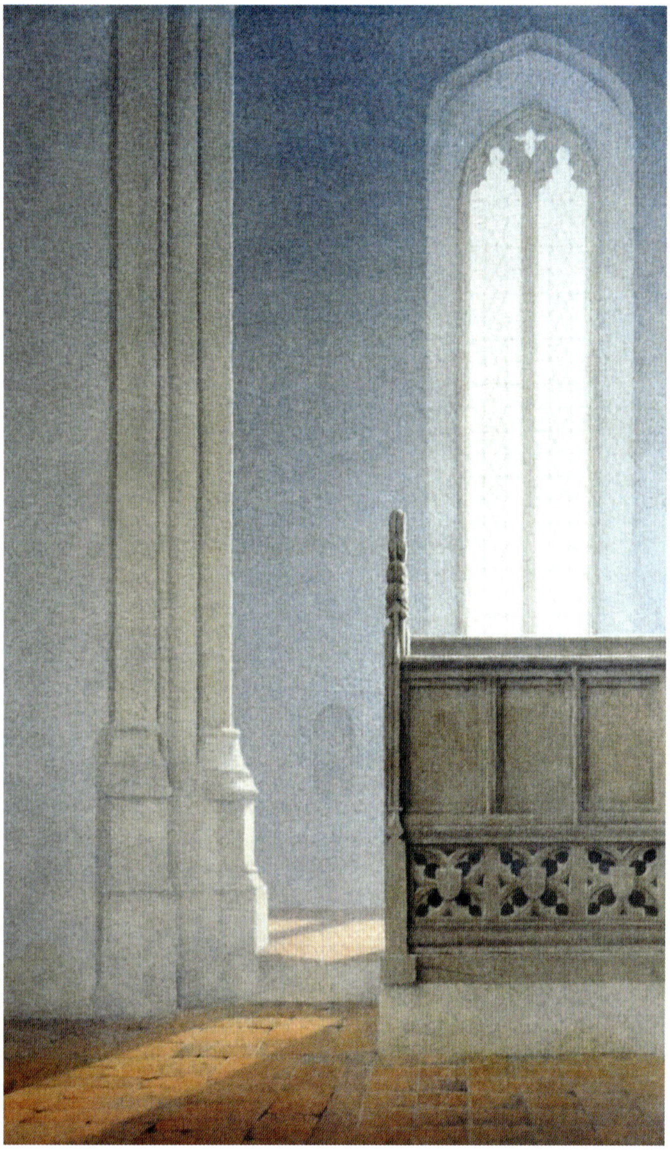

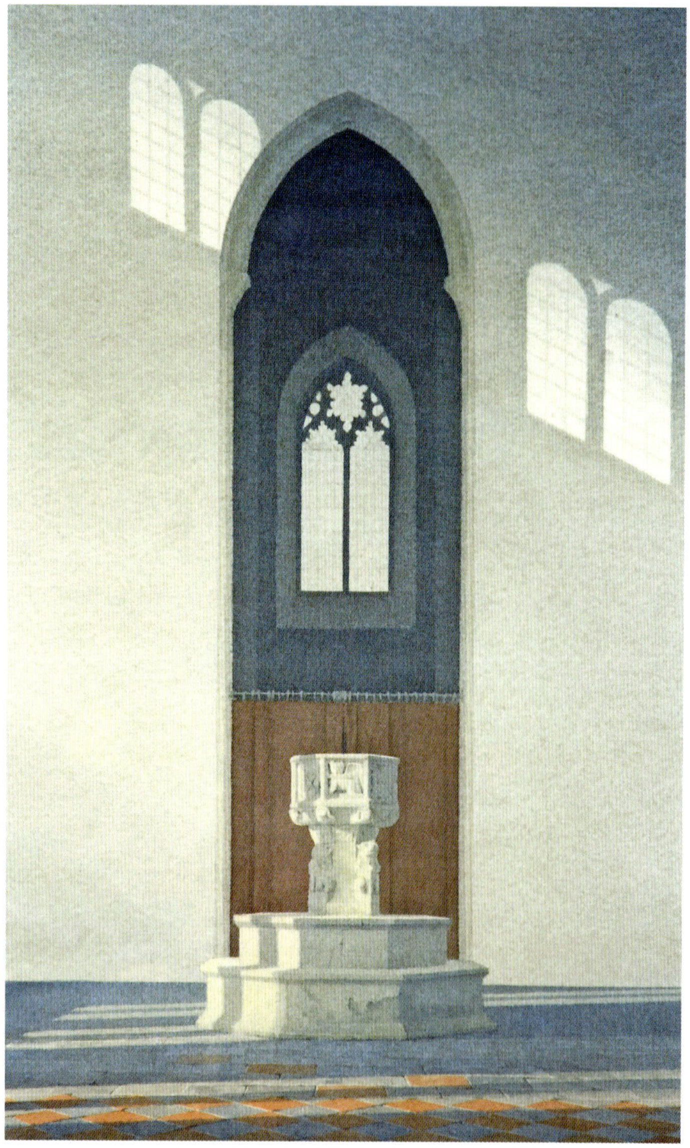

Salthouse Light I

Watercolour 2011

24 x 15 ins | 61 x 38 cm

Salthouse Light II

Watercolour 2012

24 x 15 ins | 61 x 38 cm

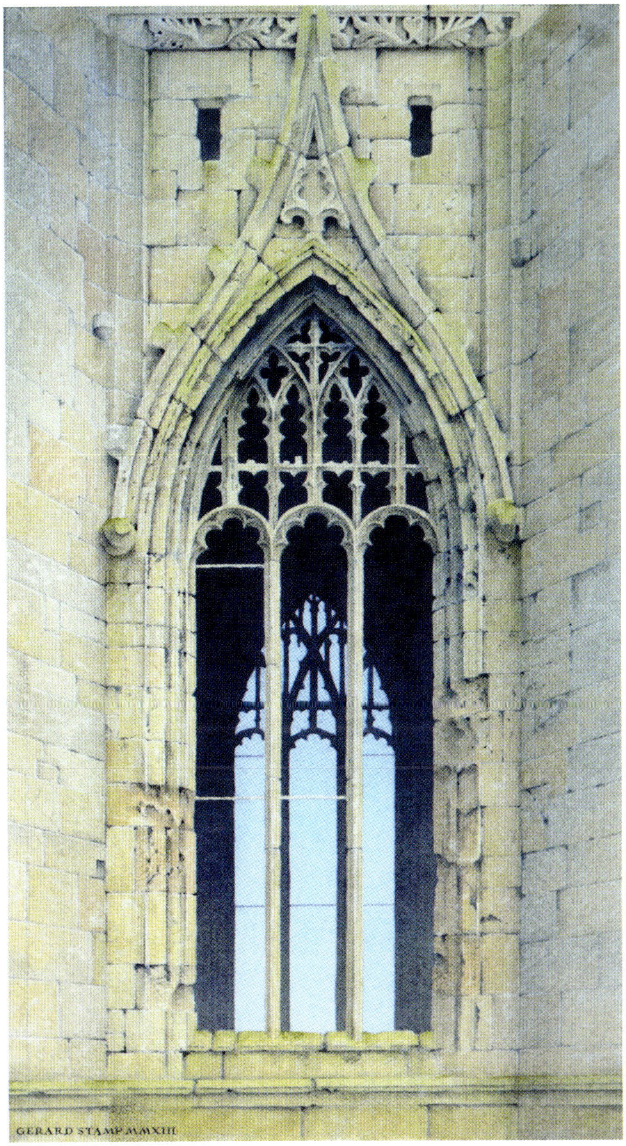

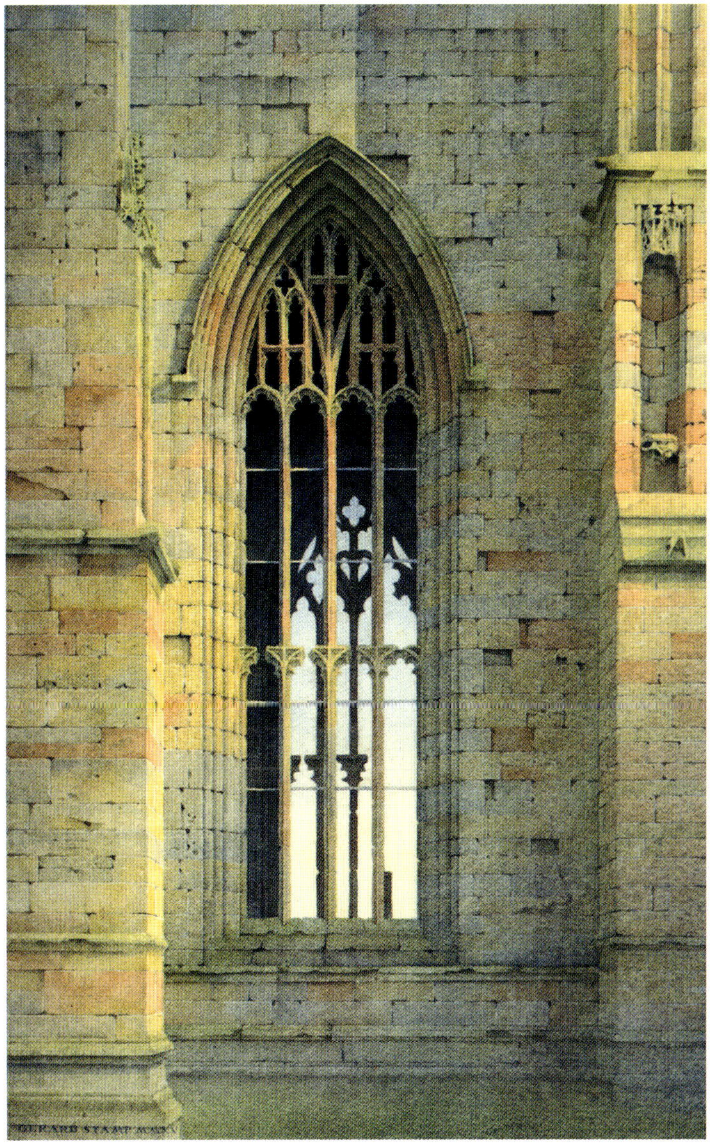

Chapter House Windows

Howden

Watercolour 2013

24 x 15 ins | 61 x 38 cm

Melrose Abbey

Watercolour 2015

24 x 18 ins | 61 x 46 cm

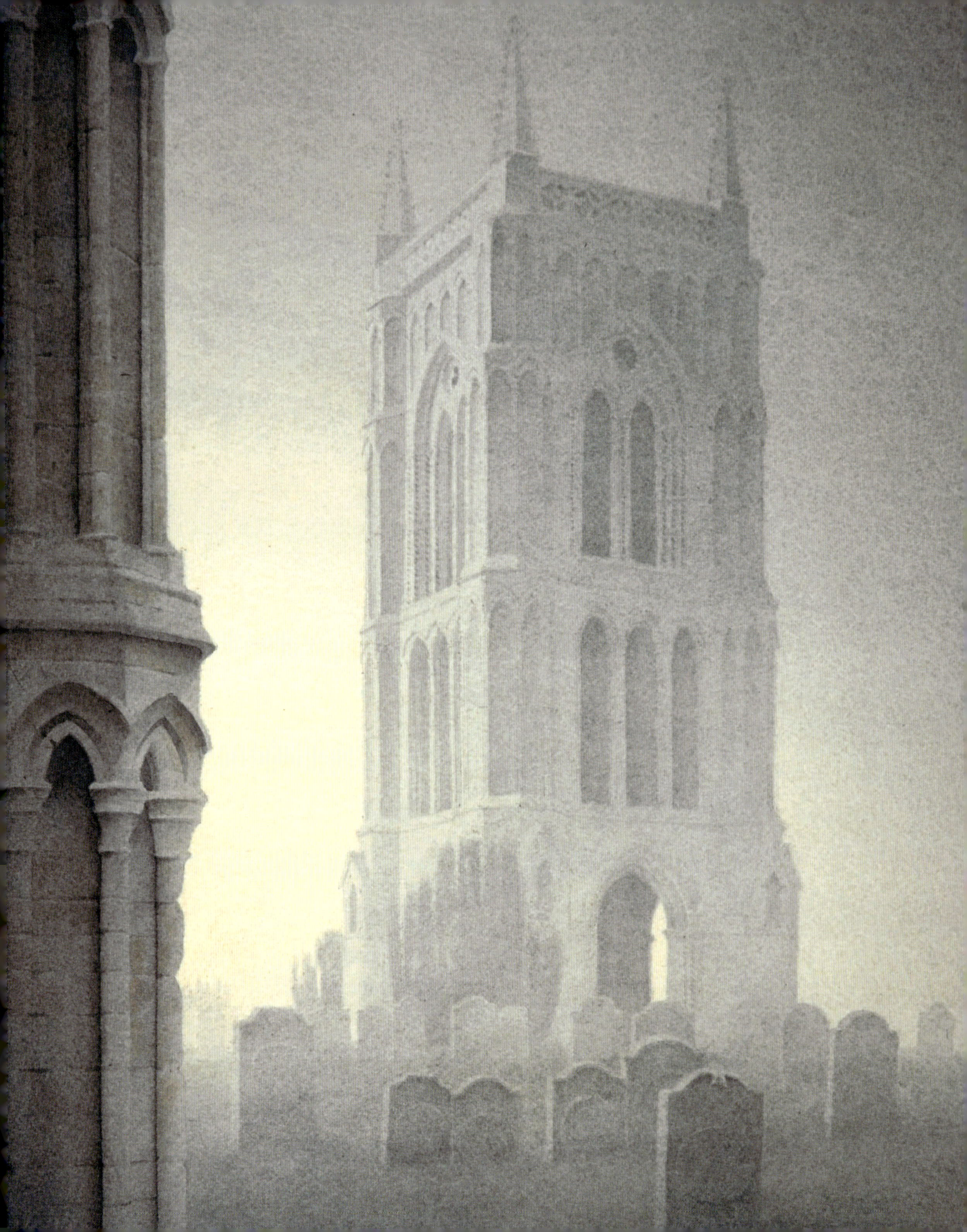

V Full Circle

Gerard's next exhibition of watercolours and charcoals was staged at Peter Low's gallery in Burnham Market in 2008. The vast majority of featured works depicted East Anglian churches – with a fresh foray into Fen towers beyond King's Lynn, set in a flat landscape which John Piper viewed as 'the best plinth for sculptural architecture in the whole country'.

Surveying beacons such as West Walton and Wiggenhall St Mary Magdalen, Piper thought it 'fanciful but suggestive to imagine that these towers have been carved out of the level Fens, and the whole area of the land round them reduced in height by a hundred feet or so, leaving them solid and whole, like some Indian rock temples.'

'How the bloody hell did you do that?'

The key difference between John Piper and Gerard Stamp as recording artists is that the former generally contended that churches in the Fens and elsewhere are distinguished as great bulks emblazoned and seemingly embattled in light. The latter homes in or out as he pleases – rendering the tough tenacity of the tower of West Walton in its entirety, but more usually the tenderness in detail most visitors may miss. His window focus at Wiggenhall St Mary Magdalen provides the cover for this book.

In another catalogue coup, the enthusiastic essayist was Simon Jenkins. The author of *England's Thousand Best Churches* wrote: 'Gerard Stamp turns architecture into art. He converts stone and brick, light and shadow, the tilt of a roof and the line of a wall into a living, exhilarating picture. His eye for the power of style is unerring, whether the fluting on a pillar or the tracery in a window. He gives depth and character to the simplest buttress or the blandest patch of limestone. Above all, his pictures evoke the mystery of English churches.

'Under his brush, buildings that have often become functional and banal are restored to their Gothic glory. He fills space with atmosphere by a shaft of light or a splash of colour.

'English churches... are dismissed as preaching boxes or social centres, properties that present their users with nothing but costly problems. Their historic role as galleries of vernacular art – and the role of their creators as artists – has long been ignored in the onward march of specialist curatorship. Most of England's finest ecclesiastical art has been removed to national museums. Only the architecture remains.

'Stamp is clearly inspired by the gallery of church architecture. He shows that the only true museum – and every church is in part a museum – is one filled by local people who have used and improved it day by day, one that embodies their memories and their achievements.'

For the spring of 2009 he delighted the Churches Conservation Trust with a plan to mark its fortieth anniversary with a fund-raising *Twelve Churches* show of watercolours and prints to be staged at Bonhams in London. The focus on buildings in CCT care ranged from Sussex to Yorkshire and Lincolnshire to Herefordshire. In an accompanying catalogue note, chairman Loyd Grossman hailed an extraordinary ability to convey light and texture in evocative paintings.

West Walton Tower

Watercolour 2008

22 x 15 ins | 56 x 38 cm

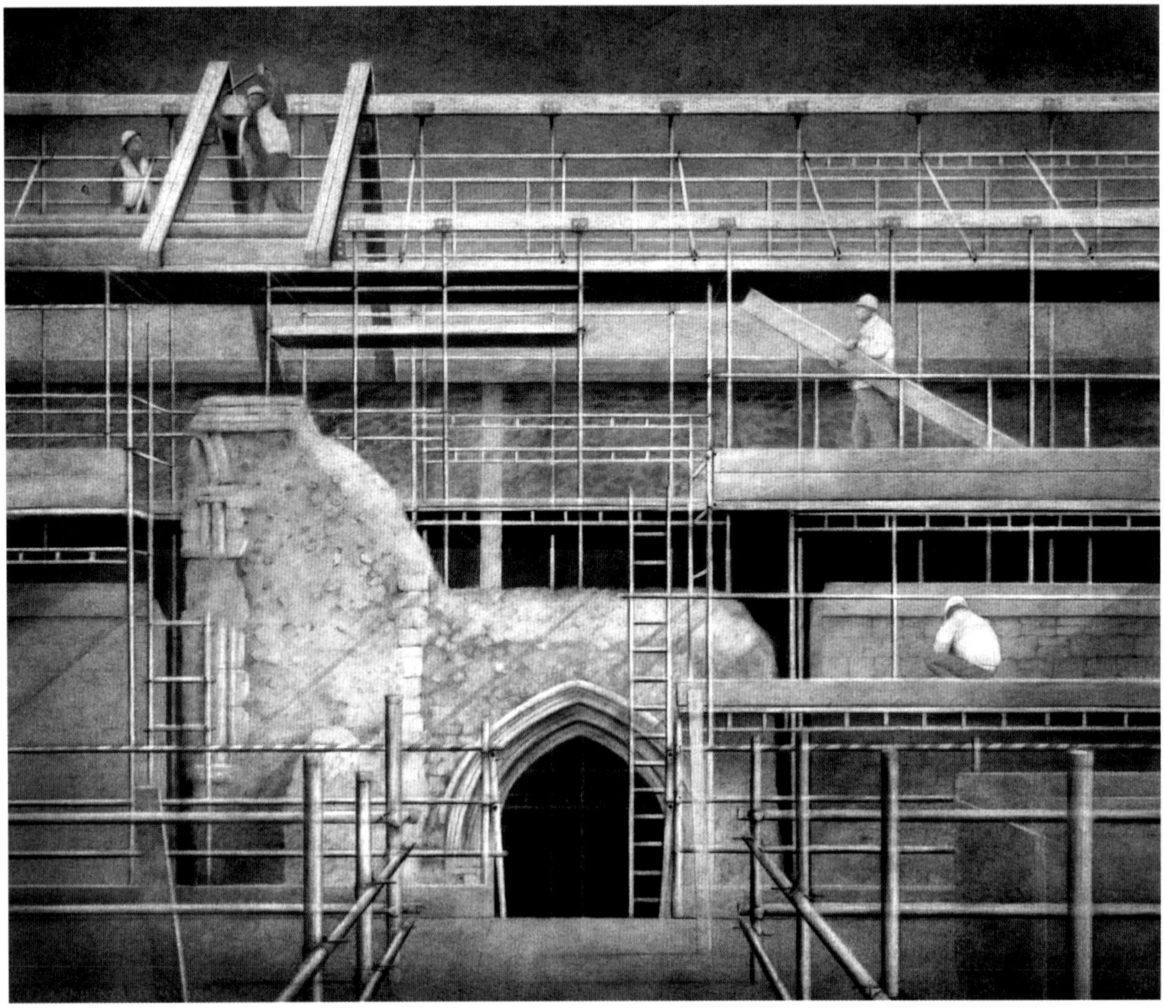

Constructing the Hostry

Charcoal 2009

36 x 42 ins | 91 x 107 cm

In May 2010 Gerard's life in the precincts of Norwich Cathedral came full circle. One of the biggest cathedral projects since the rebuilding of Coventry from wartime ruin was to be opened by Queen Elizabeth II and Prince Philip, and he was invited to stage a celebratory exhibition in the gallery part of a new Hostry.

In fact, a shop had been originally intended in the large ground floor by which the cathedral itself was to be approached. But a warning note from Her Majesty's Revenue and Customs, to the effect that the inclusion of a commercial enterprise would mean that VAT was levied on the entire £10 million project, won the day for art.

The Hostry scheme, and an earlier Refectory, won numerous awards for architect Sir Michael Hopkins. Reviving the spirit of Benedictine hospitality and education where it had formerly flourished, the designs enhanced medieval masonry and added graceful modern oak and glass constructions, like boats moored along an ancient quay. A Stamp show, adding a new twist to the historic watercolour tradition so powerfully pioneered in Norwich, was ideal for the launch.

Health and Safety concerns prevented Gerard from entering the Hostry building site, so he had to be content with sketching and photographing from the perimeter fence. He never let on that as a teenager at Norwich School, he had climbed all over the cathedral. Now he preferred to avoid the memory, even for himself, since suffering in adulthood from vertigo.

When an exaltation of an exhibition finally came together, Gerard was gladdened to present a picture to the monarch on behalf of 'all of those who love Norwich Cathedral'. He chose a lantern-like image called *Through the South Transept Screens,* and the Queen's face lit

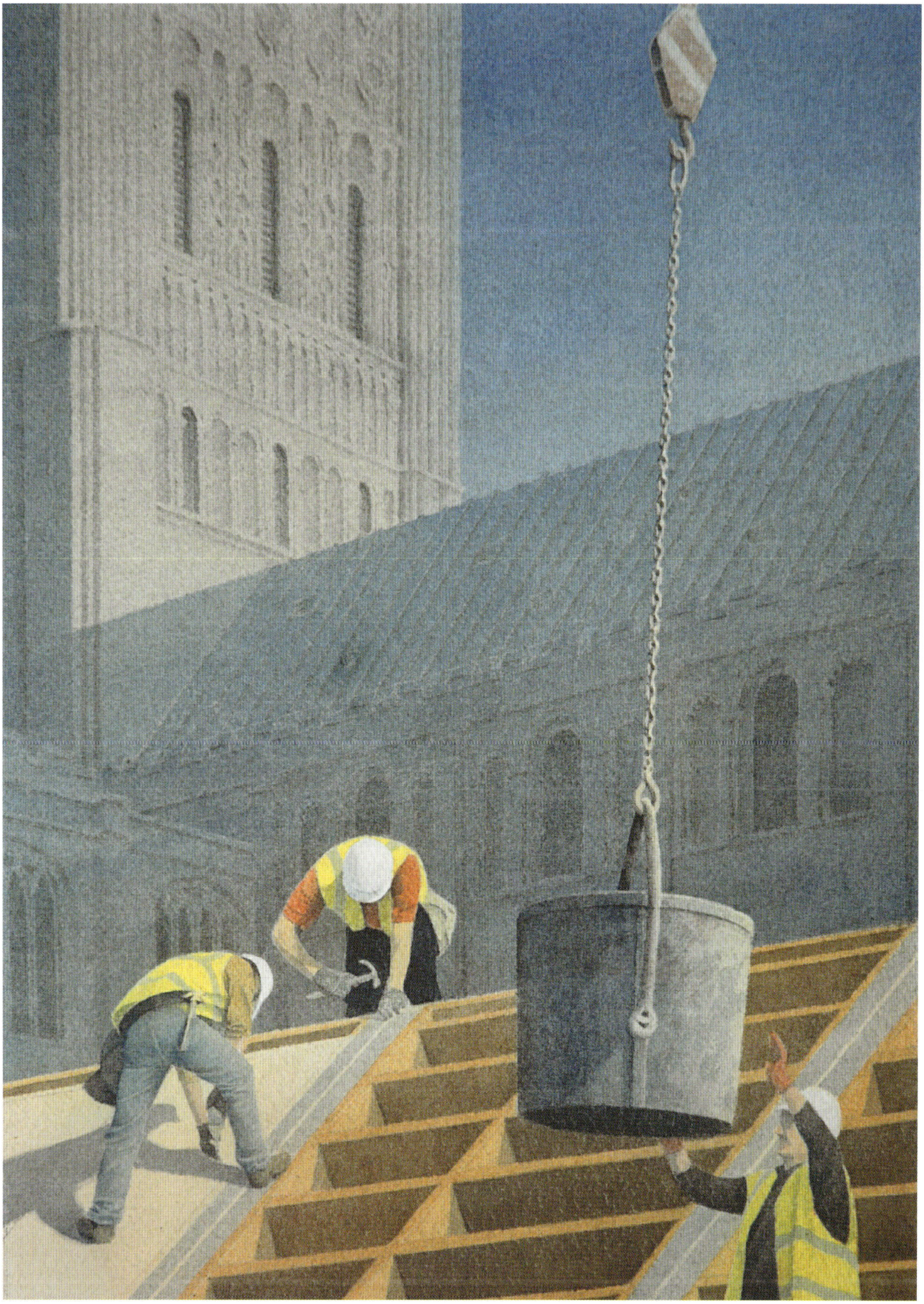

Workmen on the Hostry roof

Watercolour 2009

16.5 x 12 ins | 42 x 30 cm

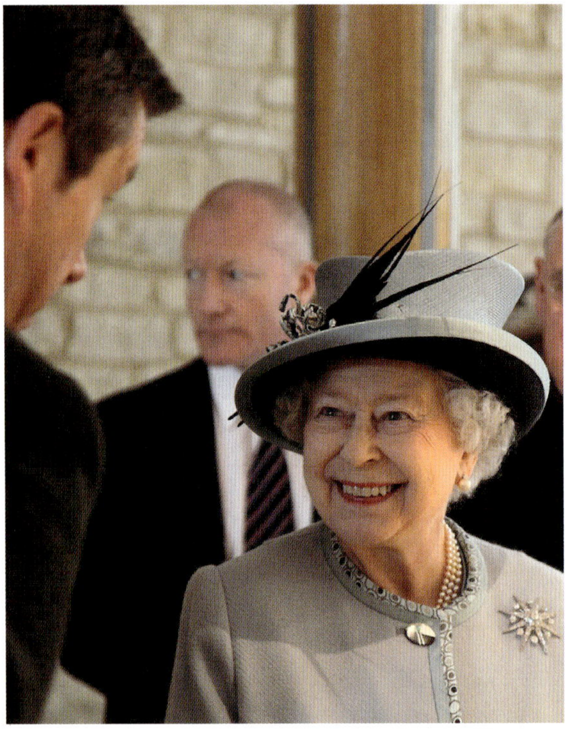

Gerard shows HM Queen Elizabeth II round the exhibition
On the occasion of the Royal Opening of the new Hostry and Refectory, Norwich Cathedral
4th May, 2010

up when she received it. 'Lovely light,' she said.

Canon Jeremy Haselock, Vice-Dean and Precentor central to the planning of the Hostry, and already a Stamp collector, witnessed the scene. 'The Queen fell instantly in love with Gerard and gazed upon him adoringly as we toured around,' he remembers. 'We had expected to put a red spot on the picture we were giving her so that it could remain in the show but not a bit of it! A member of her entourage grabbed it after lunch and off it went the same day to Sandringham where I'm told it still hangs.'

Prince Philip took a great interest in Gerard's paintings and asked him how he achieved the unique effect which distinguished his work. And, looking at one sizeable charcoal, his Royal Highness exclaimed: 'How the bloody hell did you do that?'

As usual the show proved popular with the public and now sales proceeds helped to fund a trio of stained-glass windows by abstract artist John McLean. They have coloured the air in the cathedral's north aisle since 2014.

Jeremy Haselock and Charles Spanton went on to acquire eleven Stamp watercolours, which now hang in their homes in London and France. Some were bought at and between exhibitions. One was presented to Jeremy on his retirement from the cathedral – the Dean and Chapter commissioning a picture of the eastern arm of the building from the viewpoint of his choir stall.

And Jeremy and Charles would also commission two more Stamp watercolours of the Norman interior at St Bartholomew the Great in London's Smithfield. One was reproduced in an edition of fifty fund-raising prints for the church's 900th anniversary in 2023 and formed the front cover of the scholarly book on the history of St Bart's also published that year.

Jeremy Haselock says now: 'When I look at a painting by Gerard Stamp I see – and feel – a

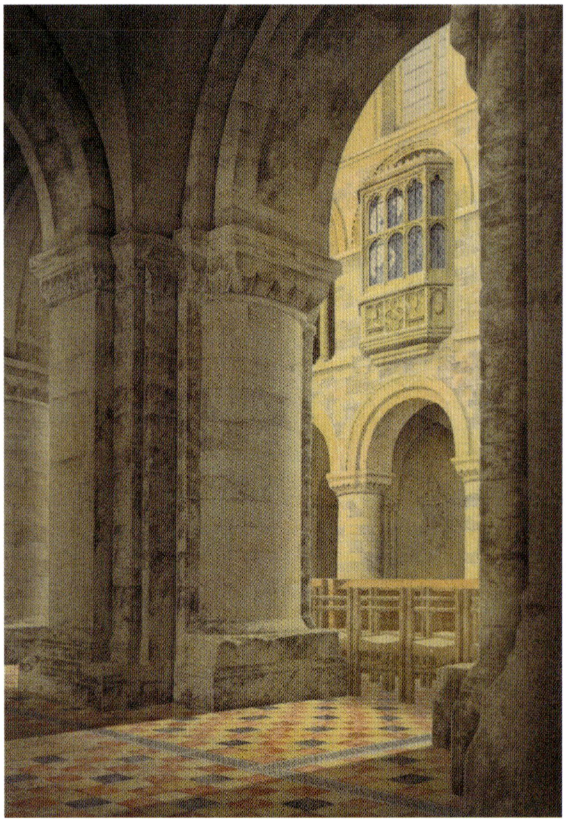

Prior's Window St Bartholomew the Great
Watercolour 2021
23.5 x 17 ins | 60 x 43 cm

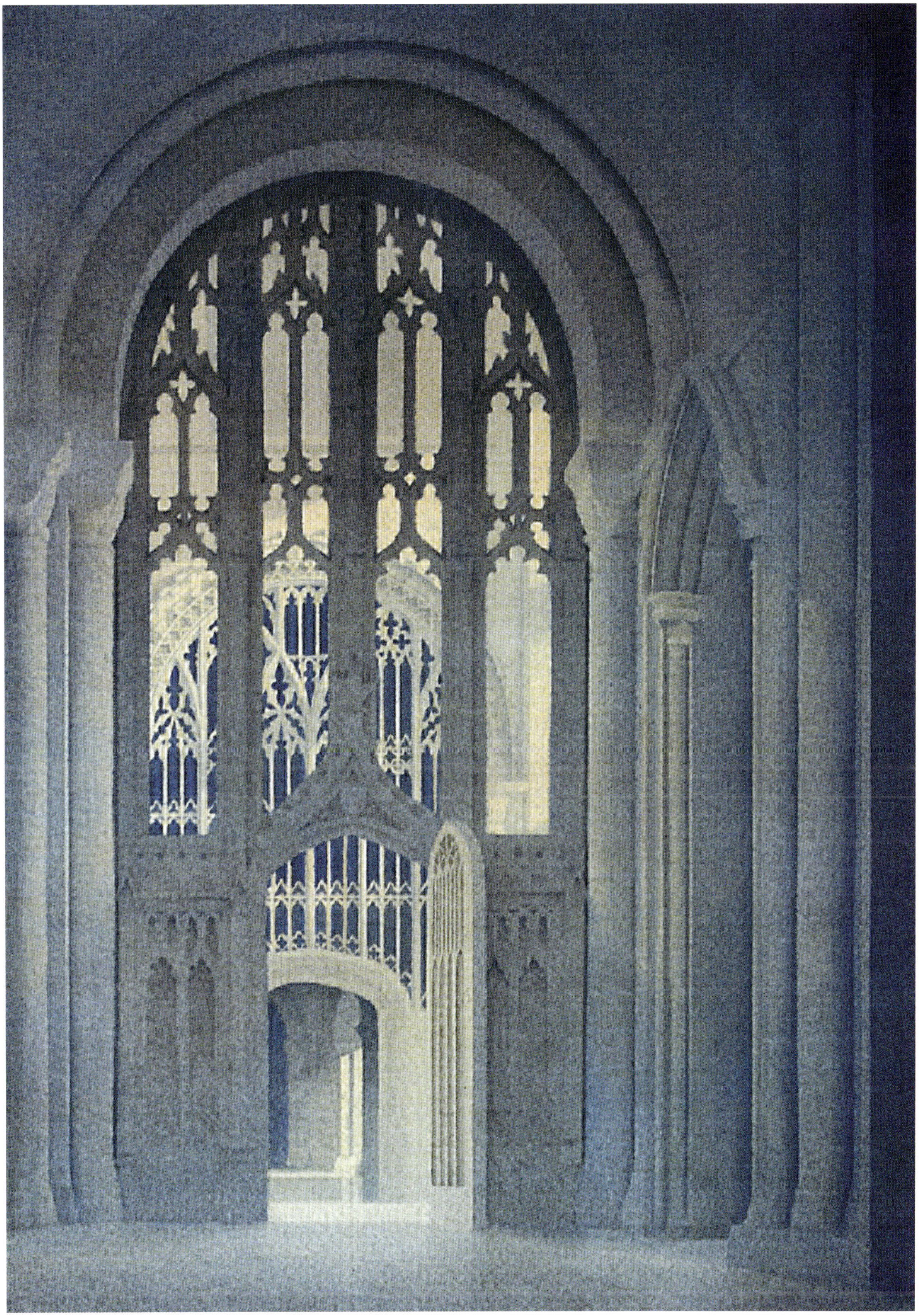

Through the South
Transept Screens
Norwich Cathedral
Watercolour 2009
24 x 16 ins | 61 x 41 cm
Reproduced by kind
permission of
the Royal Collection

stillness, the sort of stillness which is perhaps best described as a moment locked in time. History is a pattern of such timeless moments, and Gerard unerringly finds a fragment of the pattern appropriate to his subject. His pictures lie at the intersection of time and eternity...

'Next, I see texture. Gerard's depiction of architecture is always accurate and a reliable record of what is to be seen, but it is his extraordinary attention to building materials and their different textures which engages this particular viewer. Be it the crumbling of exterior lime harling, parting company with the wall it shelters – as in his wonderfully atmospheric view of the north wall of St Margaret's, Hales; or the faceted surfaces of knapped flints contrasted with limestone, in the flushwork to be found in so many Norfolk churches; or the rubbed, red bricks with which many walls

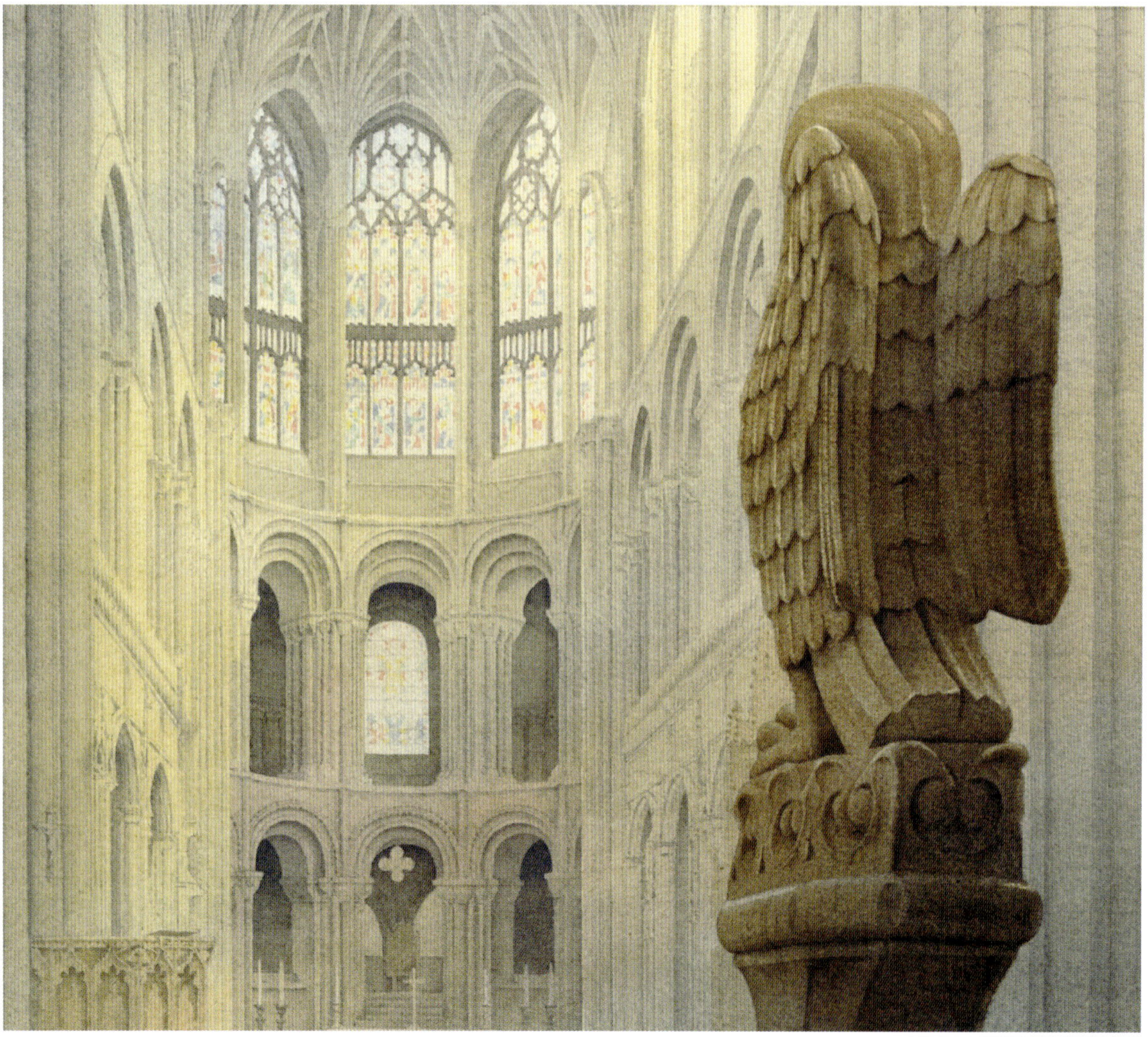

Norwich Cathedral from the Precentor's Stall

Watercolour 2017

17 x 19.5 ins | 44 x 50 cm

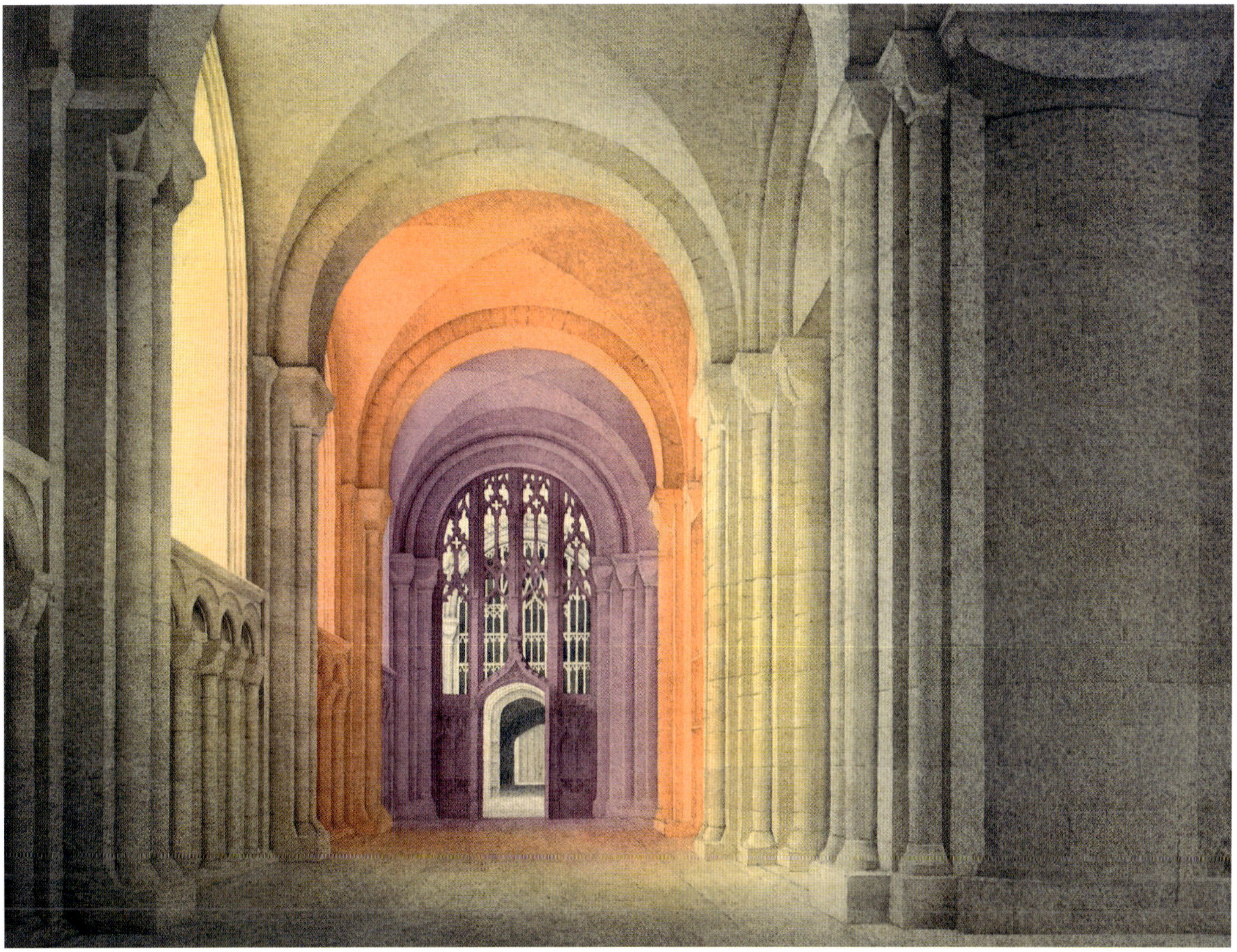

Light from the McLean Windows Norwich Cathedral
Watercolour 2014
20 x 27 ins | 51 x 69 cm

were repaired; or the plain-glass, leaded windows, each diamond quarry set at a minutely different angle from its neighbour; the complex patterns of tracery, the worn surface of carved ornament, the red pamments of the church floors... all are lovingly but gently drawn to our attention.

'Finally, there is light. Gerard unerringly finds the right position from which to view his subject. Sometimes we meet an elevation face on, but the light comes from an angle so that our attention is drawn subtly to the architectural detail by light and shade. Again, a view might be through an opening or arcade where the succeeding layers are lit differentially to give a real feeling of recession, of depth beyond the surface of the painting. Gerard might choose us to see his subject from an angle, but his viewpoint is always chosen so that the light playing on the varied textures of the building materials helps us interpret what we see. My delight is when he shows us a bright light from a window beyond the one through which we are looking, as in our painting of a window in St Peter and St Paul, Salle' (Page 103).

'Light can do strange things when skilfully managed. The three intensely coloured windows by John McLean in Norwich Cathedral have transformed a previously dull and uninspiring choir aisle into an immersive experience – a colour bath, so to speak. Gerard delighted in this from the moment the windows were unveiled and his painting of the aisle glories in the play of coloured light over the Romanesque architecture.'

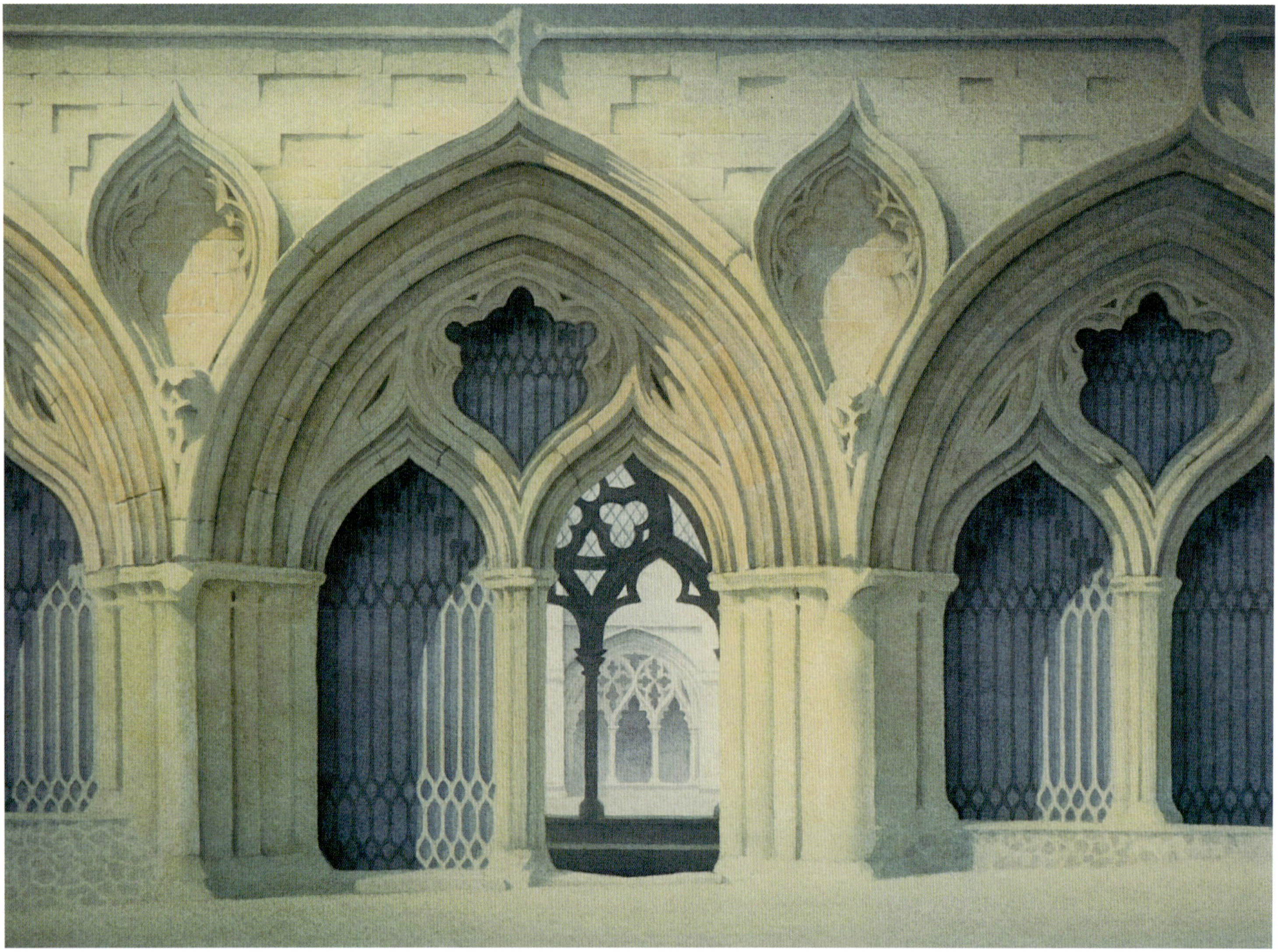

Chapter House Doors

Norwich Cathedral

Watercolour 2009

17 x 23 ins | 43 x 58 cm

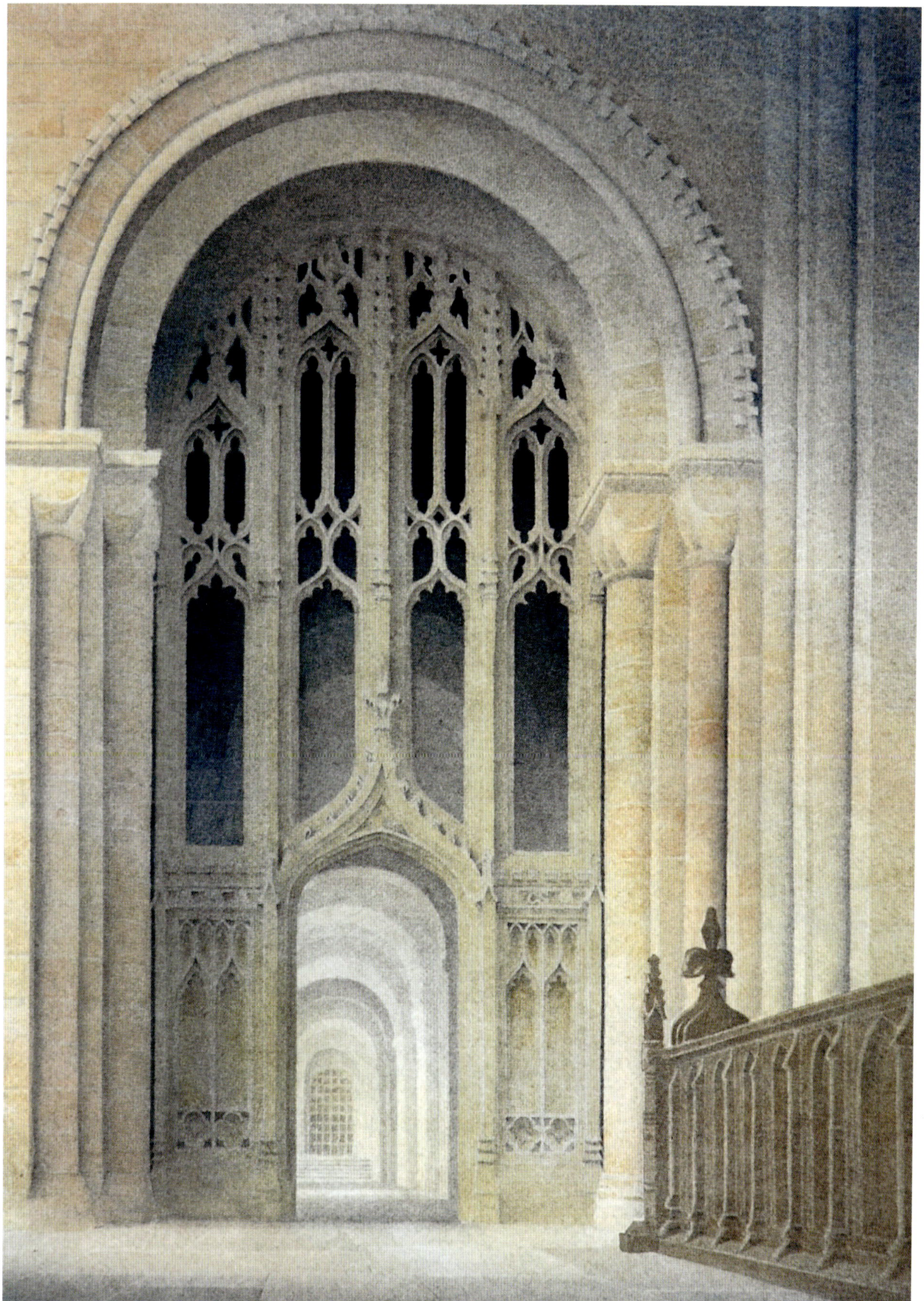

South Aisle Screen

Norwich Cathedral

Watercolour 2009

24 x 17 ins | 61 x 43 cm

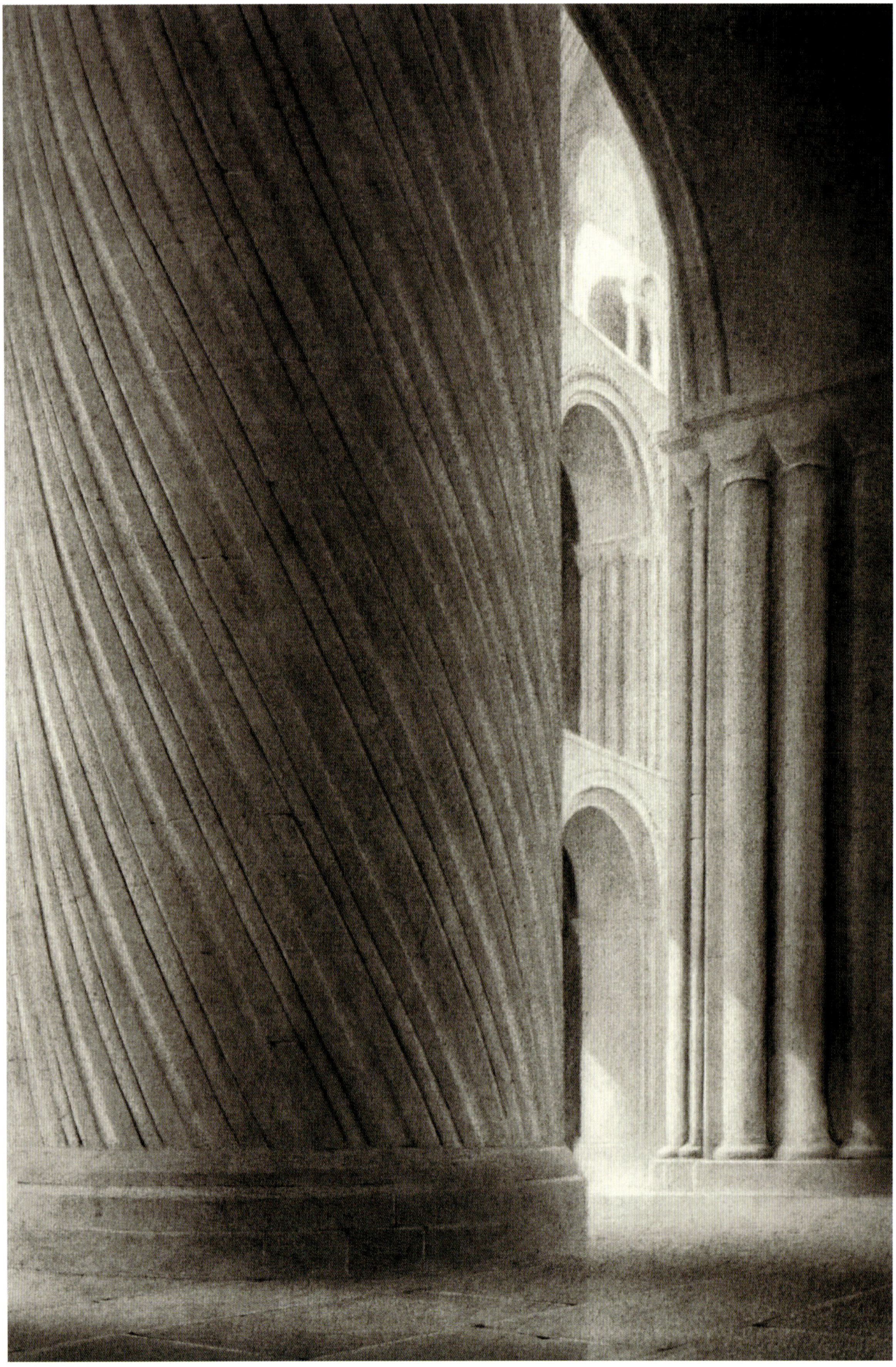

Spiral Column

Norwich Cathedral

Charcoal 2008

34 x 23 ins | 86 x 58 cm

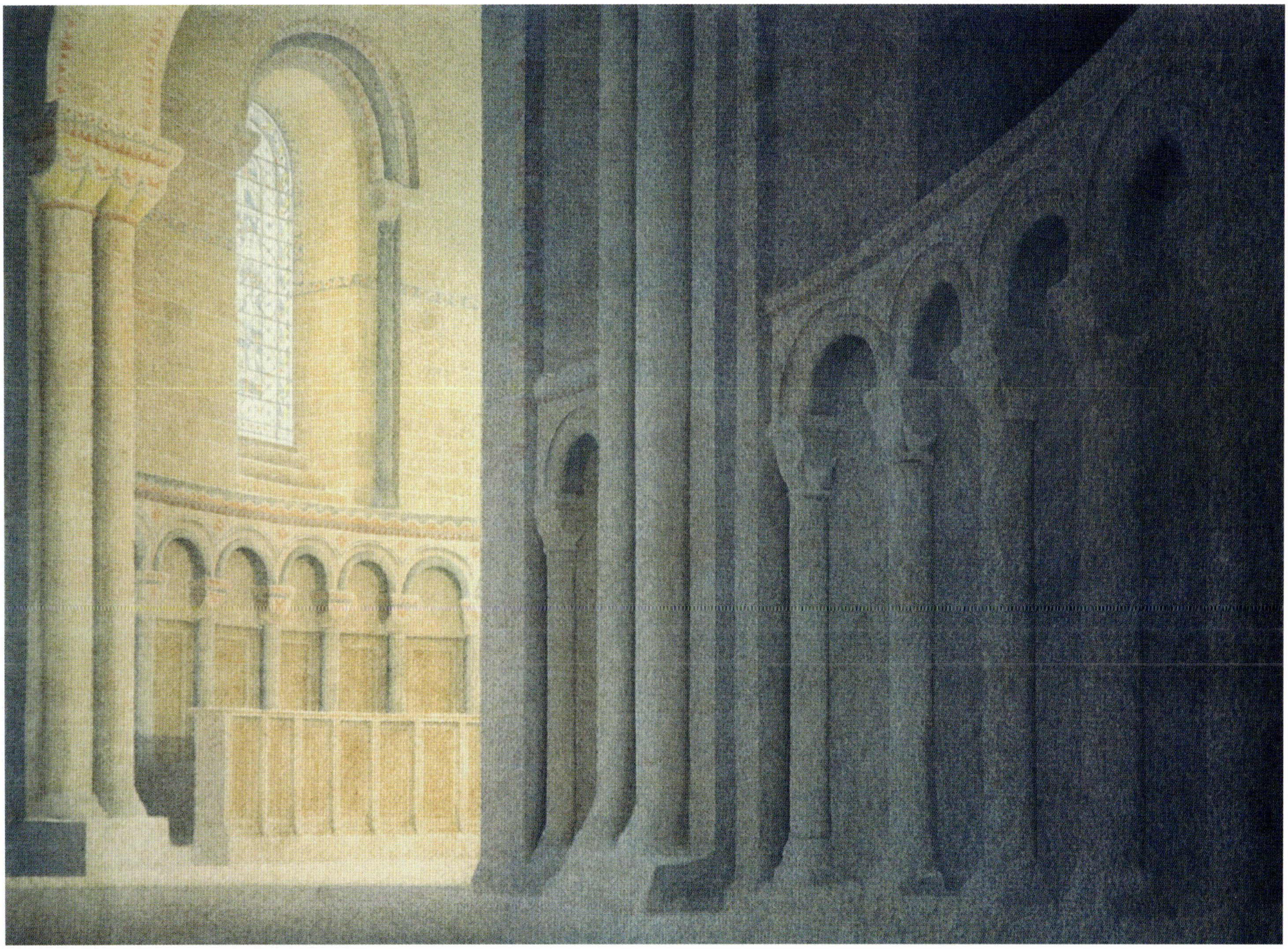

Towards the Jesus Chapel

Norwich Cathedral

Watercolour 2009

18 x 24 ins | 46 x 61 cm

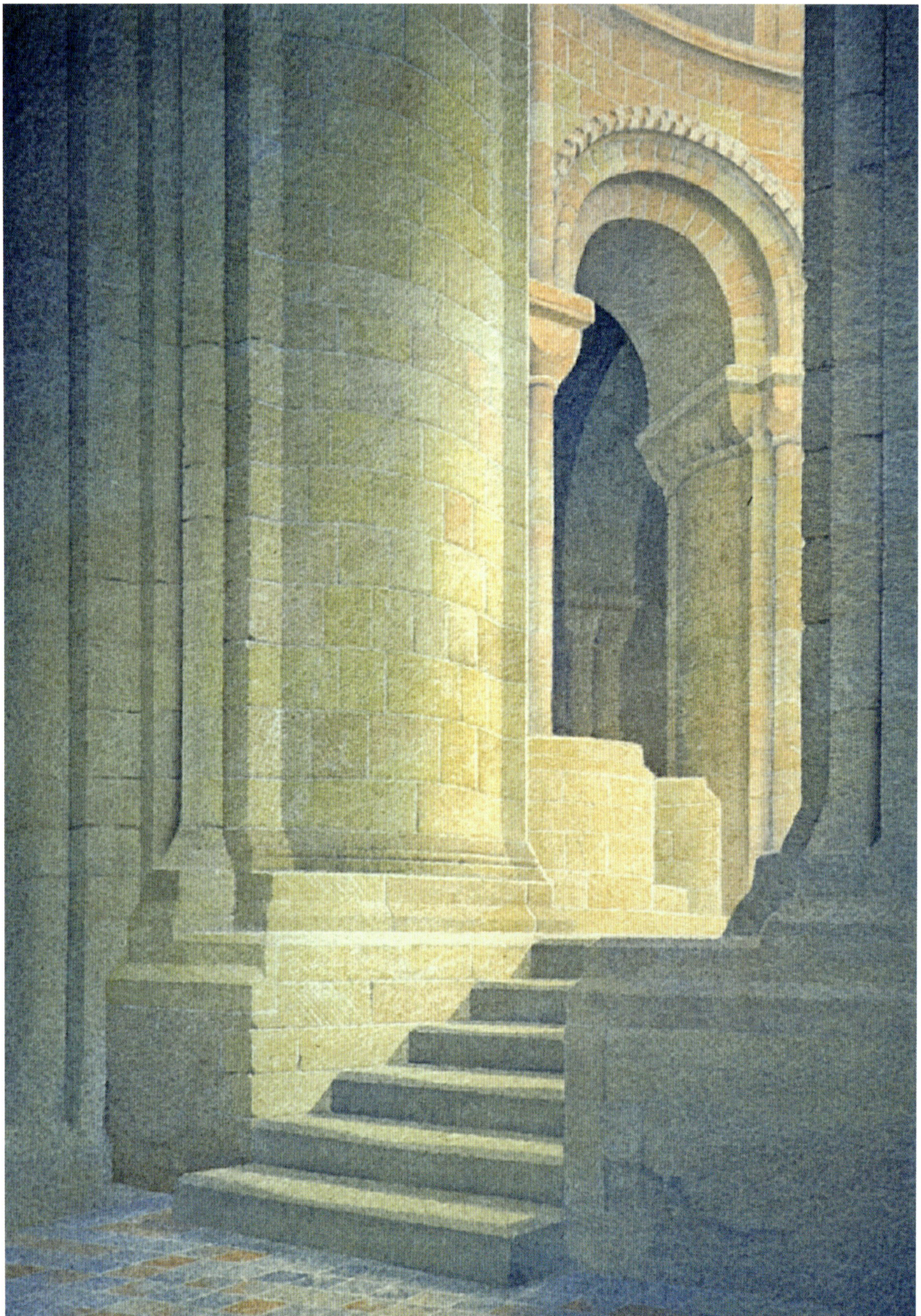

Sanctuary Steps

Norwich Cathedral

Watercolour 2009

21 x 15 ins | 53 x 38 cm

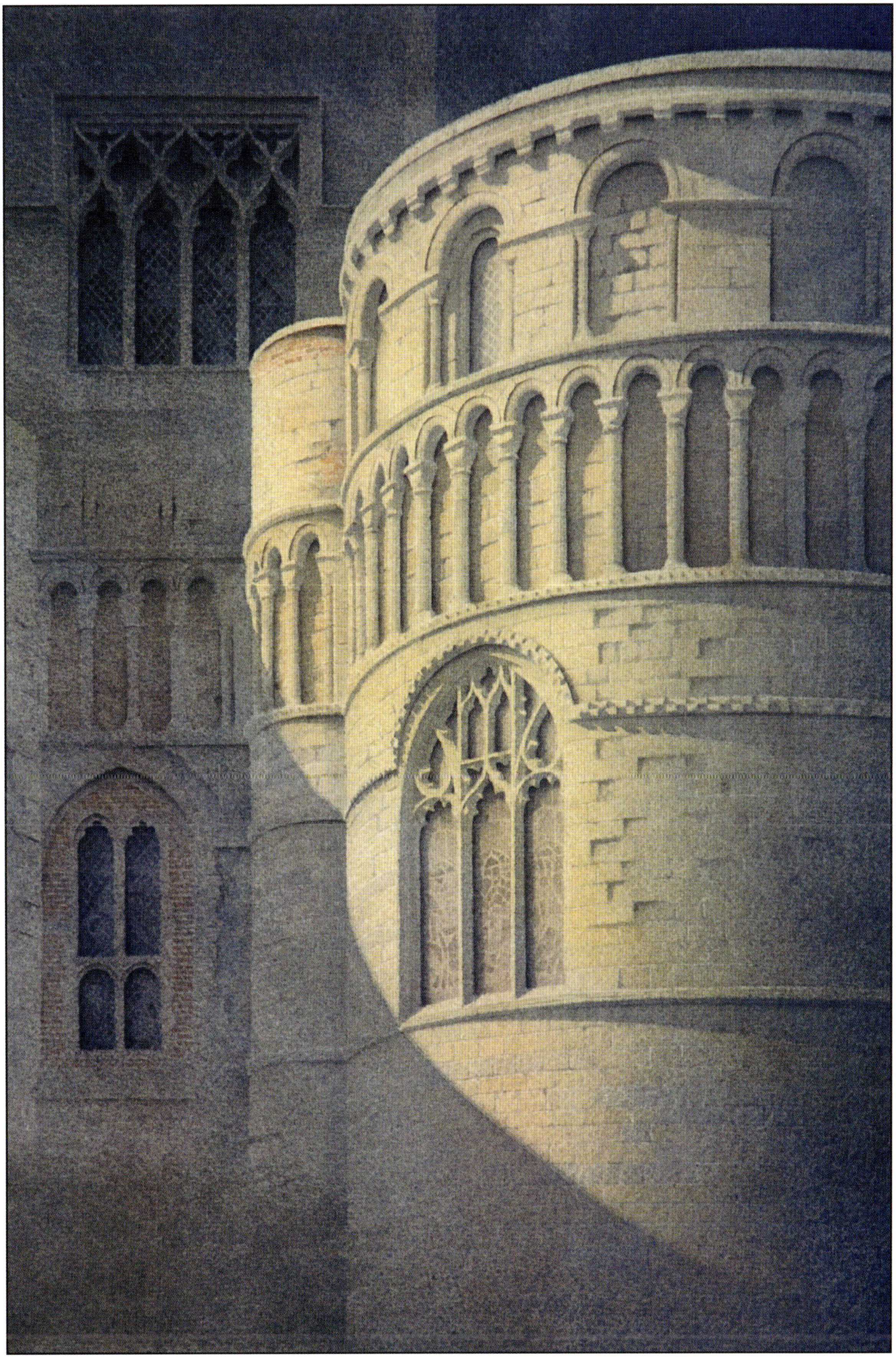

A Corner of the East End

Norwich Cathedral

Watercolour 2009

23 x 16.5 ins | 58 x 42 cm

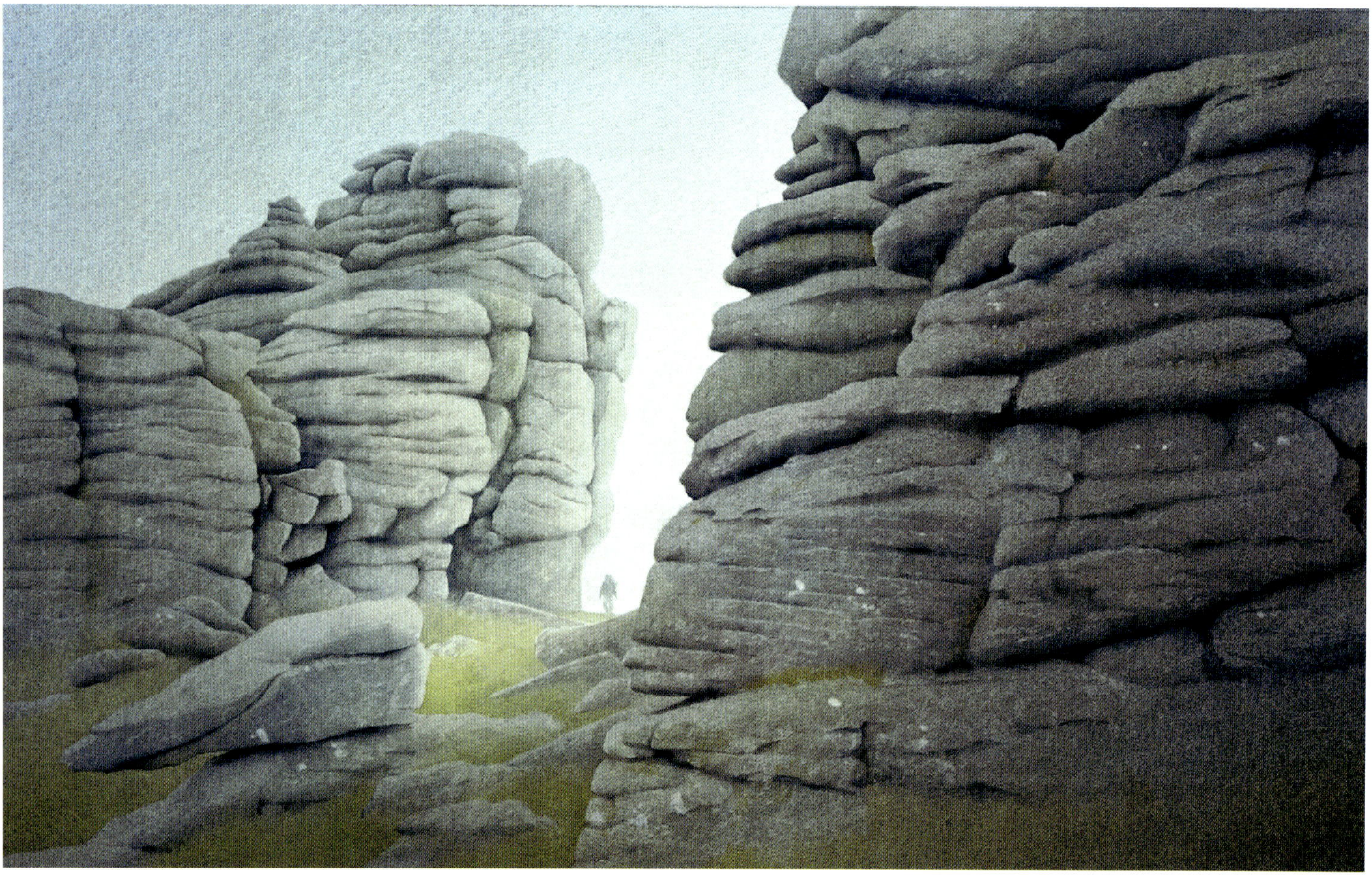

Hound Tor

Dartmoor

Watercolour 2014

21 x 24 ins | 53 x 61 cm

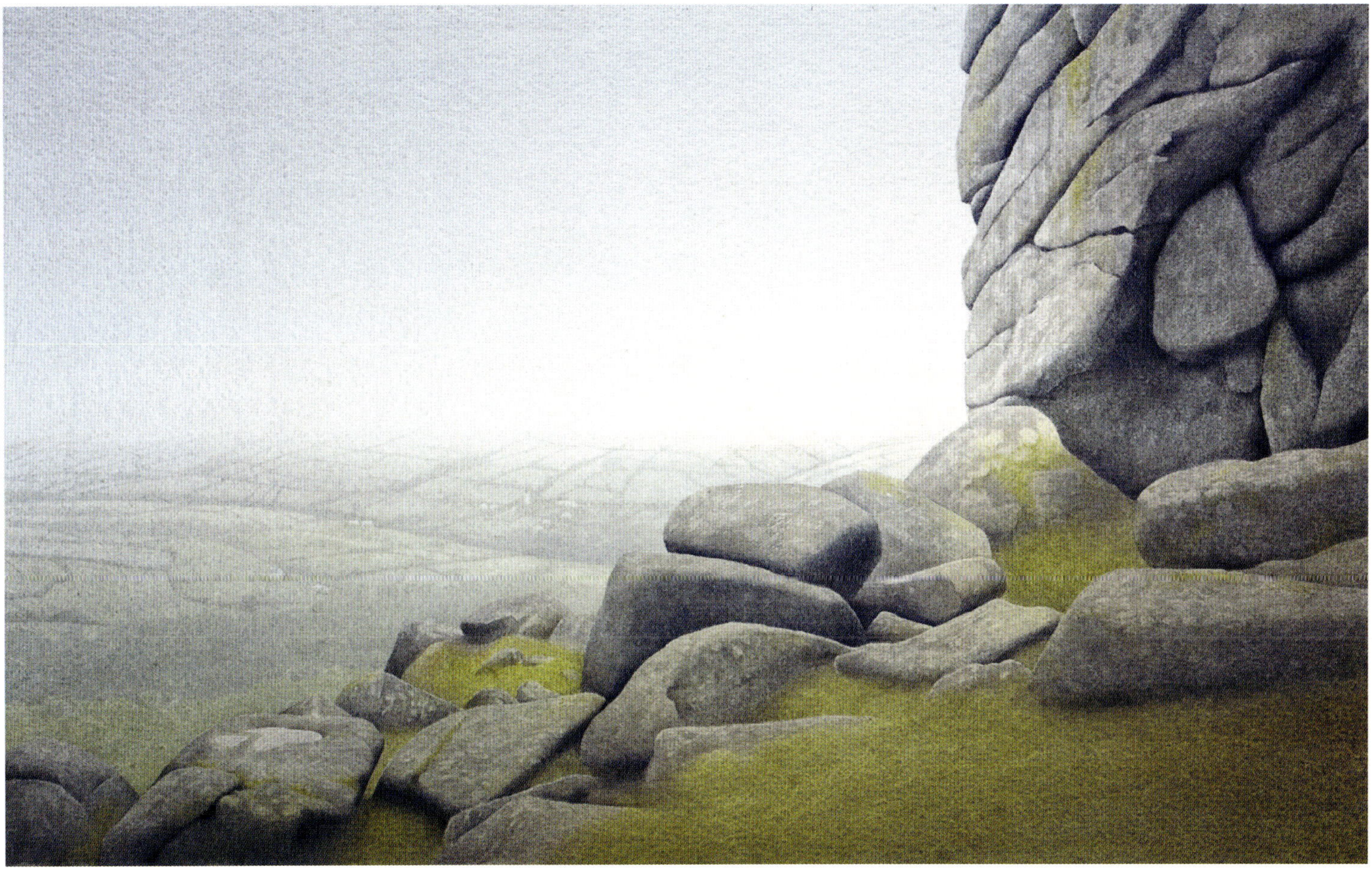

Bonehill Rocks

Dartmoor

Watercolour 2014

21 x 24 ins | 53 x 61 cm

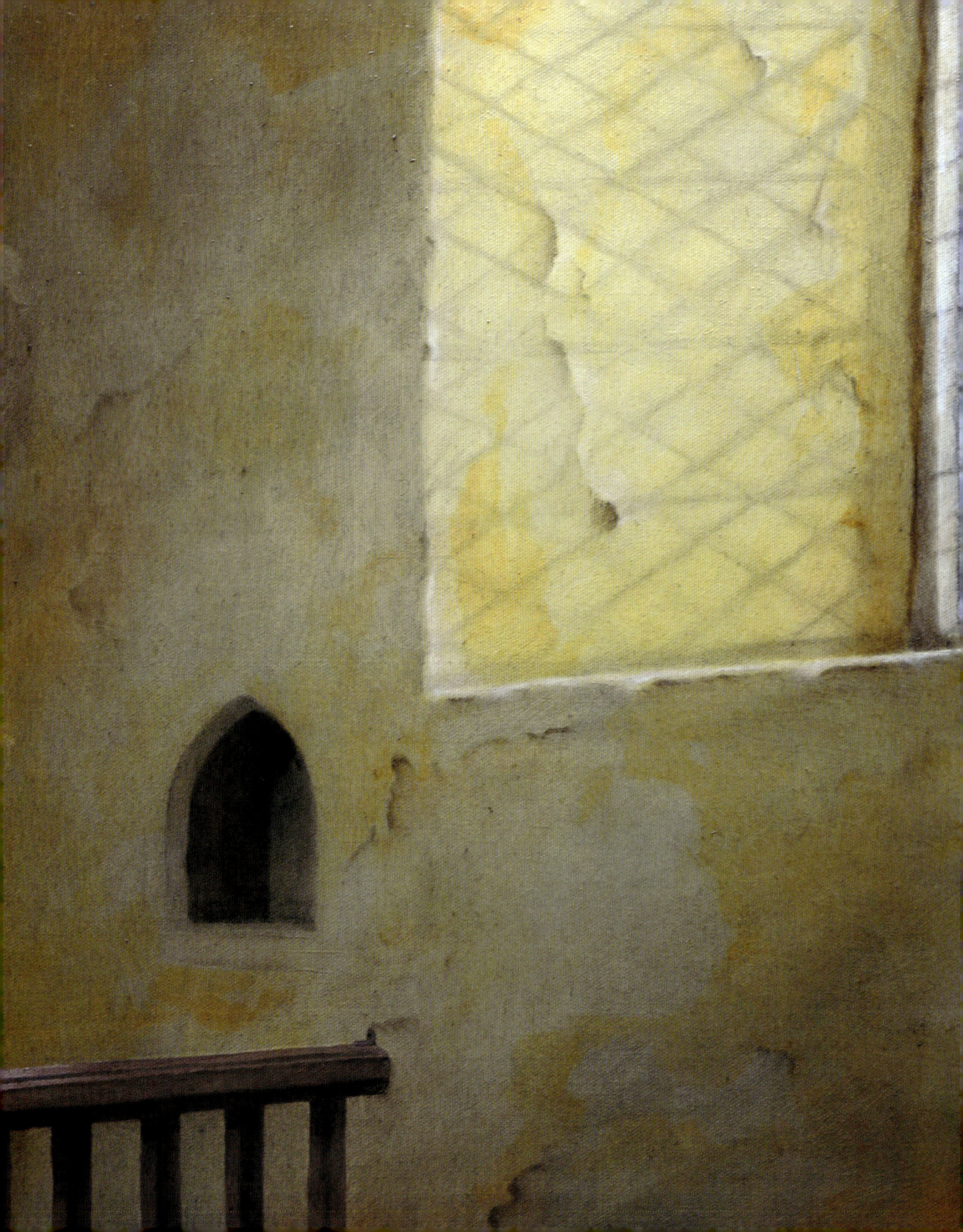

VI Fresh Horizons

From 2016 Gerard sought a fresh challenge by revisiting watercolour subjects for oil paintings. The first attempt was a relatively simple version of Waxham Piscina on the North Norfolk coast, and then he tried the window at Wiggenhall St Mary Magdalen in the Fens. As his confidence grew, he tackled a bigger rendition of Saltmarsh Dawn.

'I find oil much more of a technical challenge,' he says, 'and more frustrating because of the time it takes to dry. I use glazes which are very similar in technique to watercolour but the underlying surface does have to dry out first.'

Although sure he was advancing when revisiting the Norwich pictures *Flint Flushwork, St Michael Coslany* and *Steps to the Triforium, Norwich Cathedral* (page 38), the oil flow halted when a return to one of his favourite subjects, Hales North Door, brought frustration. 'In the end I feel much more fluent in watercolour,' he says. 'I like its stronger sense of intimacy.'

'Painting is but another word for feeling'

Never having worked en plein air, except in initial sketches, Gerard explains that he does not seek a precise reproduction of a particular scene but a poetic interpretation. Painting is not photography. A lyrical rendition adds a touch of artistic licence.

Liking to quote John Constable's maxim 'painting is but another word for feeling', he began a 2018 lecture in Norwich Cathedral by showing how that view had led to much-loved pictures of Constable Country slyly shifting reality for better pictorial effect. Cotman and Crome had done it too. The speaker concluded by confessing his own sins against prosaic exactitude. An arresting 2017 watercolour of Redenhall showed a South Norfolk beacon tower rising so impressively above a rolling and furrowed field because those contours lay in Bradfield, far closer to home.

Glazing in Wiggenhall St Mary Magdalen (our cover image) had been artistically improved, and the wall patina on a Hales church painting was actually lifted from Hellington twenty miles away. Sunlight could be genuinely glowing, glancing, dancing or dazzling – but it might also simply shift direction, as if by magic, to slant towards the artist's purpose. Evoking the spirit of a particular place demands fidelity to a deeper truth.

'Artistic licence occurs at any time,' he says. 'From the starting point of sketching in front of a subject, a lot can be left out.' He will sketch a scene from a certain angle and take dozens of photos from other angles. Then in his studio he uses a computer – being a big fan of Photoshop – and perhaps return to his sketchbook while breaking up the picture: moving things forward and back; subtly shifting the components of a scene and reducing to essential elements. The essence of a composition is secured before he begins to draw out the painting.

A lot of what is left out in a characteristic Stamp picture is – or was – other people. Jeremy Haselock says: 'Seldom are there people in his pictures which to my mind is good because their presence would overwhelm the silence, populate the moment, break the spell.'

The artist himself explains: 'When I visit a building, a ruin, a marsh, I like to be on my own. I'm irritated when someone is in a remote church

Waxham Piscina

(detail)

Oil on canvas 2016

16 x 22 ins | 41 x 56 cm

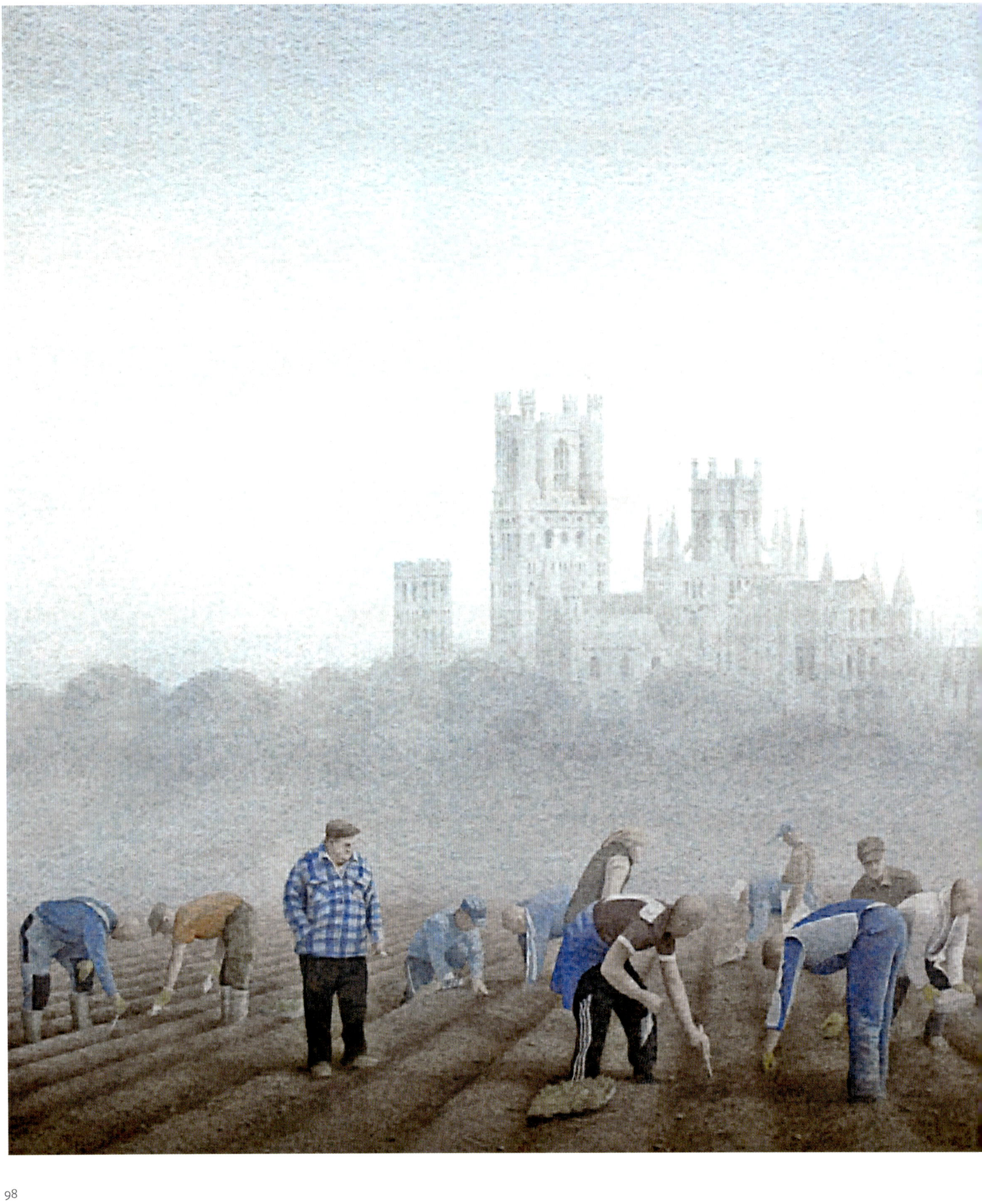

Fen Gang

Watercolour 2009

27 x 34 ins | 68 x 86 cm

when I'm visiting, for instance. So I want my paintings to be solitary too. Also, when you put people into a painting they become the subject, or at least detract from the subject. I want the viewer to put themselves in the picture; they don't need a stranger in there as well.'

But he has changed his mind on special occasions, having painted *Fen gang* in 2009 and pulled off one of his best pictures. The great Ely Cathedral looms mistily beyond foreground farm labourers – an immense symbol of spiritual peace now recast as a result of back-breaking and sometimes lethal toil. Even one of the Victorian restorers, George Basevi, fell to his death from scaffolding inside the west tower.

It is one of the great images of a landscape so flat that the grandest monument rises ever more loftily – where still-sinking land was once reclaimed from water at vast cost; where Celtic and Saxon resistance to foreign invasion gave way to diehard marshmen who murdered seventeenth-century workers for Dutch engineers in their drainage ditches. A spectacular and sinister spirit, also caught in the Graham Swift novel *Waterland*, and in a brilliantly rendered panoramic *Sugar Beet* watercolour by Edward Burra, elevating field-tenders into gaunt ghosts.

And in 2011 Gerard painted his only recognisable portrait. The elderly man with a walking stick, sitting on a pew in an aged church interior, shares the scene with a font and a bell rope. The figure might have been taken for a retired bellringer but for the title of the piece: *Church Crawling with Dad*. It was a poignant gesture of gratitude to Barry Stamp for an inherited love of visits to church buildings.

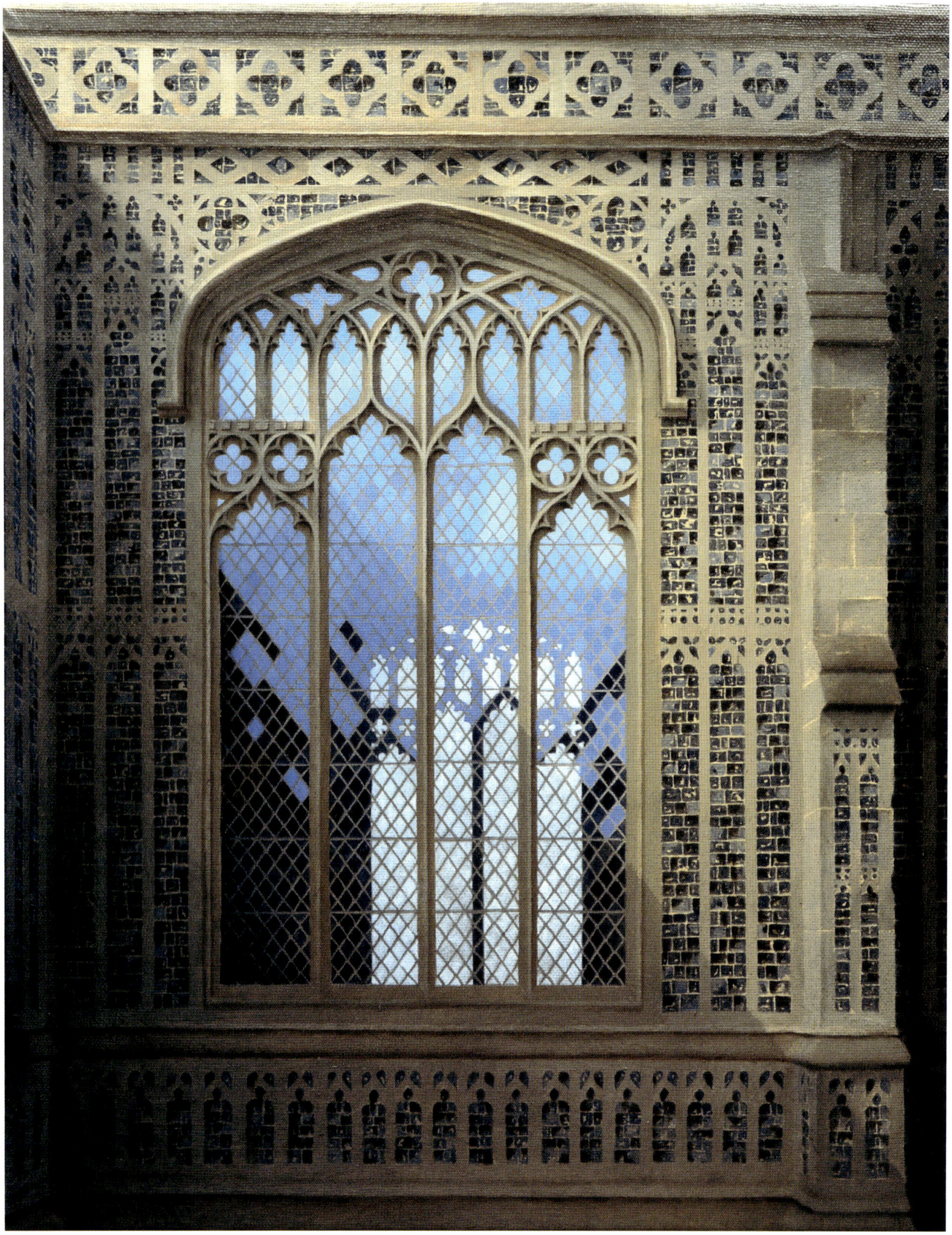

Flint Flushwork, St Michael Coslany

Oil on canvas 2017

20 x 16 ins | 51 x 41 cm

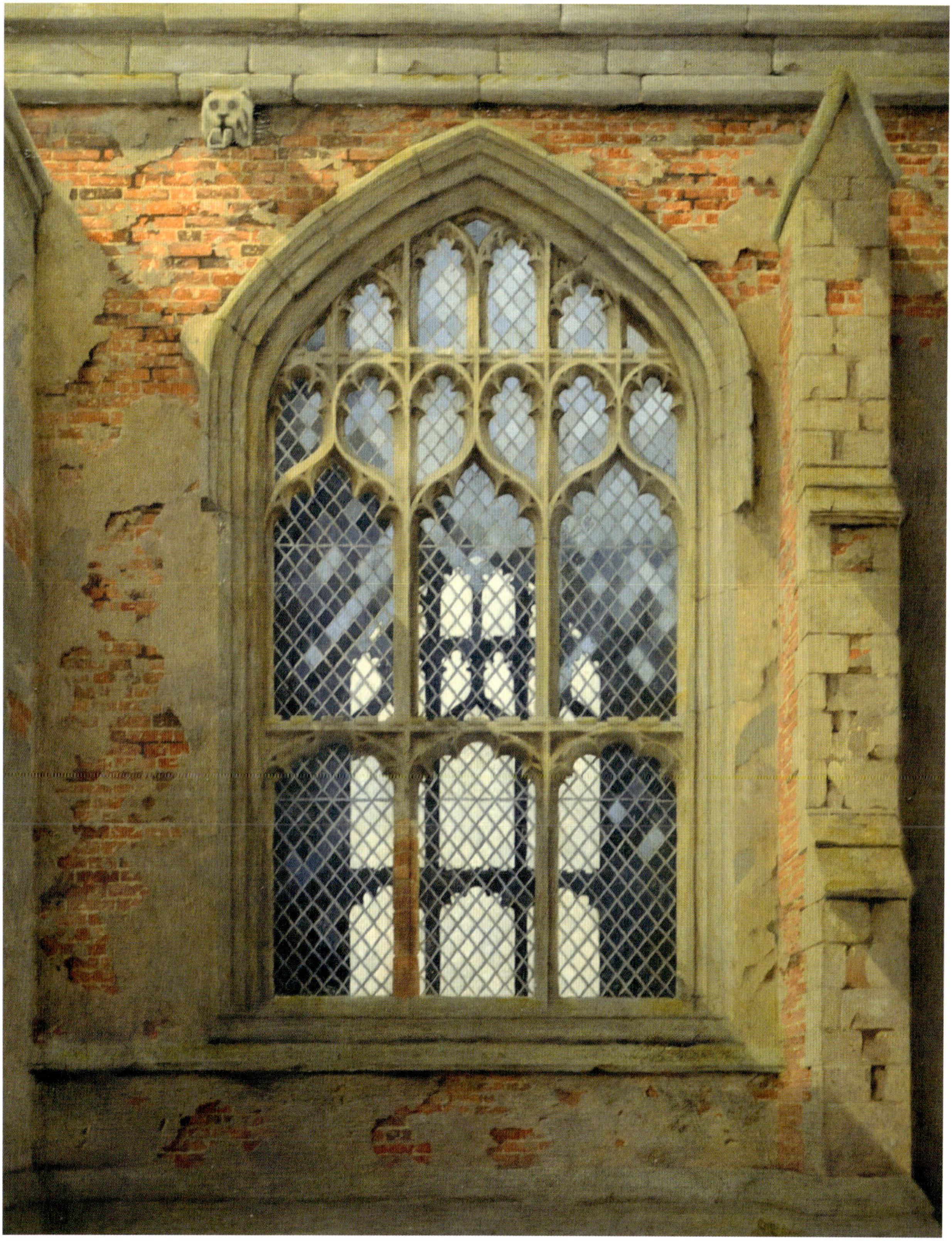

Magdalen Windows

Oil on canvas 2016

20 x 16 ins | 51 x 41 cm

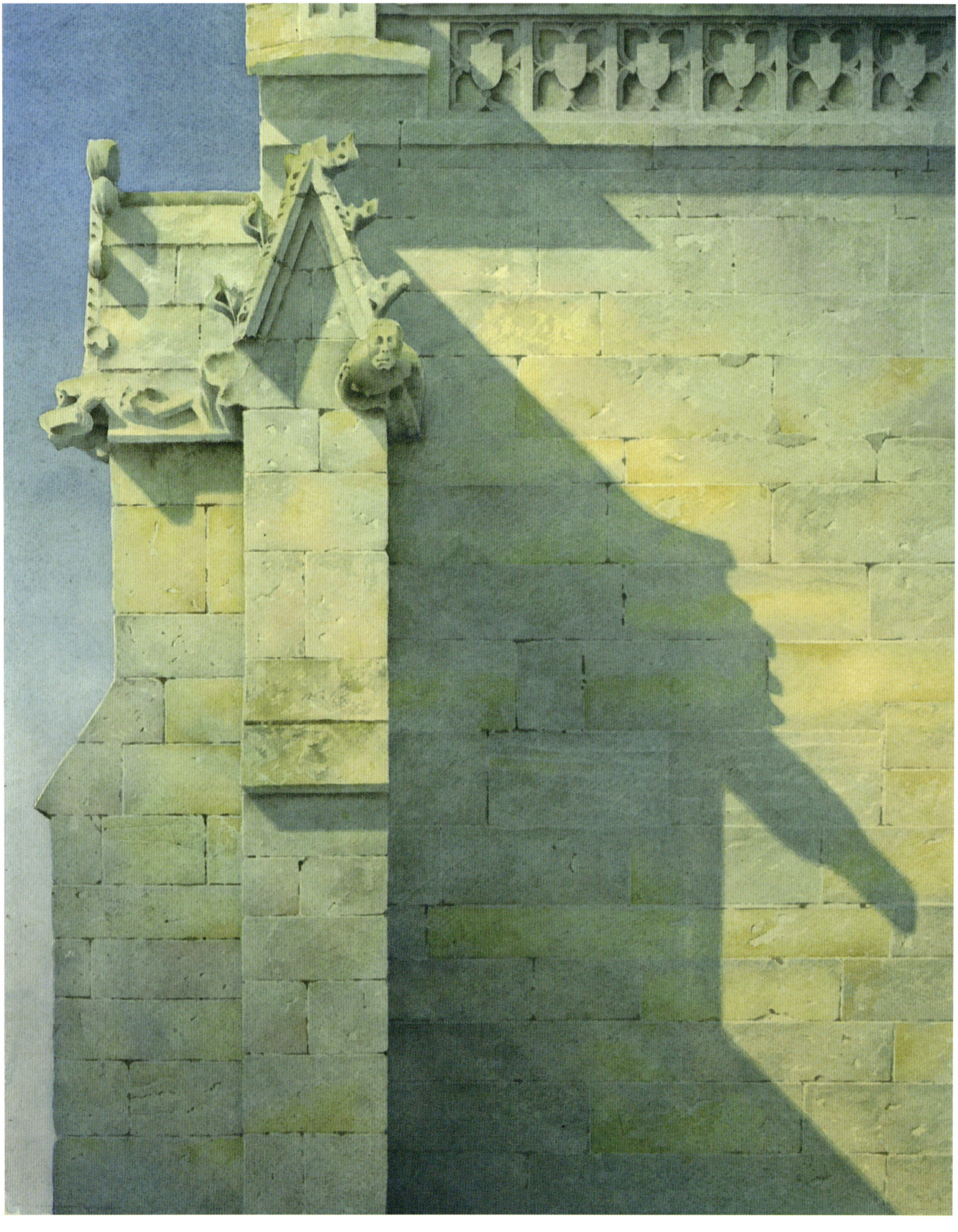

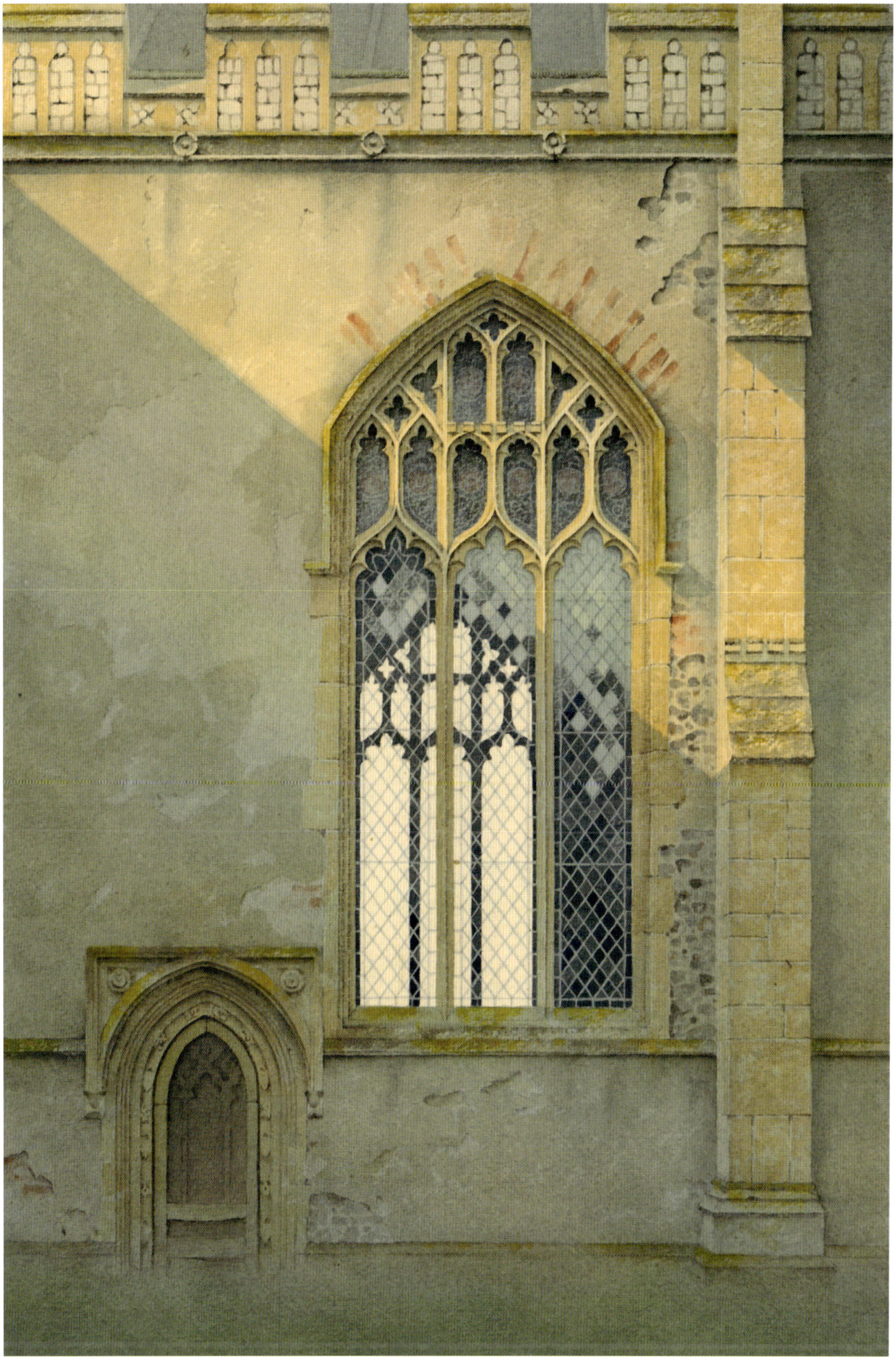

Grotesque Shadows

Heckington

Watercolour 2021

21 x 17 ins | 54 x 43 cm

Salle Windows

Watercolour 2023

23.5 x 15.5 ins | 60 x 40 cm

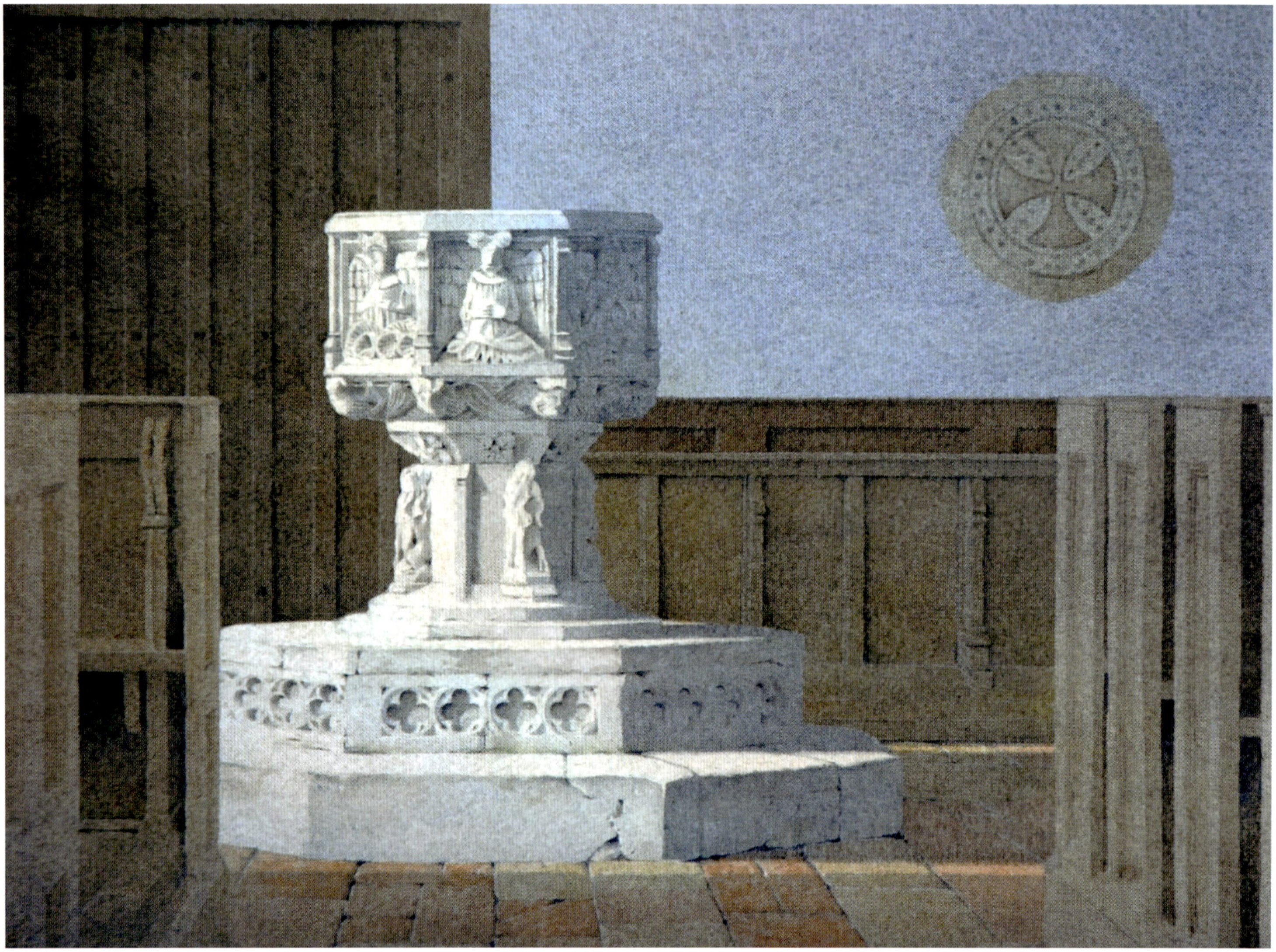

Hardley Font

Watercolour 2011

15 x 20 ins | 38 x 51 cm

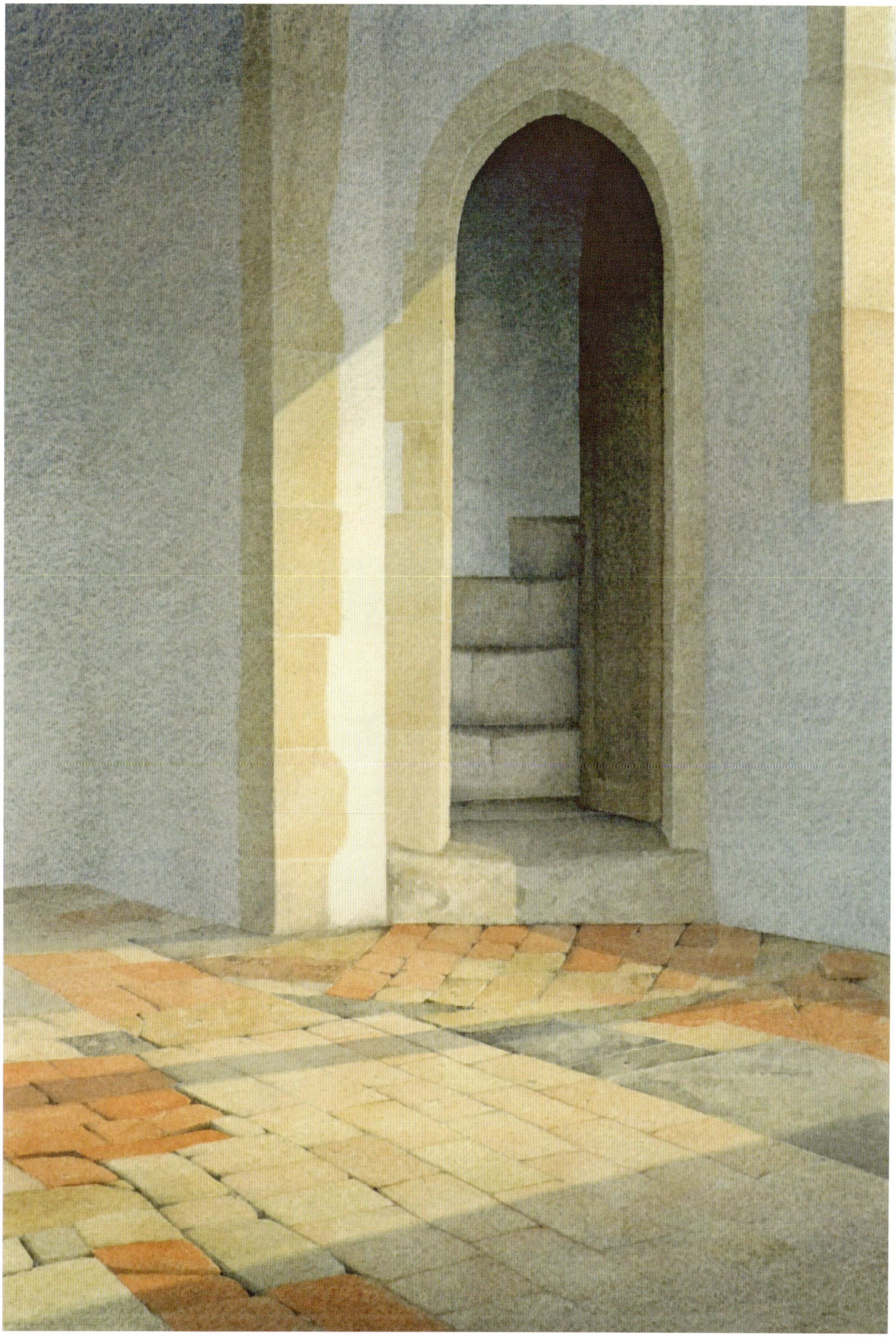

Blythburgh Steps

Watercolour 2012

20 x 14 ins | 51 x 36 cm

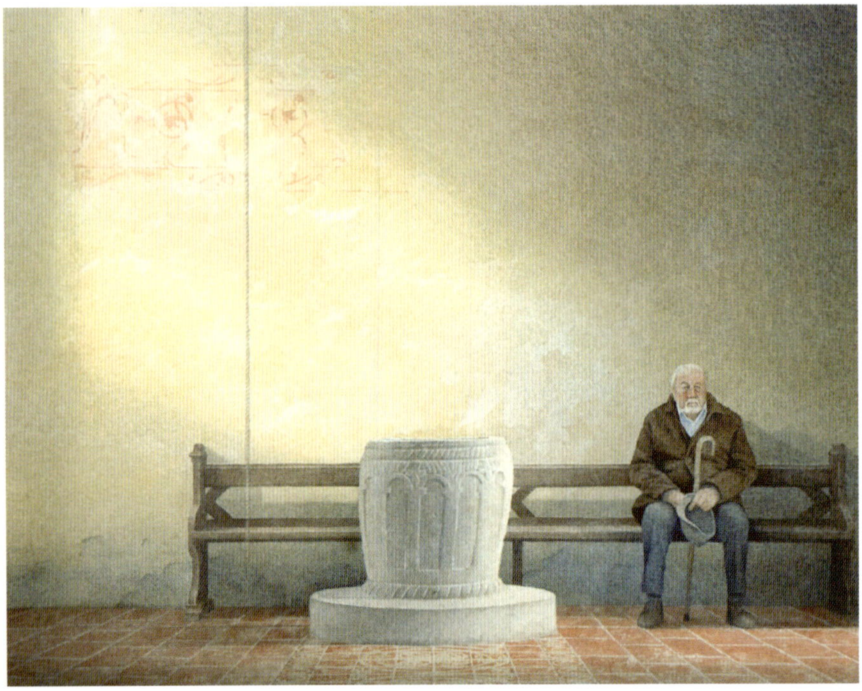

Church Crawling with Dad

Watercolour 2011

17 x 23 ins | 43 x 58 cm

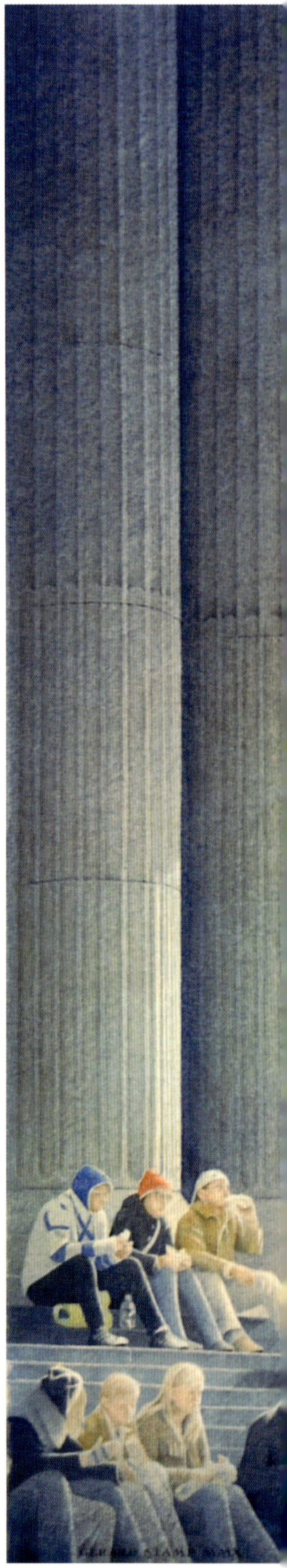

Lunch Hour on the Steps of St Paul's

Watercolour 2010

44 x 49 ins | 112 x 124 cm

Turning to St Paul's Cathedral, as one of the artists invited to show in a *St Paul's in the 21st Century* exhibition to mark the building's 300th anniversary – he decided to break once more with his normal pictorial rule of human exclusion. A building so central to capital and national life, and now with

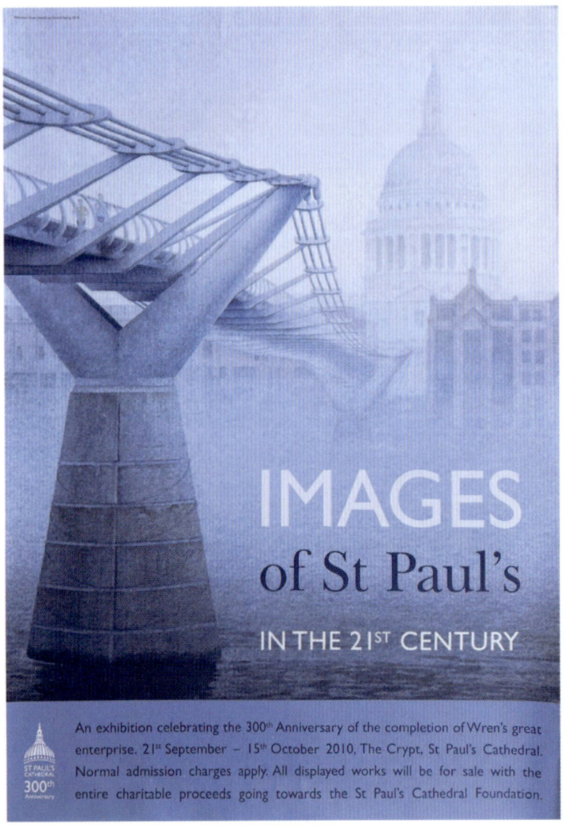

almost two million visitors from all over the planet annually, is Britain's most famous exercise in principled and architectural defiance.

Gerard had already tackled what many believe to be the very symbol of Britain in stone, with the great dome rising ever stable and majestic beyond a new and no-longer-wobbly footbridge in a 2009 watercolour *Millennium Dawn*. The vantage point was very near to the Thames-side lodgings of architect Christopher Wren, where he watched his domed design emerging from the ruins of the Great Fire of London over thirty-five agonised years. He lived to attend the dedication service.

This captivating image now became the poster for St Paul's sixty-four-artist birthday show. It also provided a one-work preview in the front window of Coutts Bank in the Strand before joining three more Stamp pictures among the array in the cathedral crypt.

The survival of St Paul's in the Second World War was a priority for Winston Churchill (whose funeral, like Nelson's, would be held there). Hit by two high-explosive blasts and dozens of incendiary bombs, the Wren masterpiece turned phoenix thanks to heroic effort by hundreds of fire fighters as the surrounding cityscape was levelled.

If ever a Stamp picture needed the human

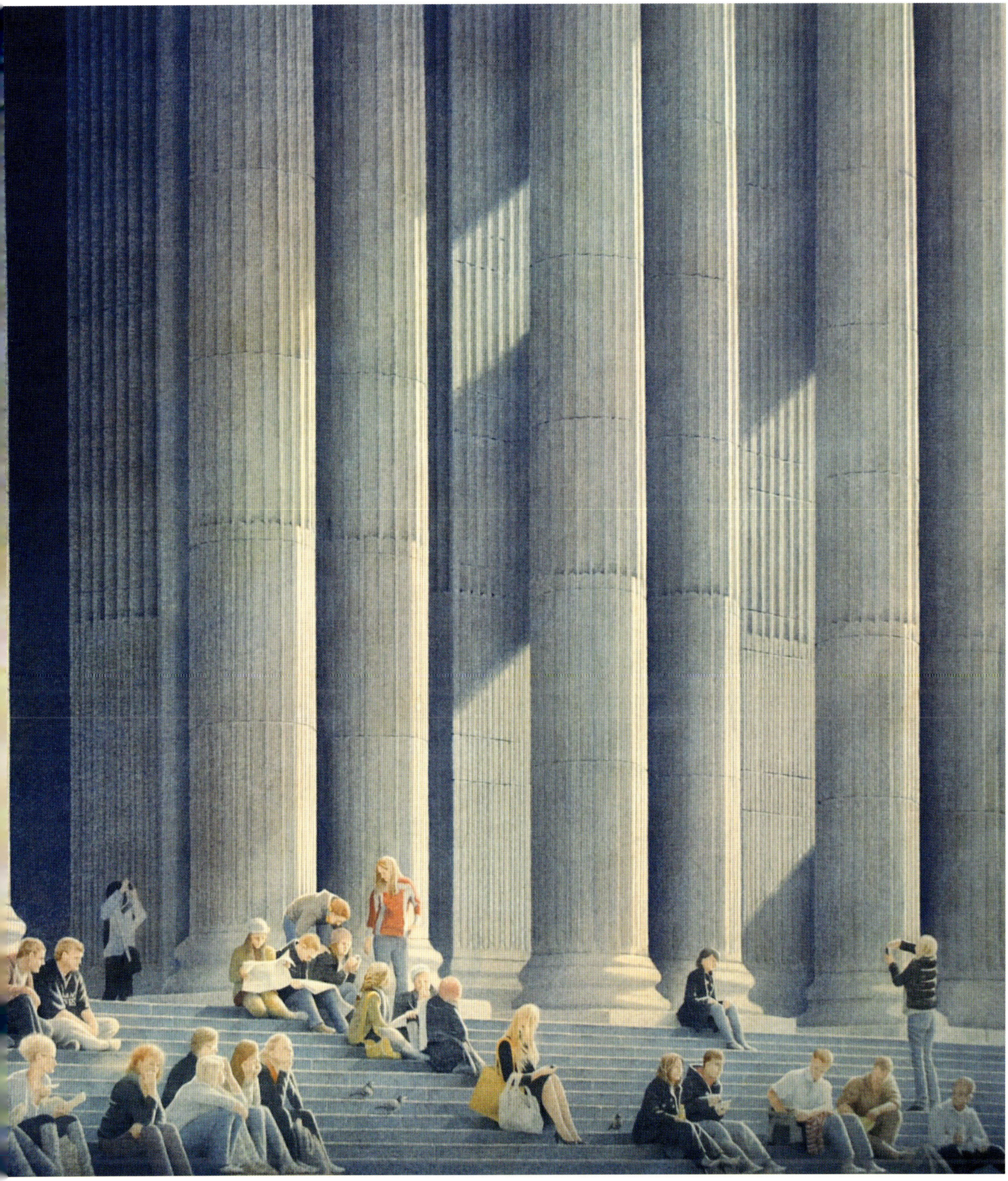

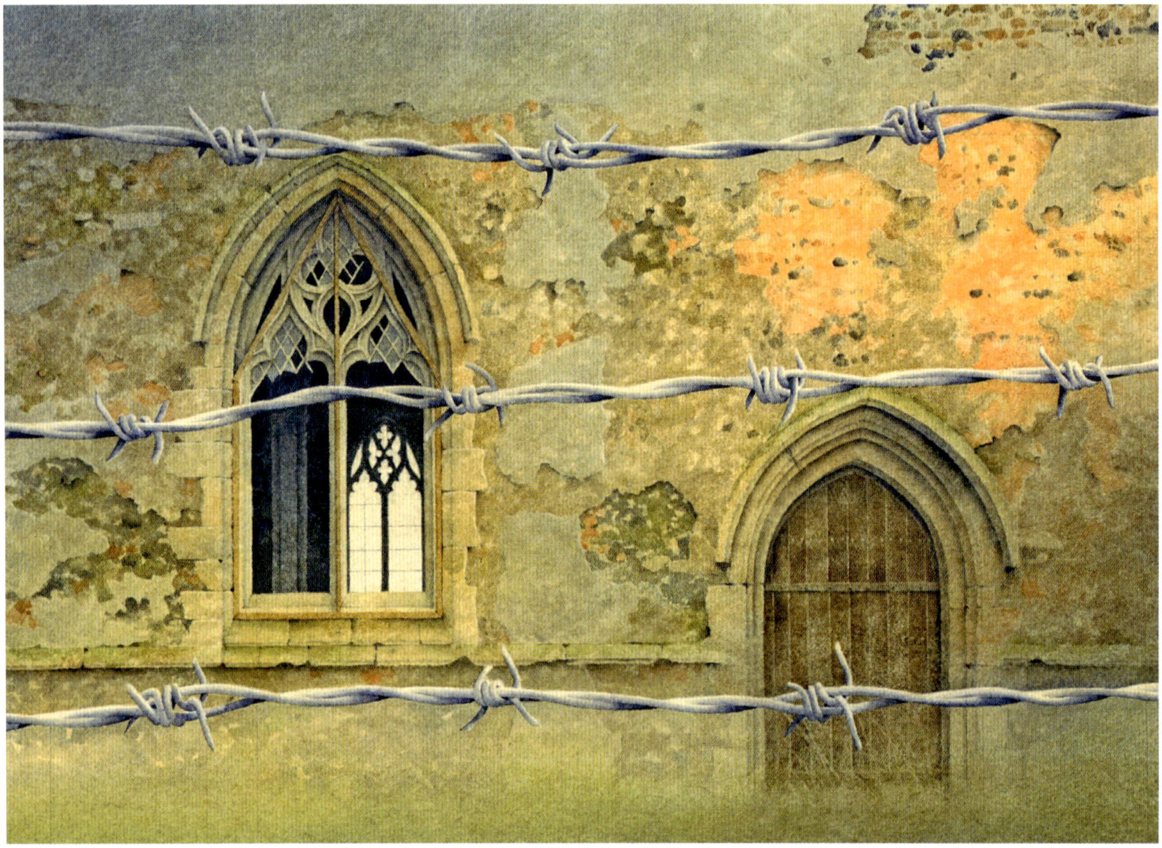

Out of Bounds to Troops

Tottington

Watercolour 2015

18 x 25 ins | 46 x 63 cm

element, this was surely it. Gerard now views the properly populated *Lunch Hour on the Steps of St Paul's* as one of his best paintings. The depicted leisure has been very hard won.

But, crucially, every church portrait by Gerard Stamp is about humanity even if apparently emptied of people. 'What is it about these places I love?' he asks. And he answers: 'Their architecture, of course, but also the sense that you can touch the past; the stories they tell of a community and its craftsmen; the fact that they belong to everyone.'

As Ronald Blythe, the great chronicler of rural and spiritual life, wrote of partly or wholly deserted East Anglian churches:

'These are the walls within which everything was said: centuries of birth words, marriage words, more words, death words, gossip, the language of the hymn poets and the song writers, of the Latin and English liturgists, and the immense Bible translation language.

'All this language said here in the local accent. This place is witness through the year to the very creation of literary and colloquial English as getting on for a thousand years of sermons battered away at human nature. So it is a house of words as well as a house of wood and stone. No old church can be understood if one omits the eloquence factor.'

It is that whispered legacy of language – so silent now that most of us cannot detect it – which Gerard Stamp hears from 'echoes in the wind'.

In the summer of 1942, residents of six Norfolk villages near Thetford heard that they must lose their homes to help win the Second World War. A military plan to depopulate 30,000 acres of Breckland anticipated feigned battles in preparation for D-Day landings and the liberation of continental Europe.

The people ordered to evacuate within three weeks would never return; they were rehoused but their ancient communities were lost forever. The story fascinated Gerard Stamp, especially since four abandoned medieval churches were still standing within the exclusion zone – protected by blast-proof roof coverings.

In what is now called STANTA, the Stanford Training Area, mock German and Afghan villages

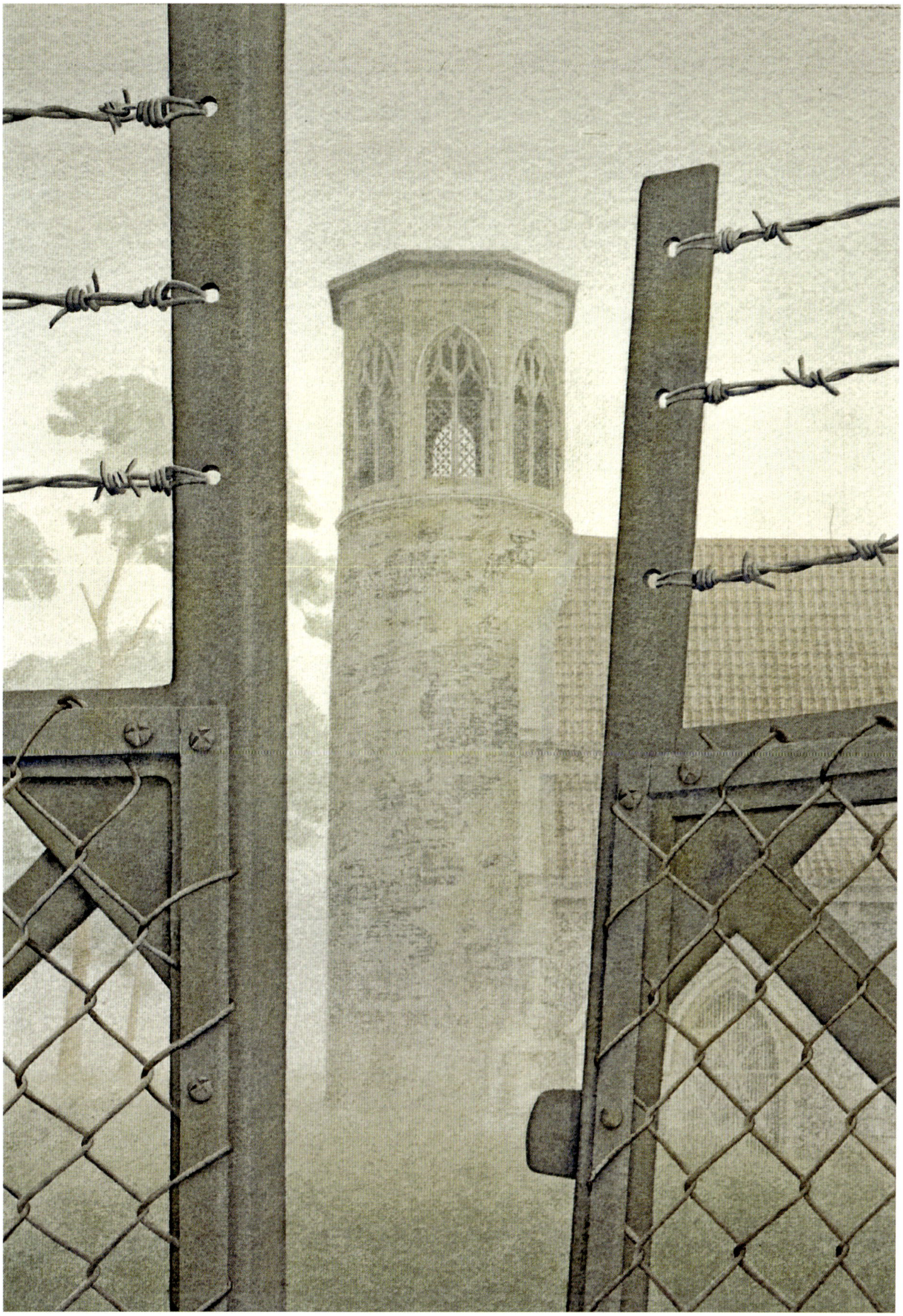

Out of Bounds to Troops

Stanford

Watercolour 2015

24 x 17 ins | 61 x 44 cm

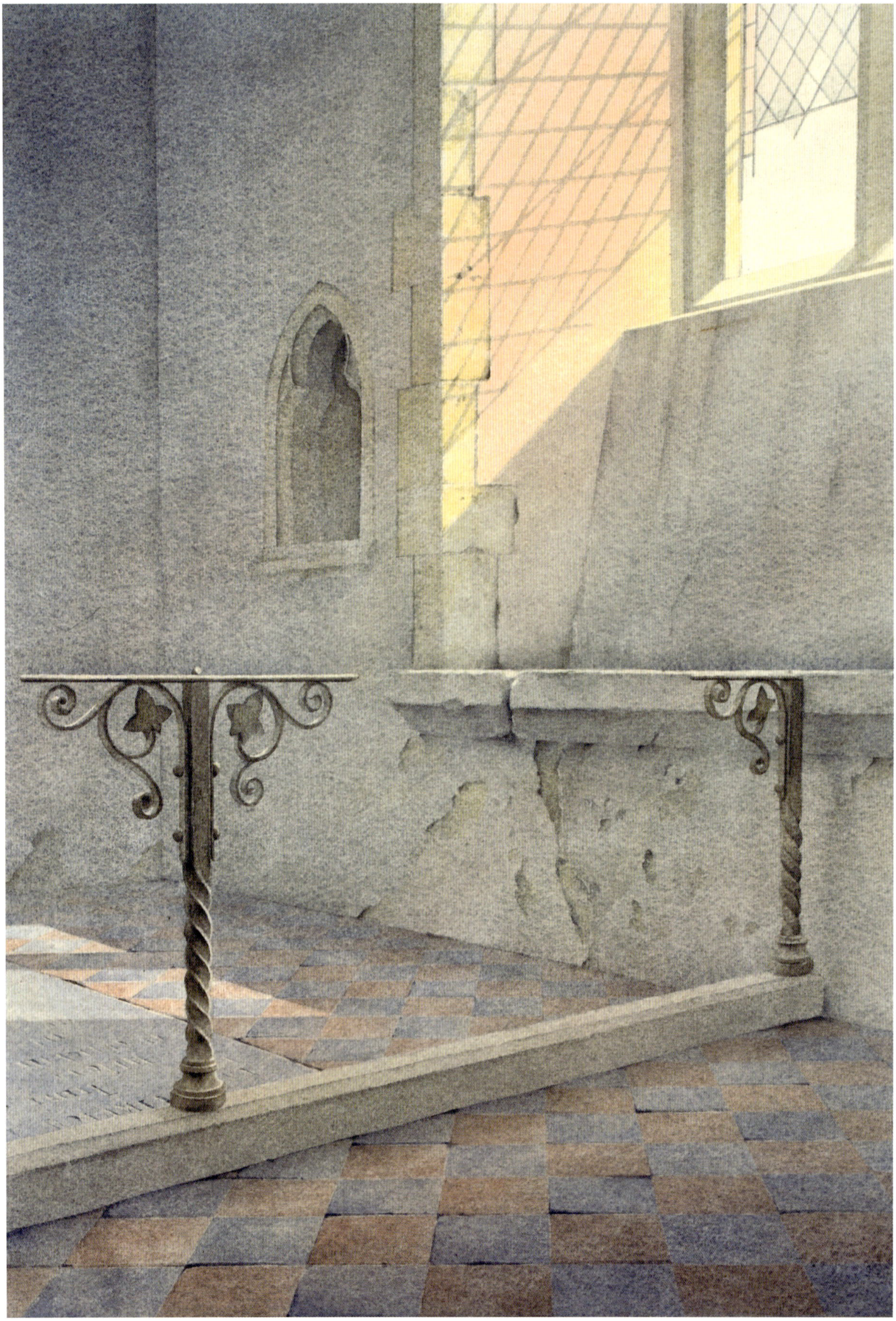

Communion Rail

Pillars, Langford

Watercolour 2015

23 x 16 ins | 58 x 41 cm

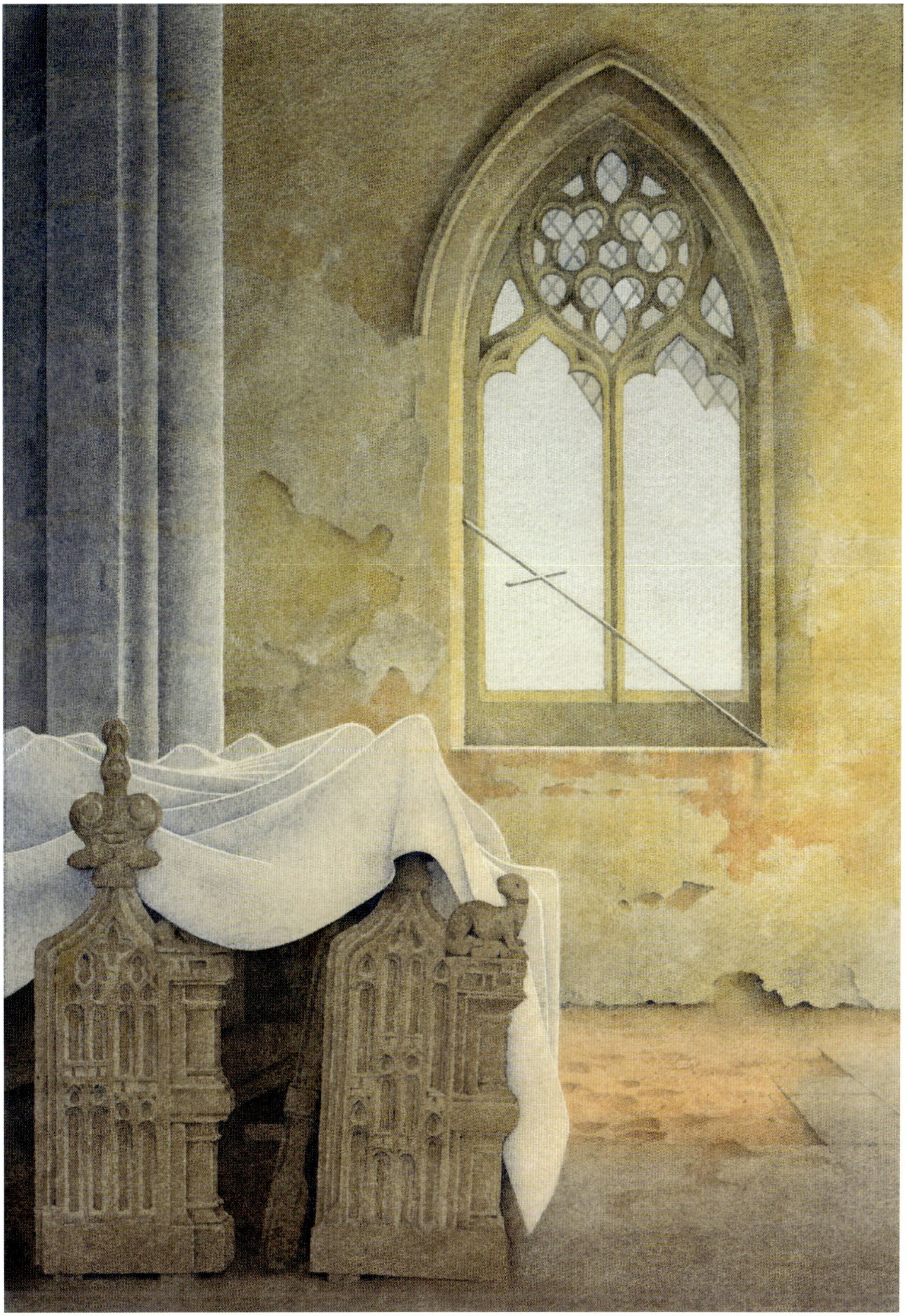

Tottington Pews

Watercolour 2015

25 x 18 ins | 63 x 45 cm

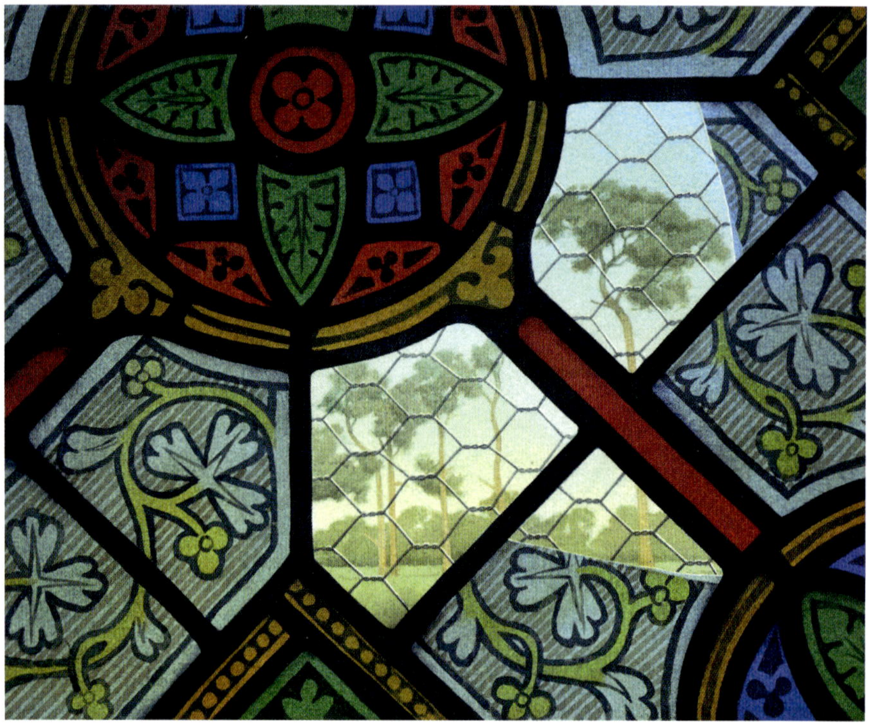

Stained Glass
West Tofts
Watercolour 2015
16 x 21 ins | 41 x 53 cm

were built down the decades complete with church and mosque. More recent manoeuvres have involved training Ukrainian troops for trench warfare. Millions of television viewers were granted indirect access to this forbidden domain of forest and heath from 1968, thanks to filming permission for *Dad's Army*.

Gerard was allowed to follow with sketchbook and camera for two days in 2015 – the start of what became a Ministry of Defence presentation the following year in St Peter Hungate church in Norwich. 'The experience was unforgettable,' he says, 'poignant, utterly quiet (this was during a break in military exercises!) and with a melancholic beauty normally experienced in a ruin – although, in its way, this is the ruin of a whole community on a vast scale.' At Tottington he depicted crumbling fifteenth-century masonry and gaping window frames behind barbed wire, shunted and sheeted pews bearing wondrous carvings and a fenced and grassed porch before a disused entrance door bearing the ironic notice 'CAUTION UNEVEN FLOOR'.

At Norman Langford he alighted on a broken Victorian communion rail, while at Stanford an ornately rounded stone tower was depicted through a metal enclosure. And at West Tofts – substantially enlarged by Pugin in the 1850s – breaks in Victorian stained-glass windows allowed a view not only of wire mesh but of beautiful pine trees beyond.

As the artist commented: 'There has been another unexpected and extraordinary benefit of Army occupation: STANTA since 1942 has remained largely unspoilt Breckland countryside wonderfully rich in flora and fauna. It is now one of the largest sites of Special Scientific Interest in England.'

That led to a 2019 project, painting a dozen threatened sites across Britain, for SAVE Britain's Heritage. The tally included: a gutted and boarded Victorian Dolphin Inn in Great Yarmouth;

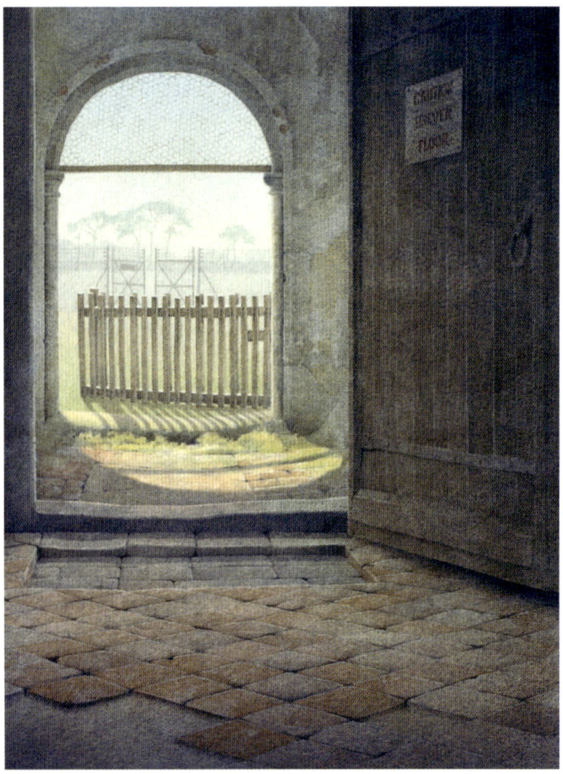

Tottington Porch
Watercolour 2015
23.5 x 17 ins | 60 x 44 cm

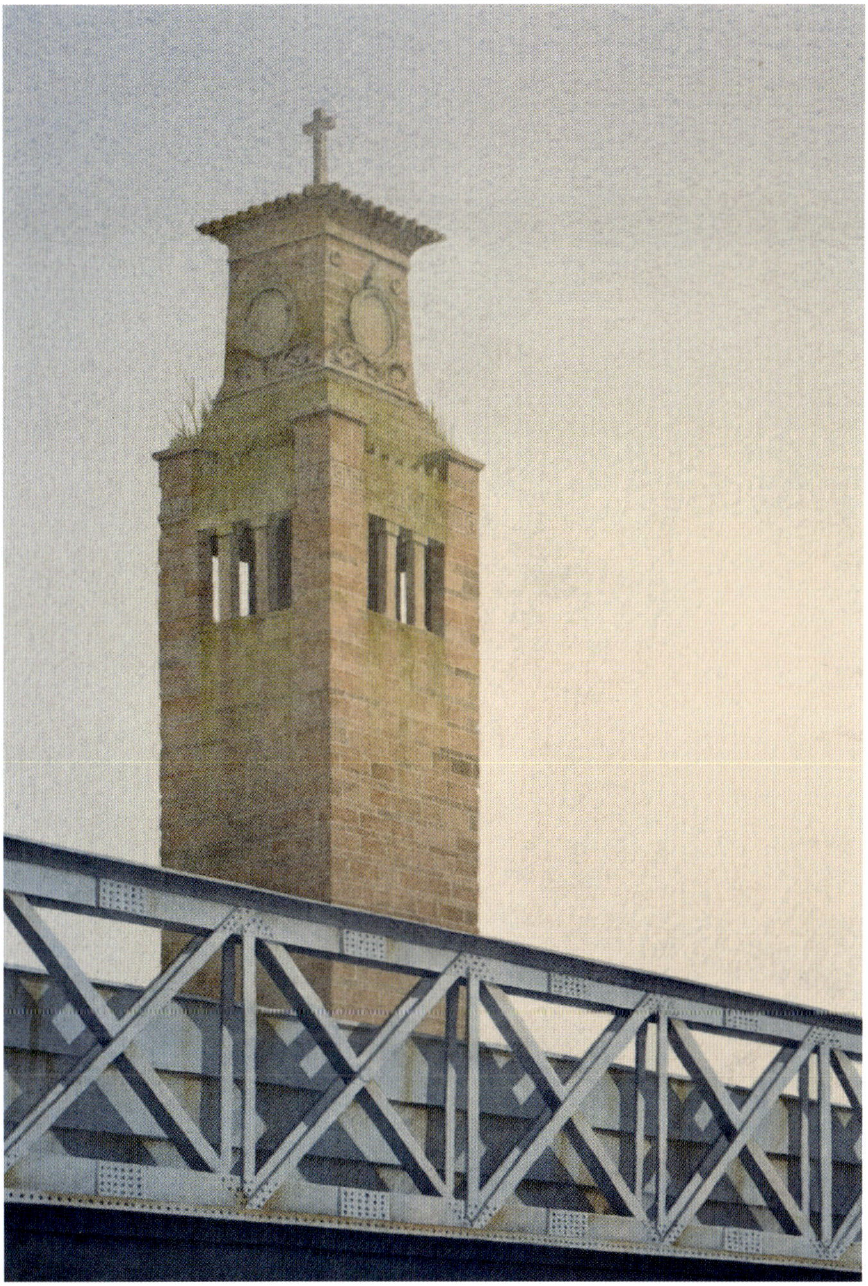

Caledonia Road Church Glasgow
Watercolour 2019
22 x 15 ins | 56 x 38 cm

Seafield House, an ex-hospital in Ayr designed by Sir William Arrol, engineer of the Tay, Forth and Tower bridges; and Caledonia Road Church in Glasgow, built by the Scottish Victorian architect Alexander 'Greek' Thomson, whose reputation Gavin did much to revive.

That same year Gerard turned to the church beside his house for a watercolour of the temple-style St Andrew's Gunton – the only complete Robert Adam chapel in England – on its 250th anniversary. The picture was auctioned at a concert of Baroque music to help repair interior stucco work. All such campaigning was very much in the spirit of his brother Gavin.

Across multifarious projects, the siblings had finally aligned for Gerard's *Isle of Light* exhibition depicting and hosted by Ely Cathedral in the autumn of 2016. Gavin contributed a wise and witty essay. 'Gerard's life and mine have gone in very different directions,' he concluded.

'The first working part of his was alien to me, but what I so admired was that, when he could, he gave up lucrative metropolitan existence and returned to Norfolk – and not just to enjoy sybaritic leisure but to devote himself to something really serious: painting.

'Even more admirable was the way he took this new (or revived) vocation so seriously, working hard and closely studying the best models, above all, the watercolours and etchings by that Norwich genius, John Sell Cotman.

'All this shows so happily in Gerard's own work which, I have to say as a bemused big brother, one that merely writes these days rather than makes, gets better and better.

'And it is now so very satisfactory that our

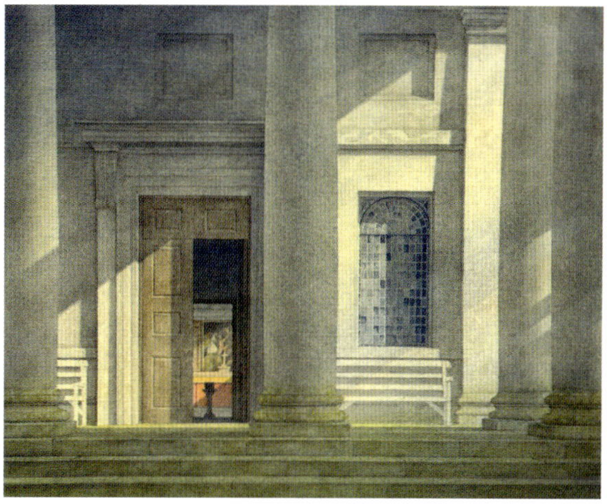

Gunton Chapel
Watercolour 2019
17.5 x 24 ins | 45 x 61 cm

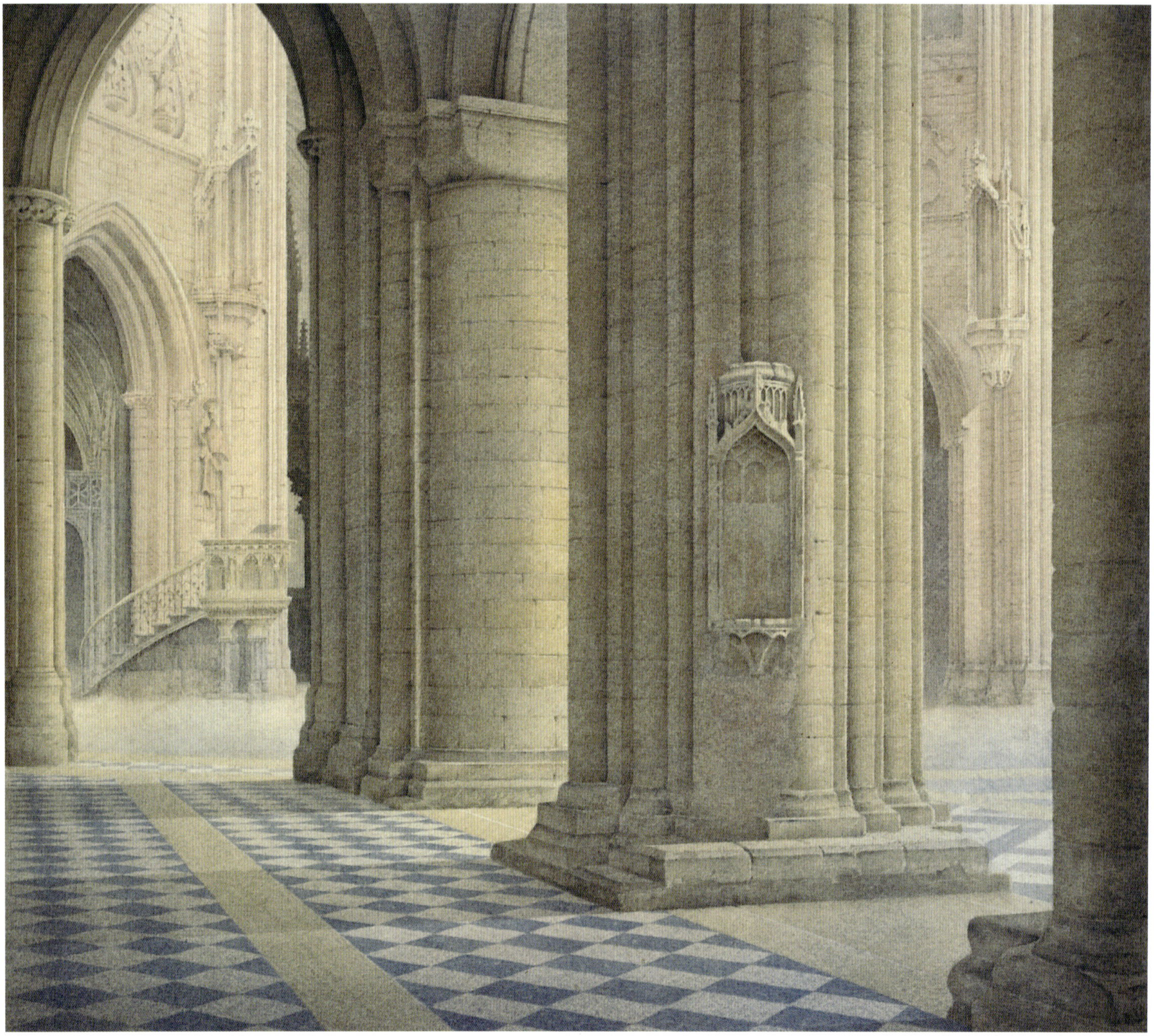

separate but compatible architectural enthusiasms should have converged on glorious, incomparably strange and yet so beautiful Ely Cathedral – the perfect subject for a romantic painter who understands and responds so creatively to great and venerable buildings.'

Barely a year after that fraternal collaboration, Gavin Stamp died, from cancer. Returning from a last meeting, on a sad Tuesday in London, Gerard had written his brother and mentor a loving and grateful letter. Recalling their heady youthful days in London, and the parties on a nunnery roof, he wrote: 'It was around this time I became conscious of the now familiar line, "You must be Gavin's brother". In my own circle I was often introduced as Gavin at dinner parties and suchlike – an easy if lazy mistake to make. But as the years progressed I must confess it got more and more irritating. After all, wasn't I making a name for myself in advertising? Hadn't I won awards for helping to sell beans and burgers?

'But then I matured a little. (Just a little.)

The Empty Niche
Ely Cathedral
Watercolour 2016
22.5 x 25 ins | 57 x 64 cm

'Gradually, imperceptibly, the moniker "Gavin's brother" ceased to be a cause of irritation, but one of pride. I started to look at the business of advertising, and my role in it, with increasing anxiety. I kept recalling how disappointed and unimpressed Mum was when I showed her my first TV commercial and she said to me, "But you were so good at art."

'And I kept watching my brother.

'So the urge to change path, to do as much as possible with the talent that I have, went from being a trickle to become a torrent. I had to see what I could do as an artist, having spent so much of my life seeing what my brother was achieving as a writer, journalist, TV presenter, historian, teacher (and artist).

'So I quit advertising in order to paint. (Paintings of our shared passion, of course: beautiful buildings.)

'And then one day at a private view, much to my amusement, someone came up to us while we were chatting, took a look at you and said, "You must be Gerard's brother".

'What I am trying to say is that without the example of my big brother I doubt I would have been pushed to raise my own game to the modest successes I've achieved.

'Back to last Tuesday. You were holding my hand, and you said to me "I've still got so much to do." That touched me, has played on my mind, and hence this letter.

'All I can say is this: just look at all you have done already – more than a dozen lifetimes combined. Frankly, if you live to 100 you will still be saying "I've still got so much to do".

'I am deeply proud to be Gavin's brother.'

Gavin Stamp died while the letter was in the post. He was just sixty nine.

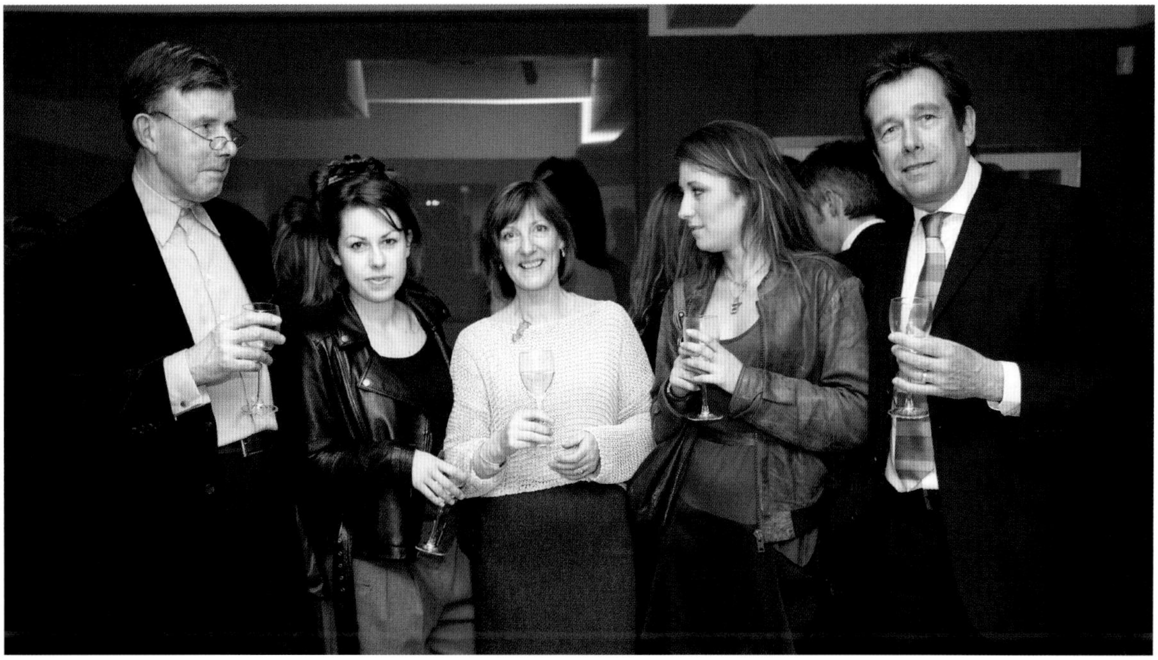

At the Churches Conservation Trust 40th anniversary exhibition, Bonhams, New Bond Street 30 March 2009

Left to right: Gavin, his daughter Agnes, Jacqui, Eleanor-Rose, Gerard

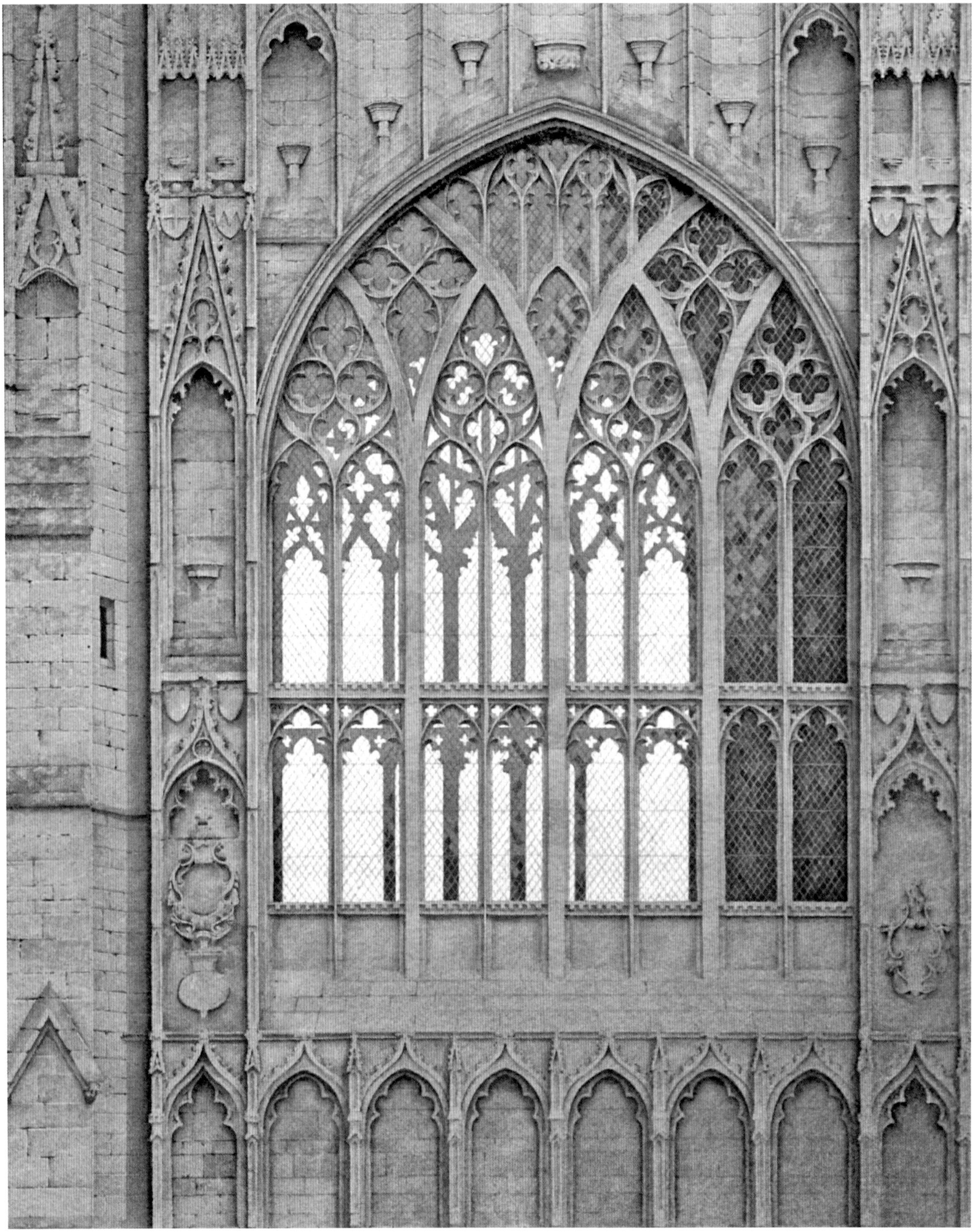

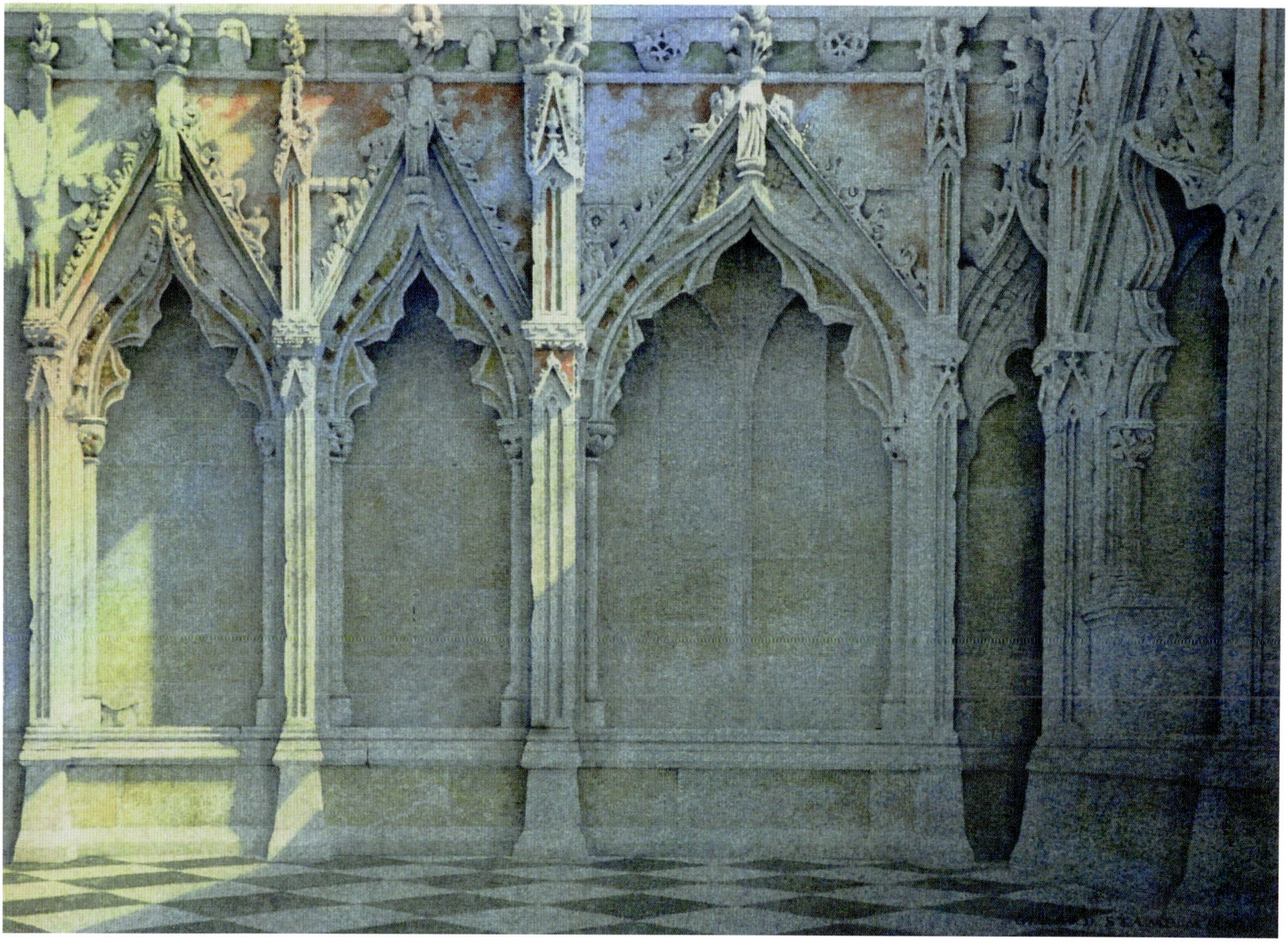

Lady Chapel Windows

Ely Cathedral

Watercolour 2015

30.5 x 24 ins | 78 x 62 cm

A Corner of the

Lady Chapel

Ely Cathedral

Watercolour 2019

17 x 23 ins | 43 x 58 cm

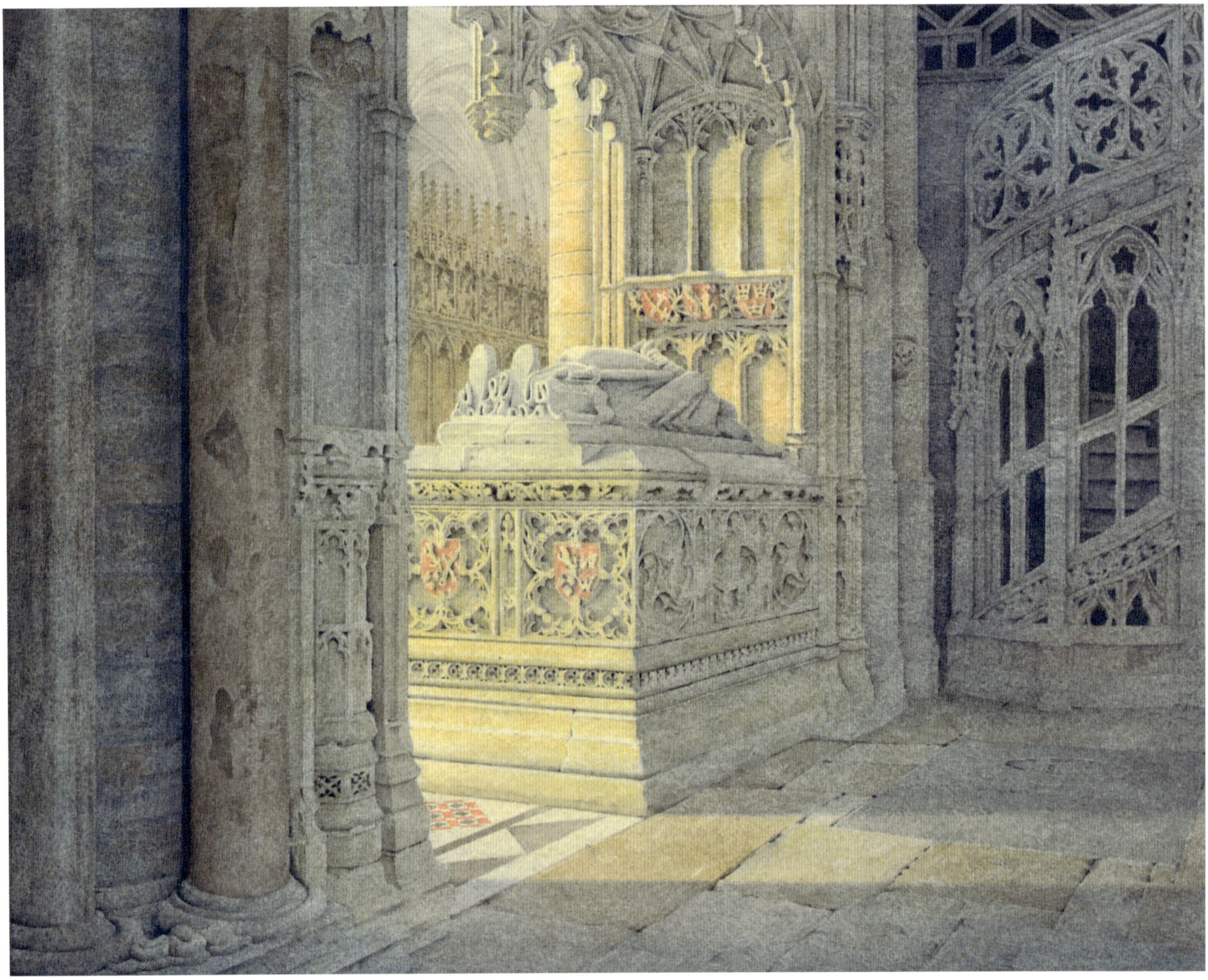

Bishop Redman's Tomb

Ely Cathedral

Watercolour 2016

17.5 x 22.5 ins | 45 x 57 cm

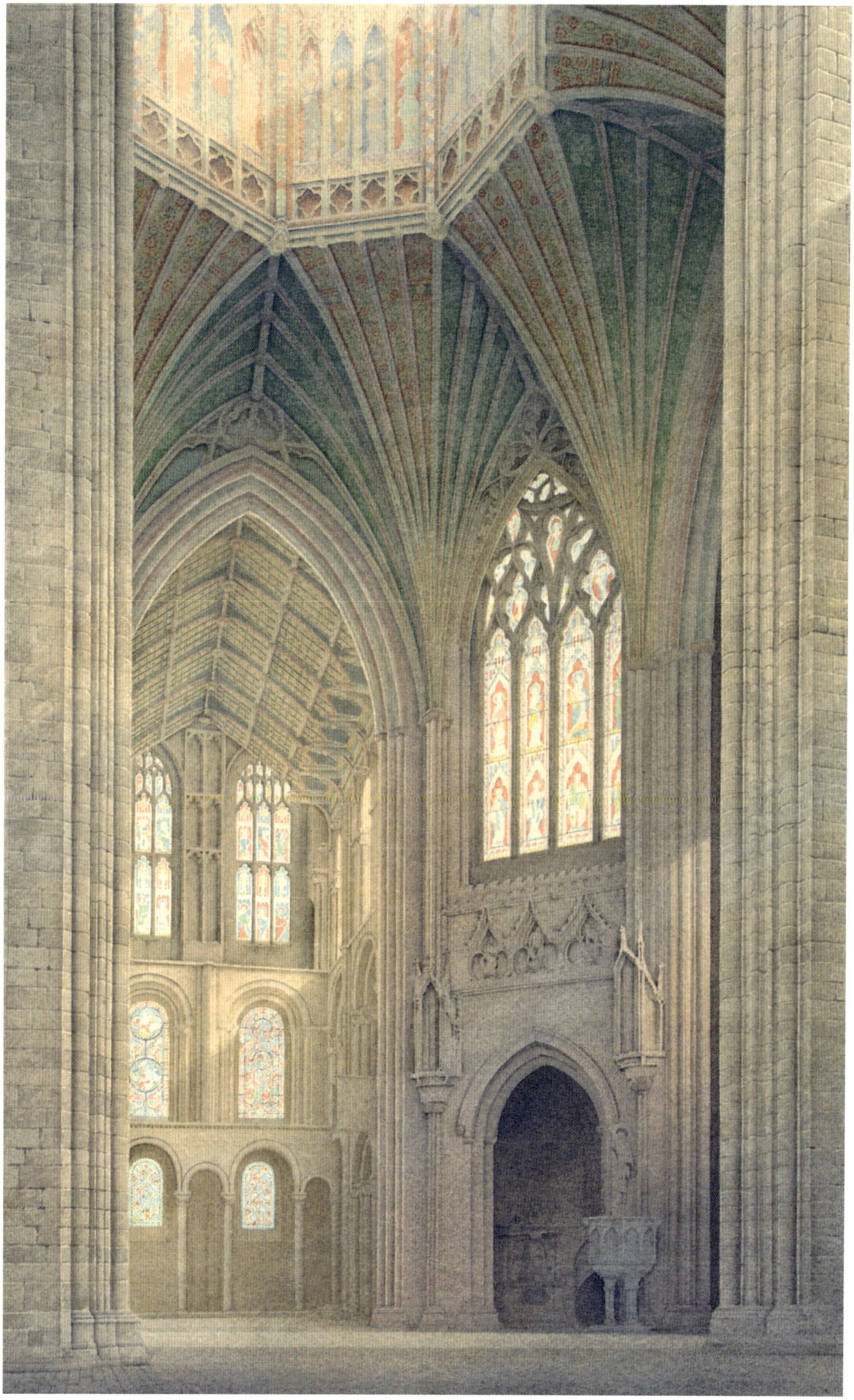

The Octagon

Ely Cathedral

Watercolour 2016

36 x 22.5 ins | 91 x 57 cm

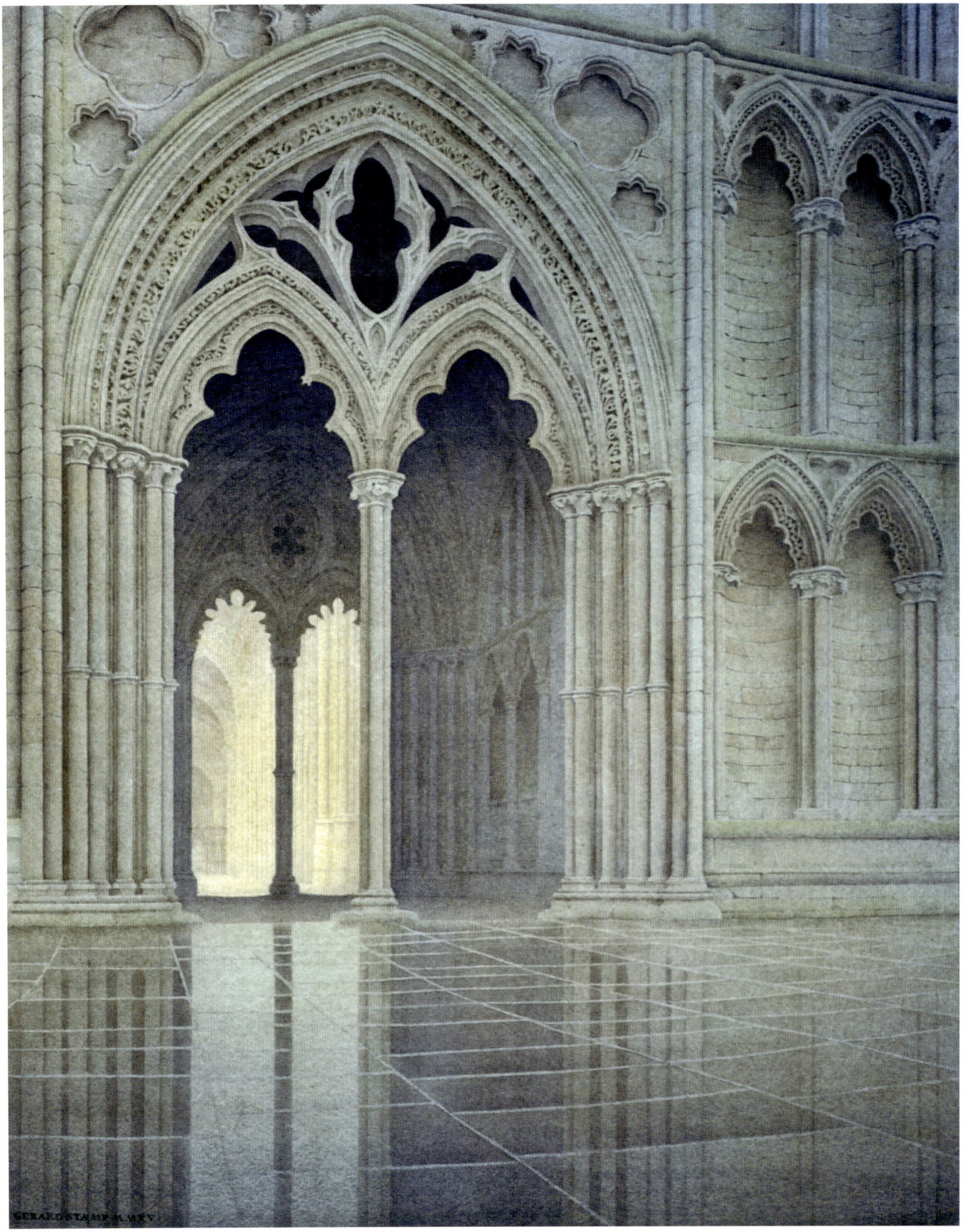

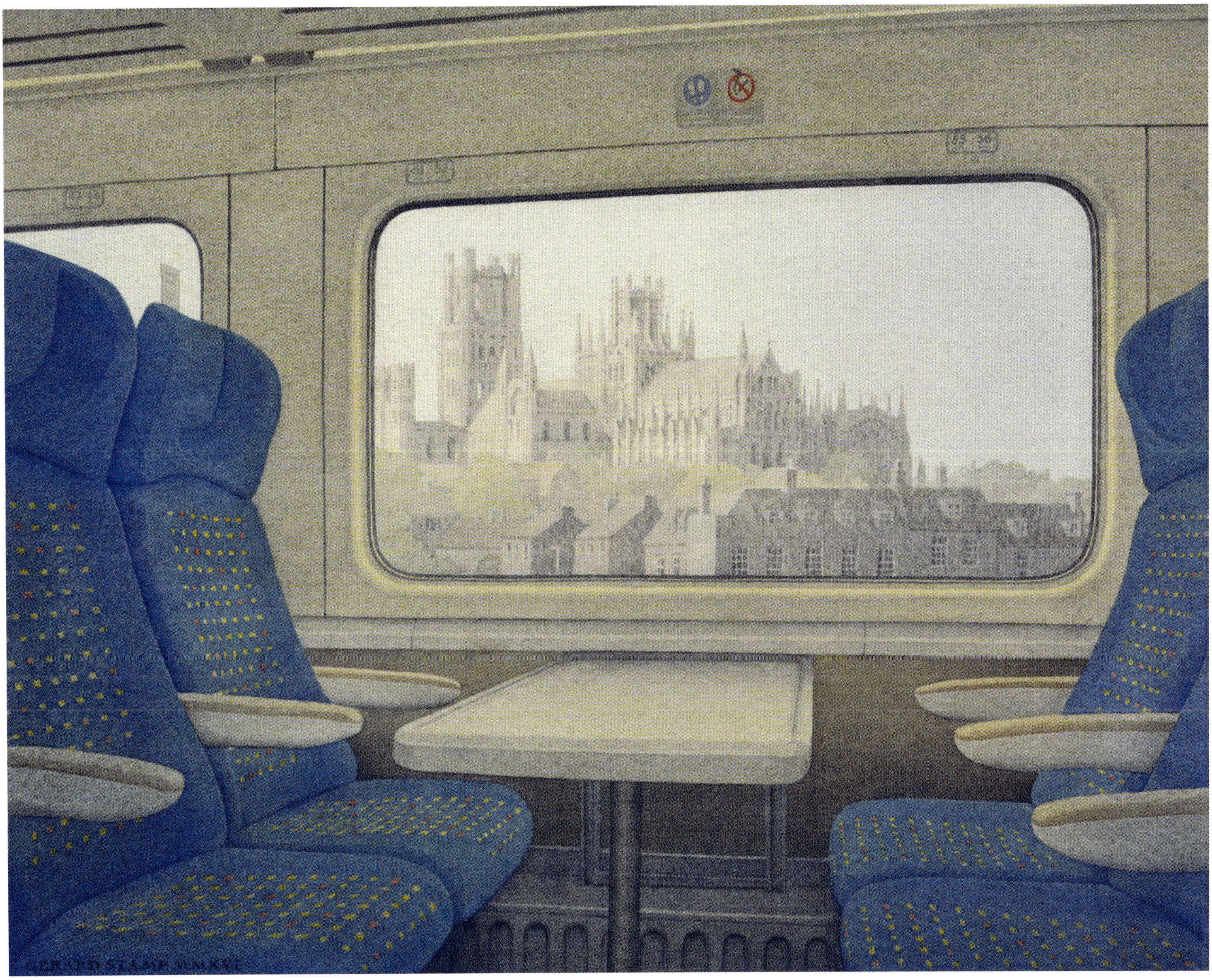

The Galilee Porch

Ely Cathedral

Watercolour 2015

32 x 25.5 ins | 81 x 65 cm

From a solo exhibition which

raised over £50,000 for

East Anglian Air Ambulance

Train Cityscape

(long after Ravilious)

Watercolour 2016

22 x 17 ins | 56 x 43 cm

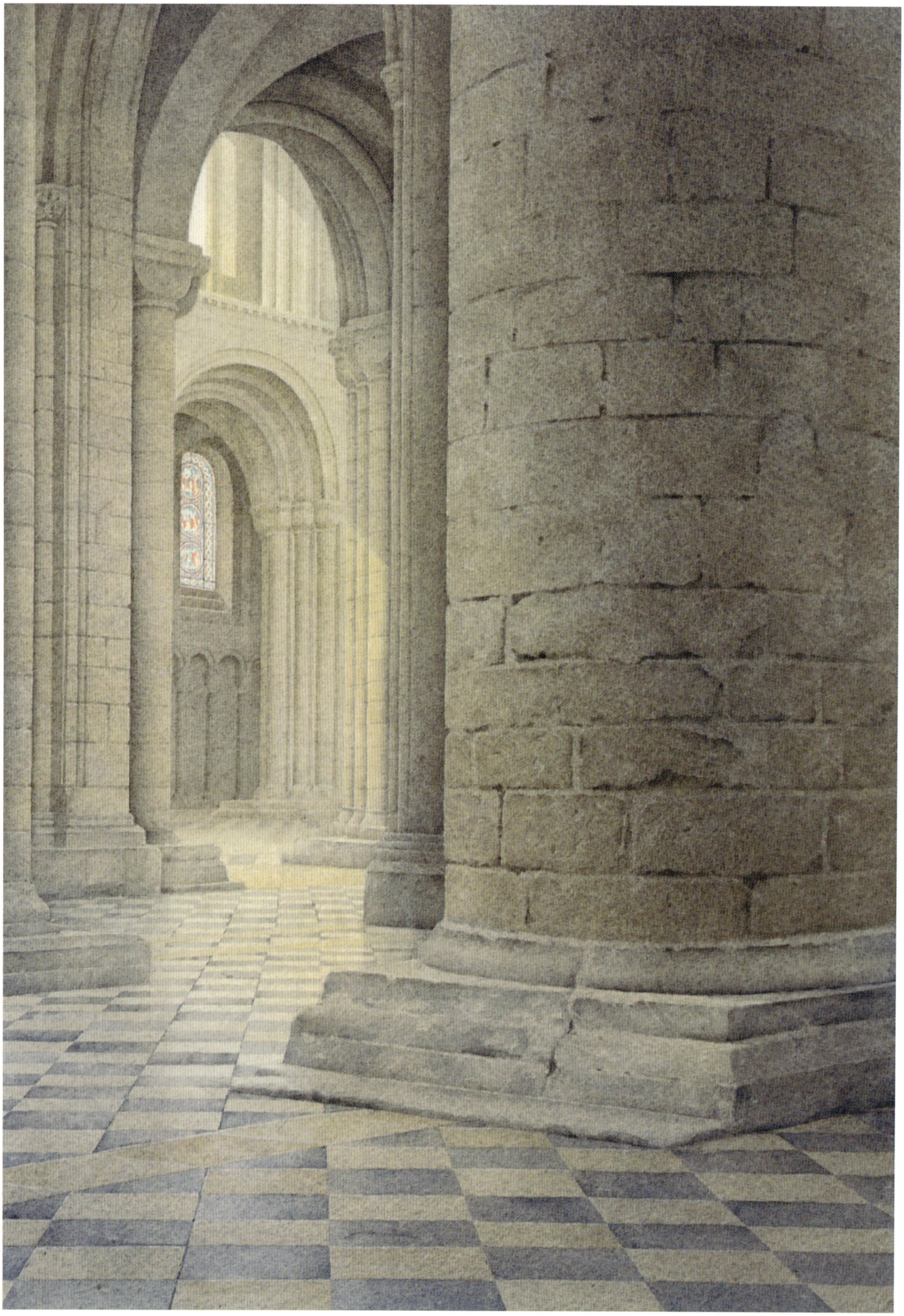

A Path to the Nave

Ely Cathedral

Watercolour 2016

22 x 17 ins | 56 x 43 cm

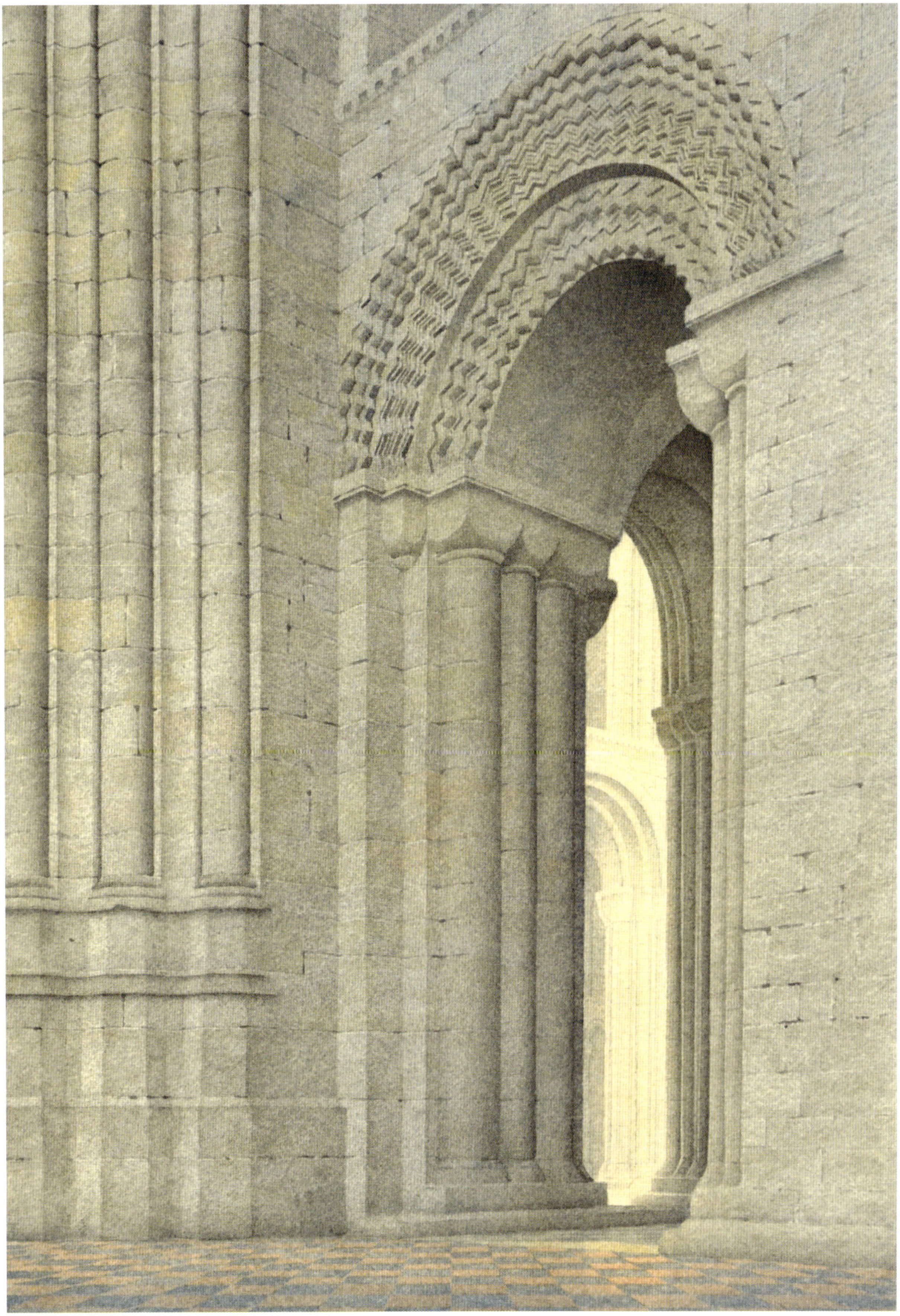

Zig-Zagging Towards the Nave Ely Cathedral

Watercolour 2015

25 x 17 ins | 63 x 44 cm

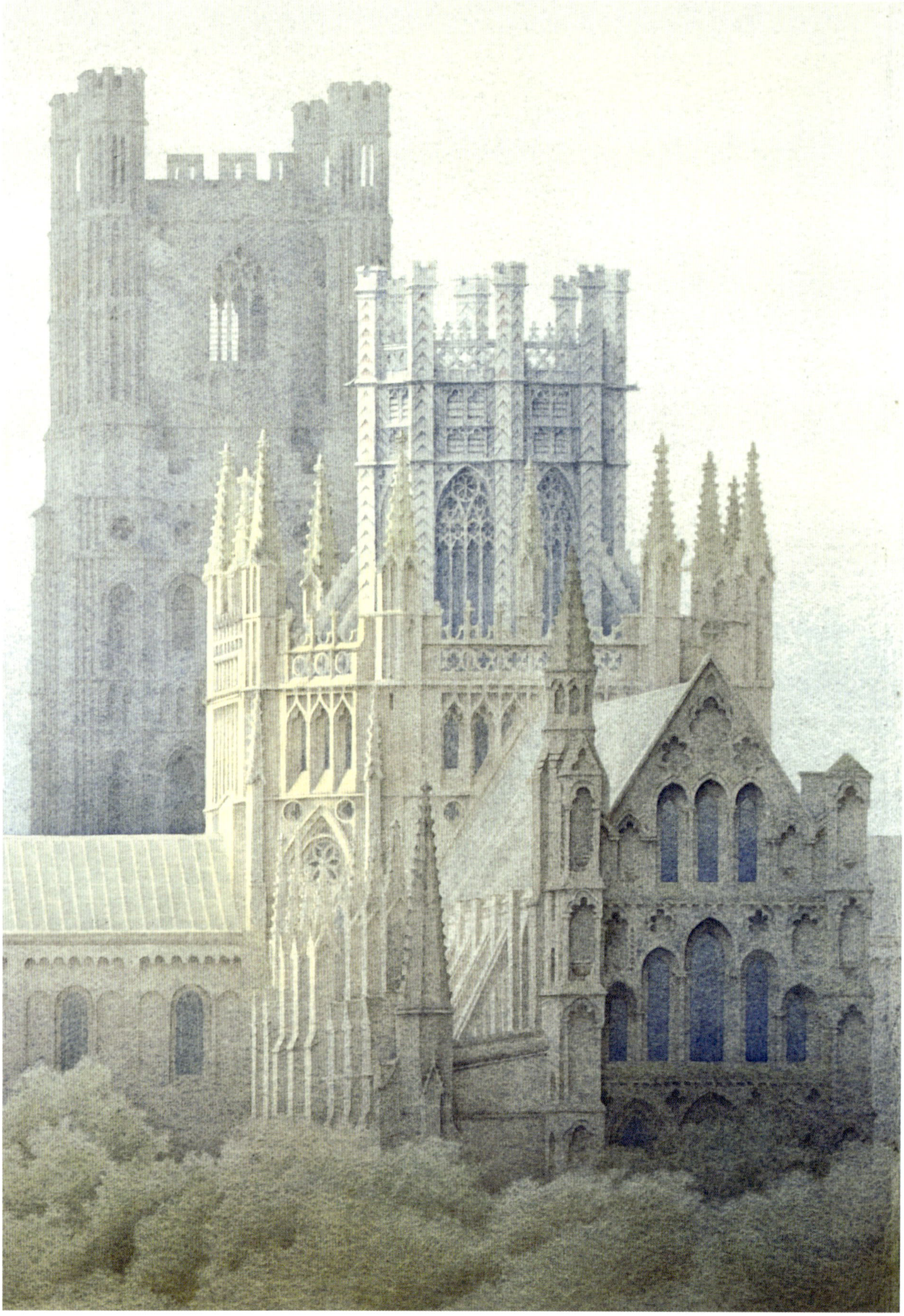

Ship of the Fens

Watercolour 2016

27 x 18 ins | 68 x 47 cm

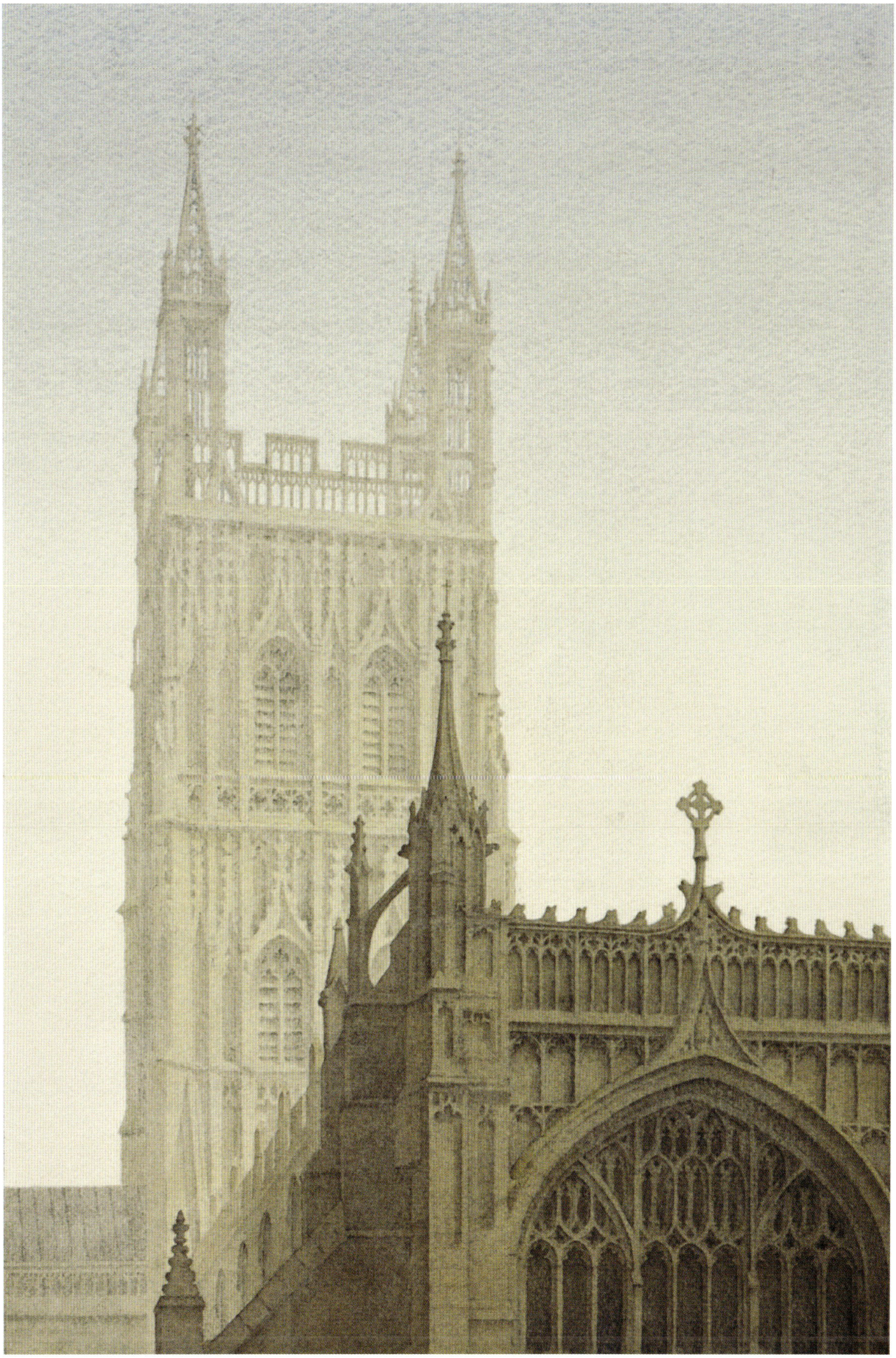

Gloucester Tower

Watercolour 2020

24.5 x 16 ins | 62 x 41 cm

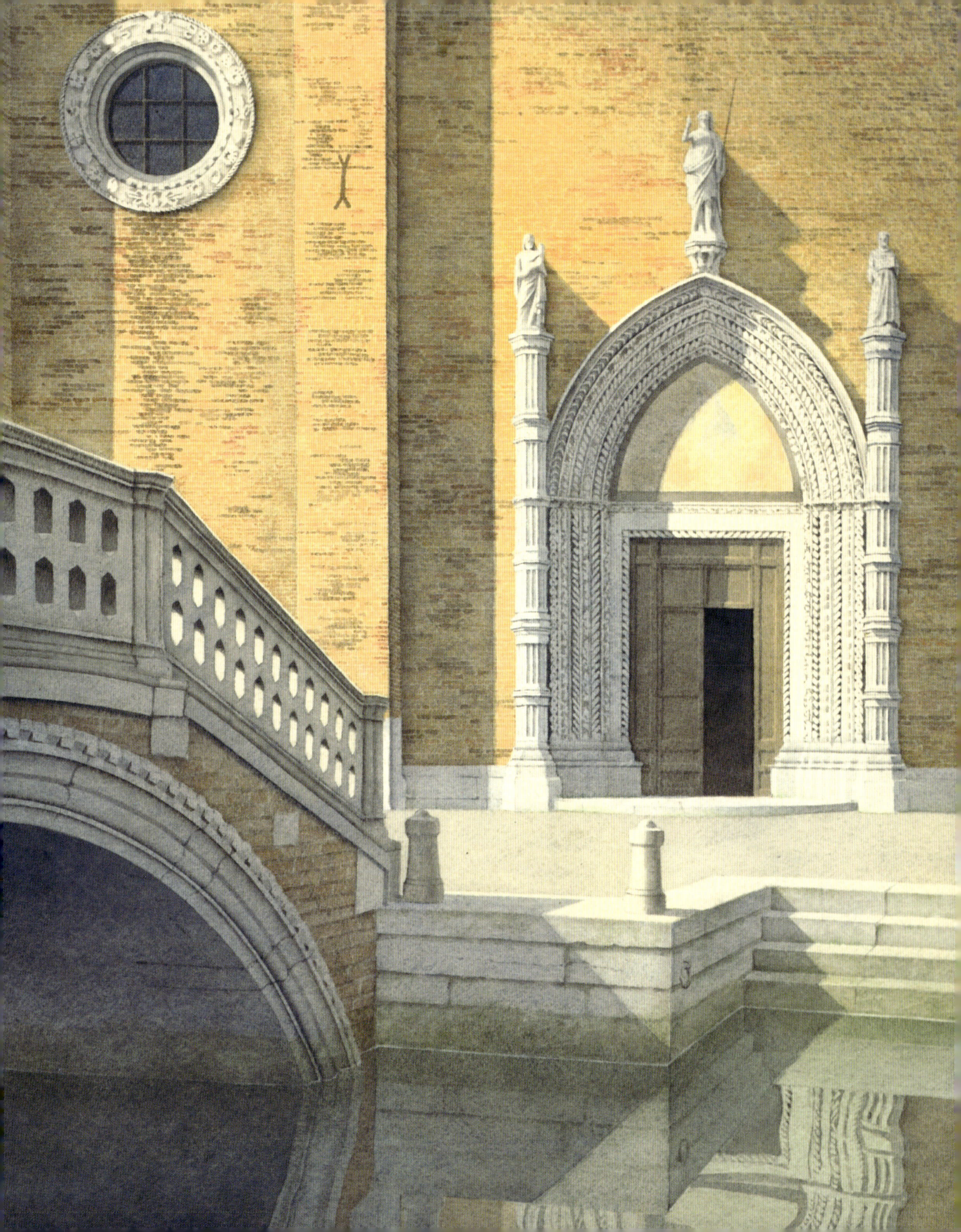

VII Echoes in the Wind

On 11 April 2019, four days before the burning of Notre Dame, a halogen floor lamp in the Stamp sitting room was accidentally left on and then nudged under a curtain. The result was very nearly the second great fire of Gunton.

Gerard opened the door of the octagon-shaped room, which had been the Georgian kitchen, and saw floor-to-ceiling flames. He quickly closed the door again and called the fire brigade. The action of starving the blaze of oxygen, plus the earlier installation of a fire-retardant ceiling, confined the blaze within the room. Flames never reached the windows, but the result was still a blackened mess of smoke and ash and an insurance bill for more than £100,000.

Painstakingly painted walls, made by the resident artist to resemble stone, had to be redecorated just as laboriously. But damage to engravings, piano and furnishings was less upsetting to the Stamps than a scorched potted palm. Jacqui had helped Gerard lug it from a former London office. 'I was so grateful that I proposed to her,' he told the *Financial Times*, where the near-disaster was recounted in a feature on insuring listed buildings. He hoped it might grow again. And it did.

The peace of Gunton Park was beyond wonderful during lockdown, and as restrictions eased Gerard Stamp painted, wrote, directed and presented a witty series of short films on church buildings, histories and legends for release on YouTube. The starting point for each one was a watercolour picture.

In 2020 he staged a *Fine English Churches & Cathedrals* exhibition at the John Davies Gallery in the Cotswolds. And in 2022, back in Norfolk, a show of his works at Wolterton Hall raised £50,000 for the East Anglian Air Ambulance. He continued to participate in mixed exhibitions and in charitable and conservation campaigns.

One happy collaboration was for a 2022 Father and Daughter exhibition at the Grapevine gallery in Burnham Market, with Gerard's landscape watercolours hanging alongside equine portraits by Eleanor-Rose Stamp. She had also followed her parents into advertising.

'I have lived and breathed horses all my life,' she says. 'I know their anatomy and their characters so well. With my background it would be impossible not to love old buildings, but as for painting them... they might look quite good but they wouldn't have that emotion that needs to come through. Now I have horses of my own not far from Gunton and Mum and I still ride together a couple of times a week.'

'Whatever you do, don't paint Venice. It's such a cliché'

Stamp cousins – daughters of Jacqueline and Gavin – would also carve out original careers as writer, artist and jewellery designer. But Rupert Stamp was to thrive as a programmer, designing computer games and projects focused on Britain's heritage, via coding – mathematically – on screen.

All the while Gerard was testing his thoughts and broadening his horizons. He had always admired the great houses and castles handed down to us by history, while never feeling the same passion to paint them as he felt for churches.

That was about to change. He had grown to love a particular statement from the Victorian art

Entrance to the Basilica dei Frari

Watercolour 2025

25.5 x 20 ins | 65 x 51 cm

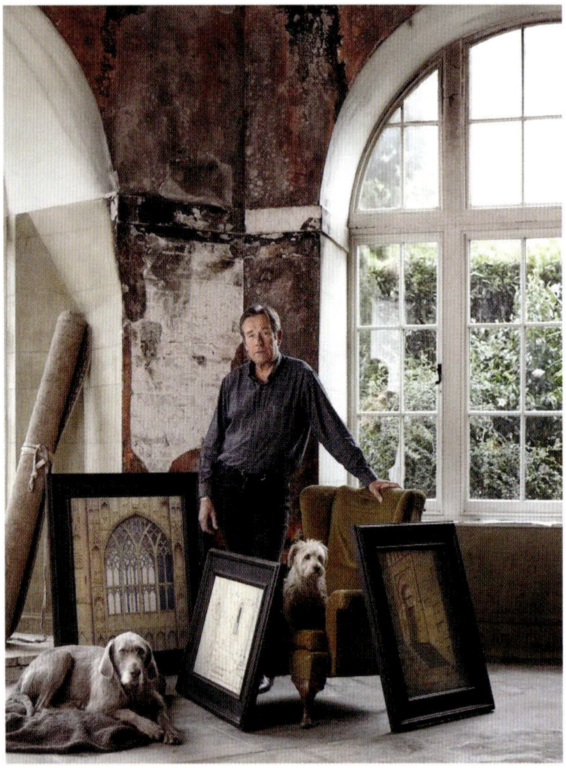

Rescued from the Flames
(*Financial Times* article on insuring historic homes 2019)
Photograph also features Viktor and Jackson

critic and artist John Ruskin: 'The greatest glory of a building is not in its stones, nor in its gold. It's glory is in its Age, and in that deep sense of voicefulness, of stern watching, of mysterious sympathy, nay, even of approval or condemnation, which we feel in walls that have long been washed by the passing waves of humanity... it is in that golden stain of time, that we are to look for the real light, and colour, and preciousness of architecture.'

Gerard responds: 'The idea that a structure made out of brick and stone can somehow impart "approval" or "condemnation" may be to the modern cynic at best unduly romantic and at worst utterly ridiculous. But it is this anthropomorphism, and the feeling of being able to touch the "passing waves of humanity", which give spirit to these places and draws me to them.'

Ruskin believed that the apotheosis of art lay in the works of J.M.W. Turner, and of architecture as arrayed in the buildings of Venice. It was that very conjunction that rather kept Gerard away from the great Italian city of stone, water and light. The deterrence hardened in an early encounter with an art dealer who said: 'Whatever you do, don't paint Venice. It's such a cliché.' Walter Sickert, who painted some highly innovative pictures of Venice, nevertheless took that done-to-death view of the lovely Stour Valley, forming the Suffolk-Essex borderland. In the wake of Gainsborough and Constable, he warned himself and others against tackling the landscape equivalent of a 'sucked orange'. He therefore missed the ongoing zest of renditions by Alfred Munnings, John Nash and Cedric Morris. Most rules have exceptions.

Gerard Stamp rather sneaked a magnificent Venetian picture into a 2008 exhibition – presenting a fresh view of the Doge's Palace between the columns of St Theodorus and St Mark's, the two patron saints of the city, in a misty morning light.

A brilliant introduction was long an outlier – though there would be a few more added over the years as the city of canals on the lagoon was visited and revisited.

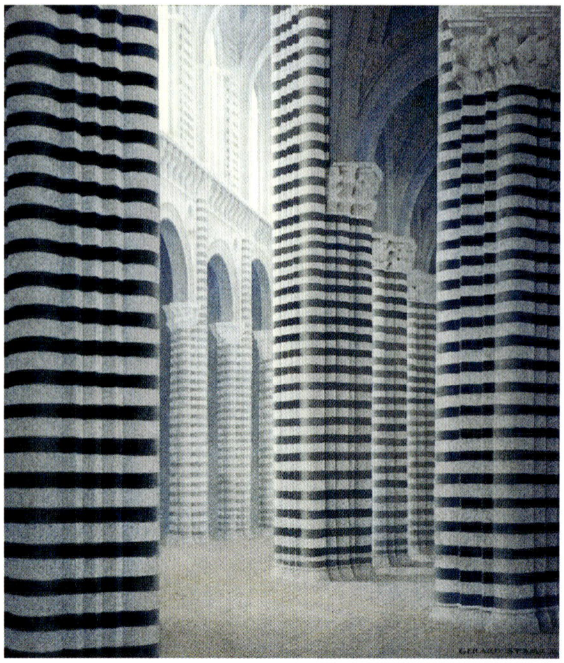

Siena Duomo
Watercolour 2011
18 x 18 ins | 46 x 46 cm

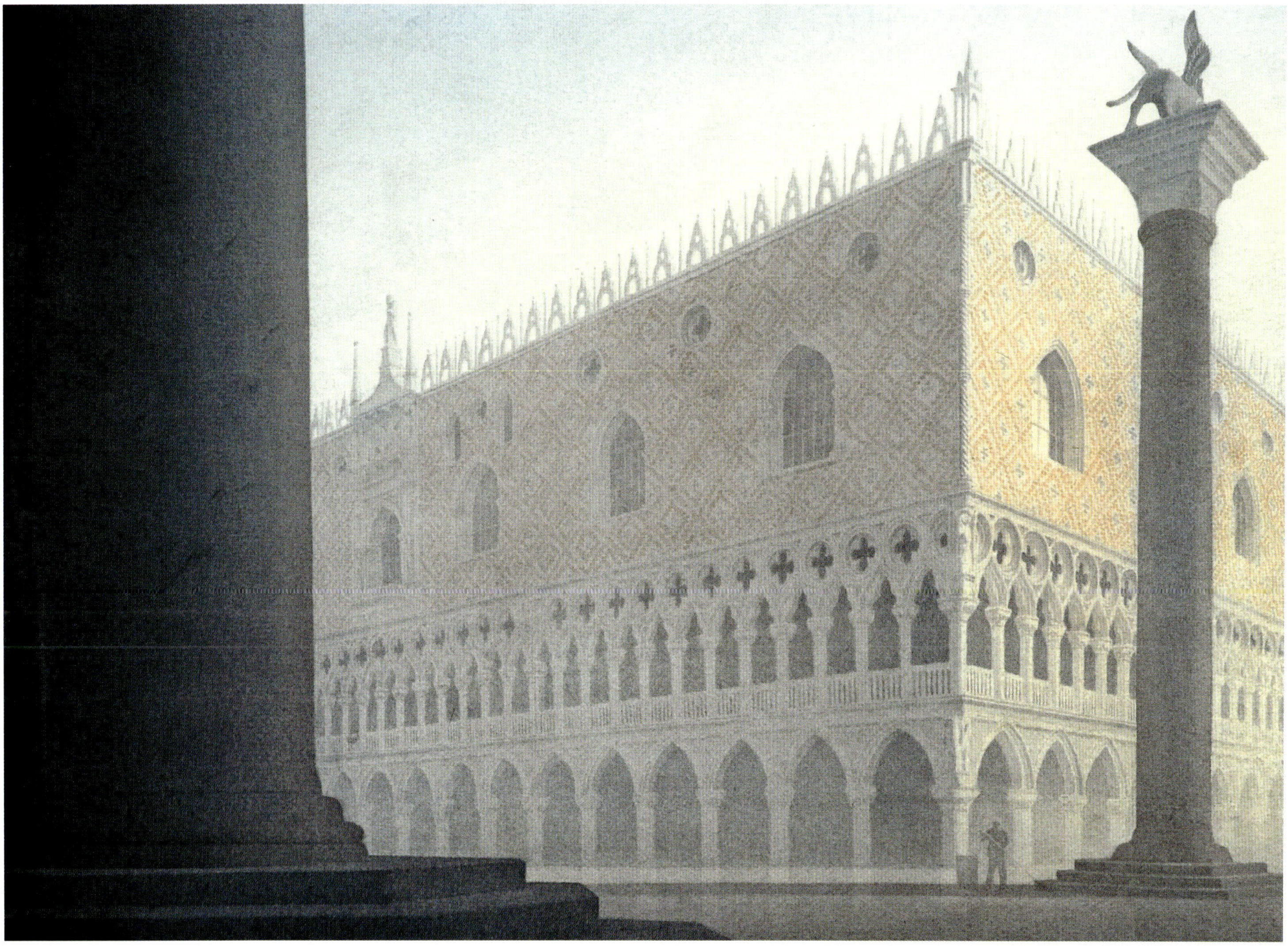

Doge Dawn

Watercolour 2008

20.5 x 27.5 ins | 52 x 70 cm

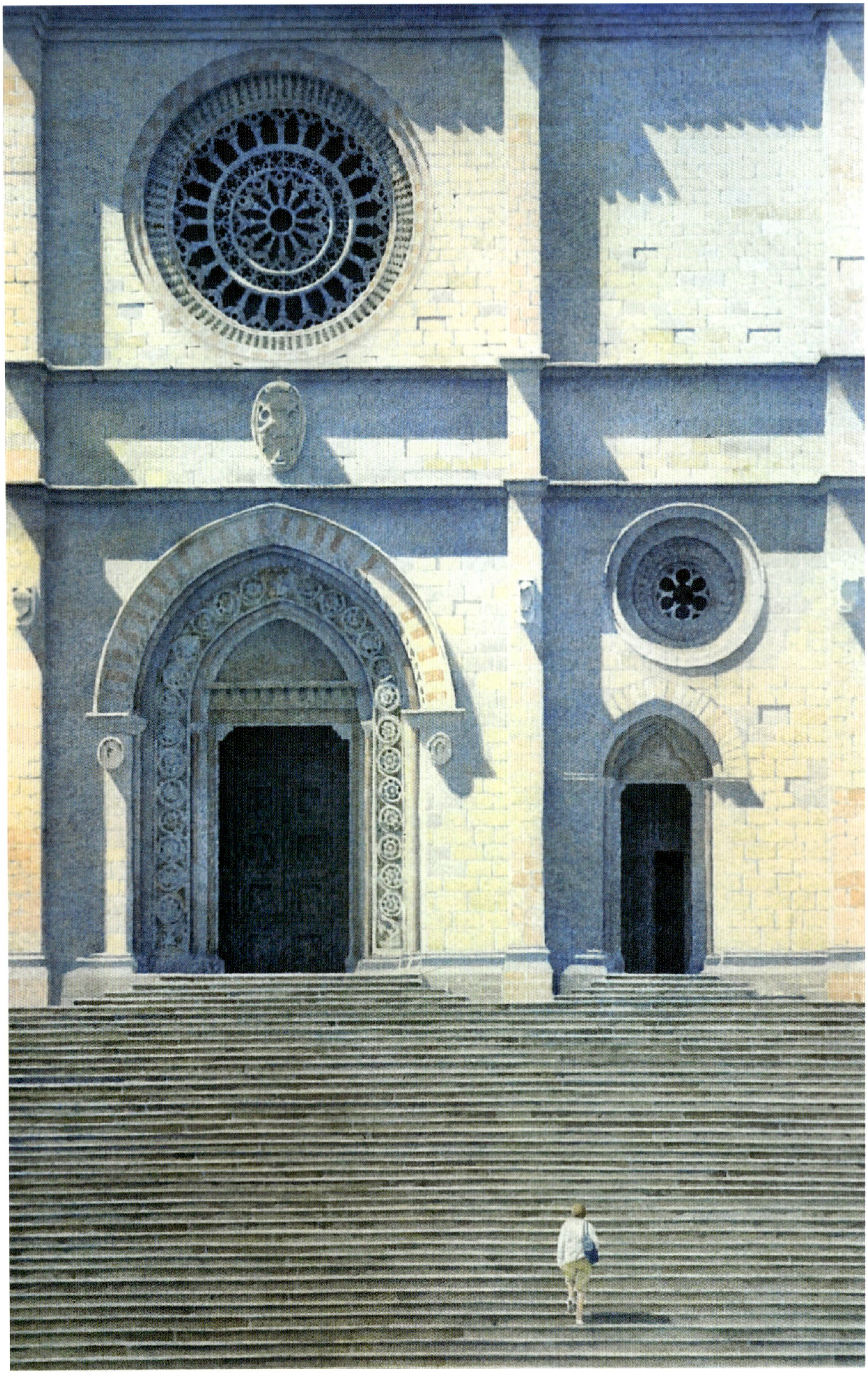

Todi Duomo

Watercolour 2011

34 x 23 ins | 86 x 58 cm

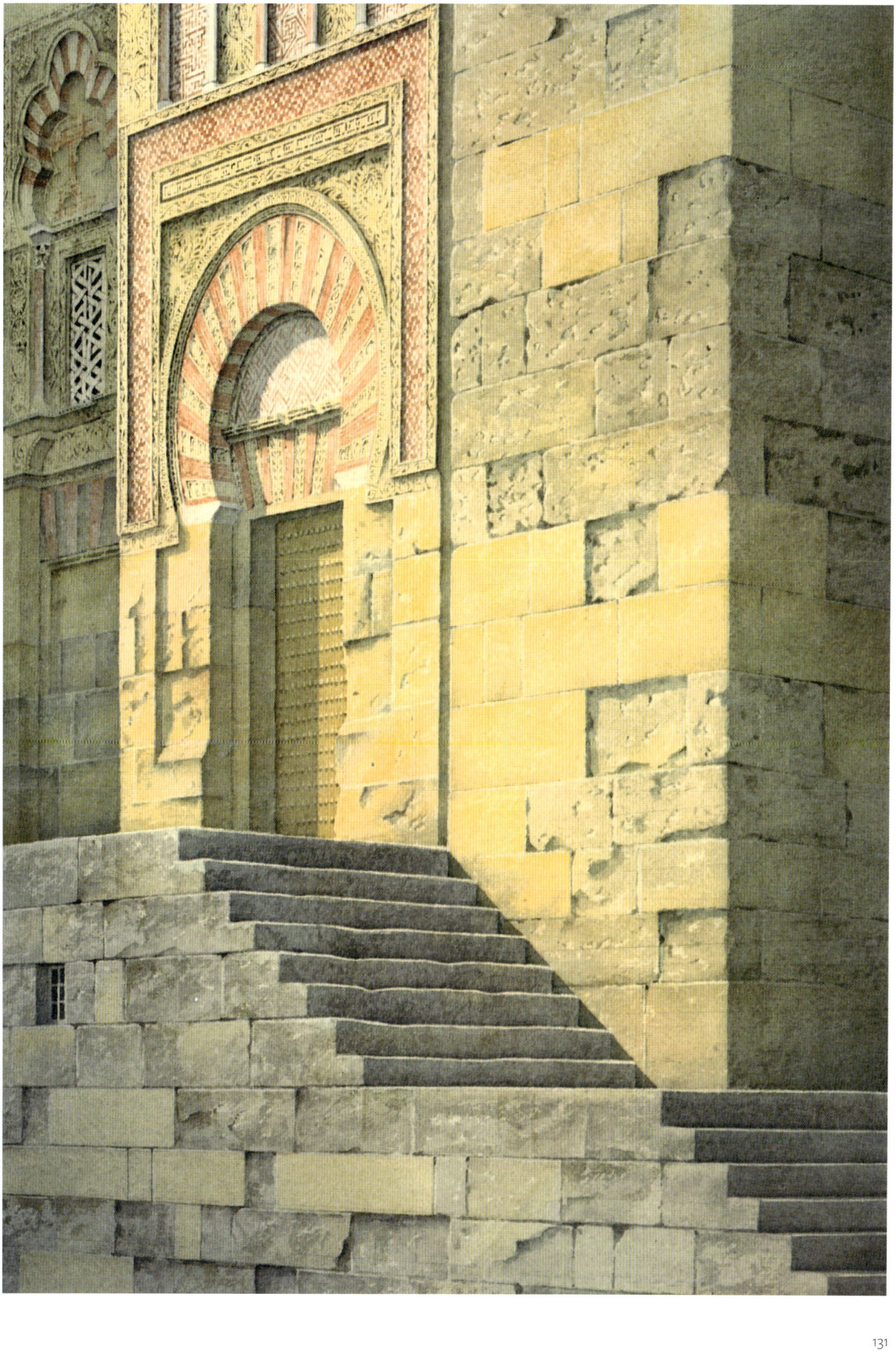

Entrance to the Mezquita, Cordoba
Watercolour 2018
25 x 17 ins | 64 x 44 cm

(Overleaf)
Valle Umbria from Assisi
(detail)
Watercolour 2018
23.5 x 33.5 ins
60 x 85 cm

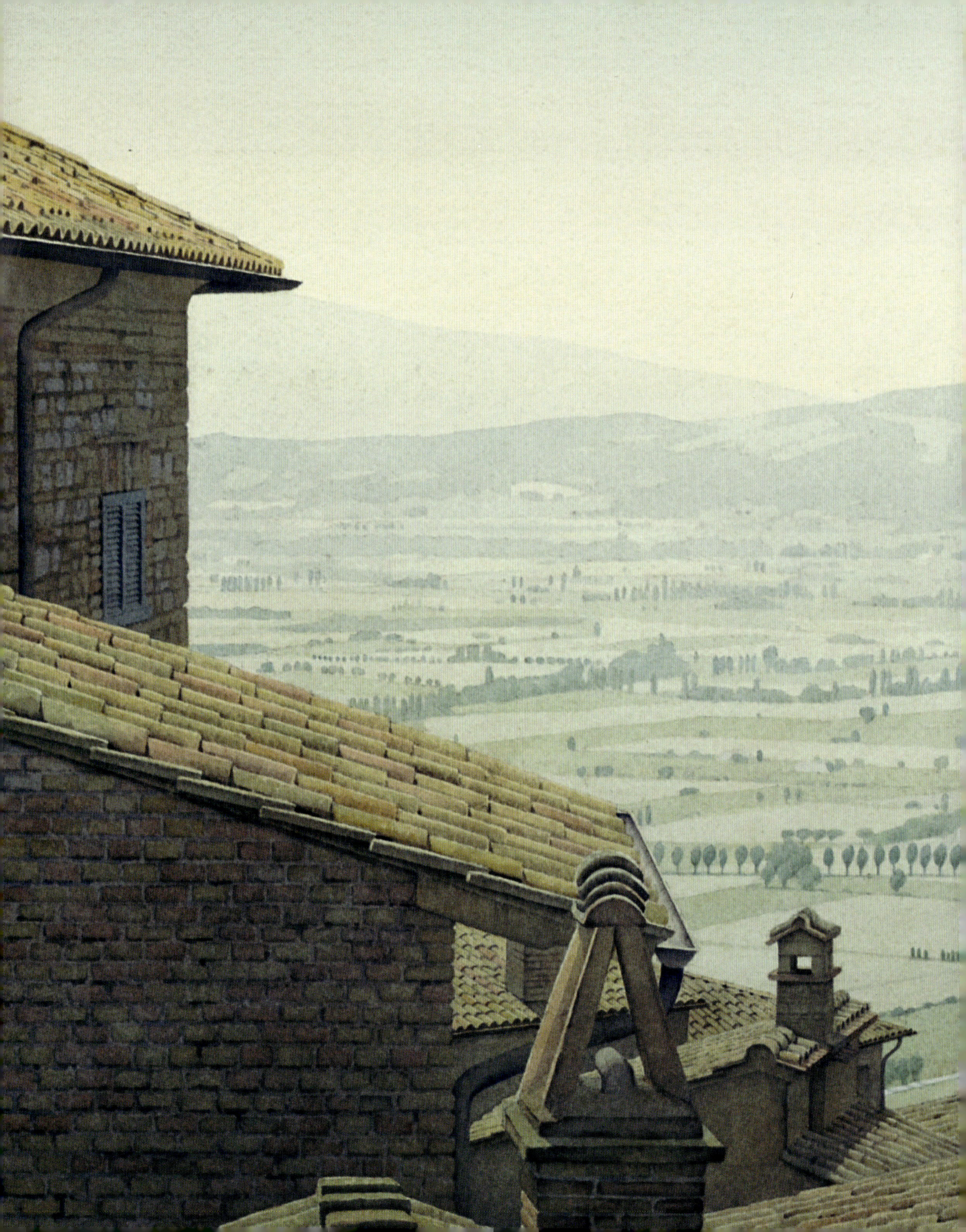

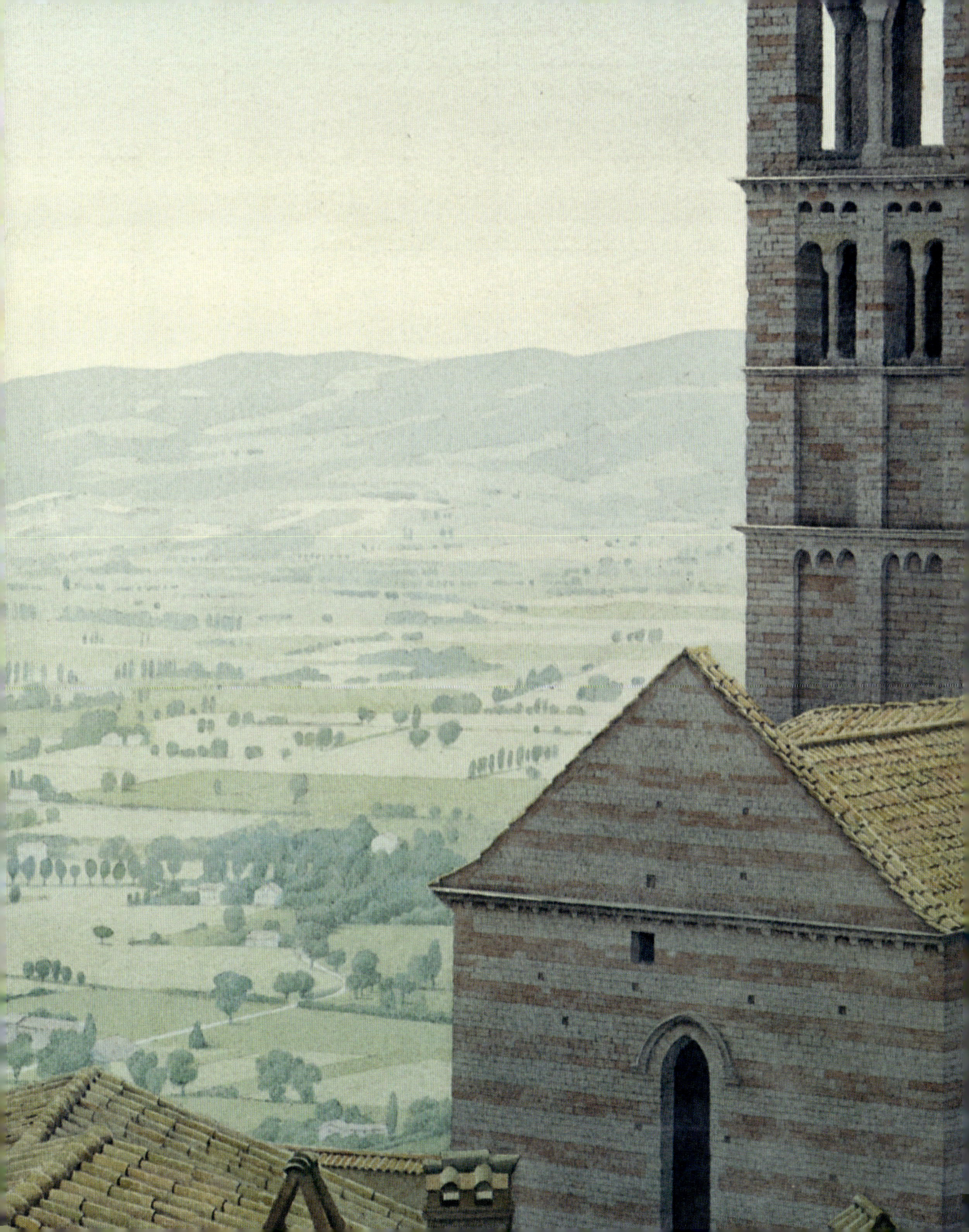

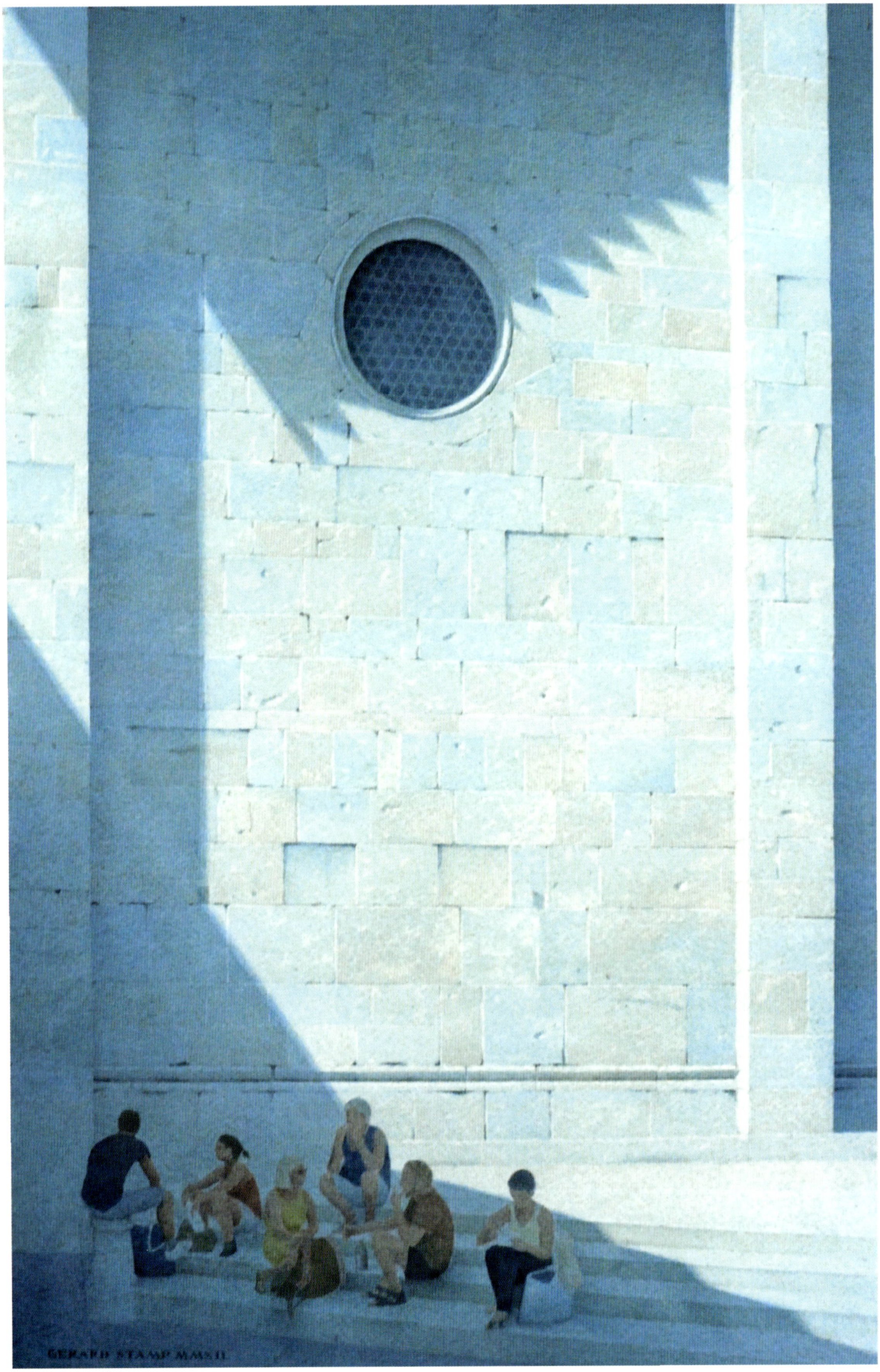

Lunchtime in Lucca

Watercolour 2012

23.5 x 33.5 ins | 60 x 85 cm

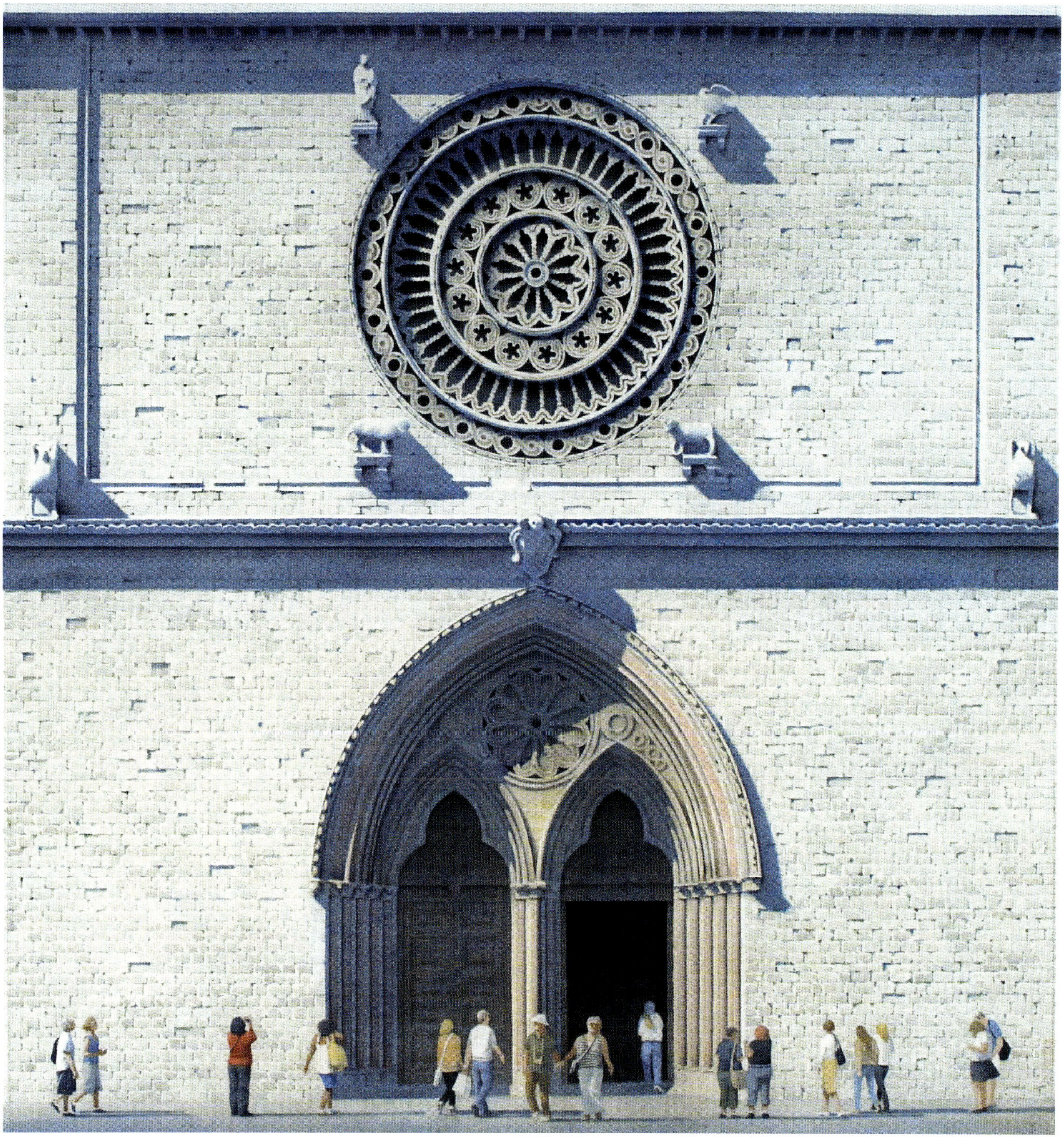

Assisi

Watercolour 2011

35 x 35 ins | 89 x 89 cm

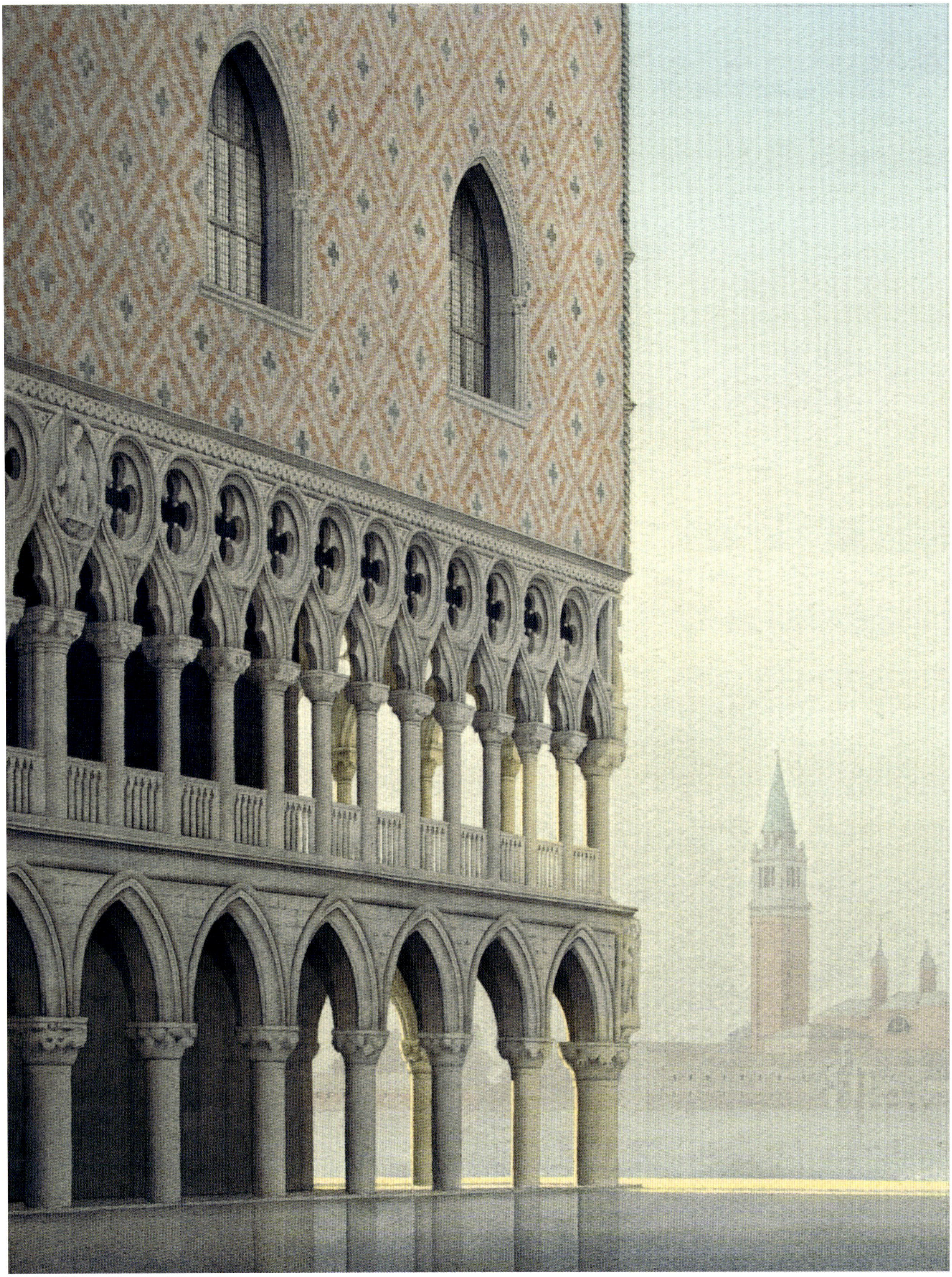

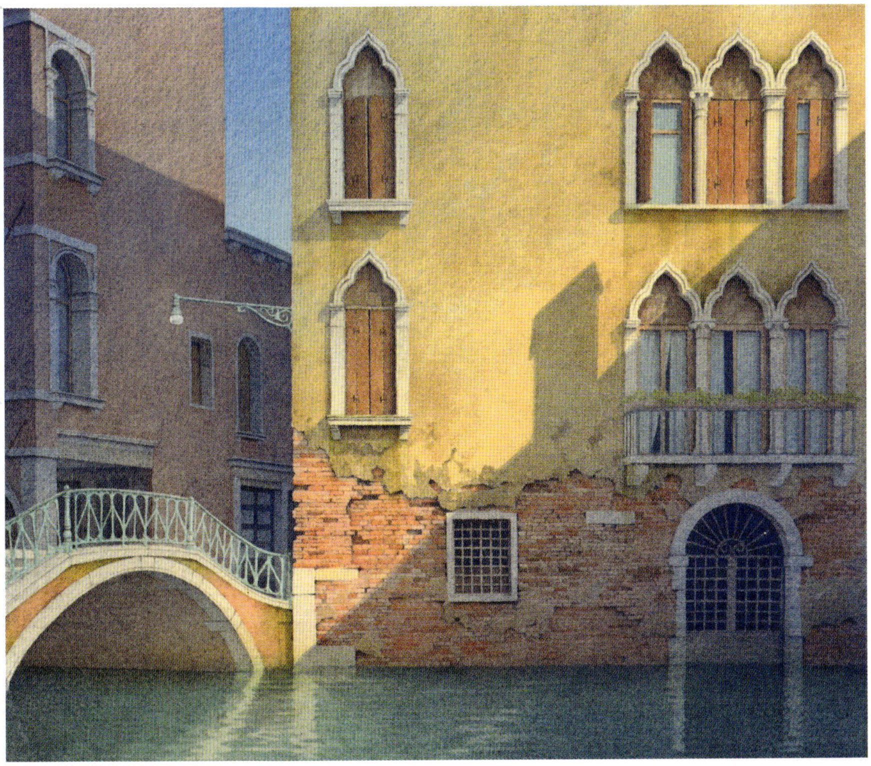

Ponte del Piovan

Watercolour 2025

16.5 x 19 ins | 42 x 48 cm

For several stints from 2009, Gerard taught painting at schools in Umbria and Tuscany, leading to extensive tours with his sketchbook and ensuing church-centred paintings. Vivid impressions of Siena, Todi, Lucca, Assisi, Perugia and Orvieto appeared like artistic milestones. The obvious destination, up in the Veneto, remained glaring in its absence.

Finally, he could resist no longer – saying: 'Venice is the most painted, photographed, selfie-sticked city in the world for a reason: it's also the most beautiful. Yes, there are thousands of clichéd images of the same view (or artist style) but there is always a fresh way to interpret it. It's also a city that belongs to us all (sorry Venetians).'

The tipping point in his case was the fact that Venice was a mighty mercantile city-state for almost a millennium until invaded by Napoleon in 1797, with a marked lack of religious zeal and wealth endowing predominately secular buildings. He wanted to move beyond a reputation as a church painter.

Stamp and Ruskin being avowed medievalists, there was also the irresistible appeal of a city passing its peak in the fifteenth century and fading gradually into the most romantic decay in history. Ruskin hailed the architects and builders of the Middle Ages as 'artists of profound and tender feelings'. For him such profundity and tenderness yielded the 'golden stain of time'. That in turn ruled out not only restoration but cleaning.

For Gerard Stamp that gold-stained standard ruled out paintings of interiors – given the cold, pompous interior designs of the High Baroque which appealed to seventeenth- and eighteenth-century tastes when money was still plentiful and Venice was in deep decline.

He says now: 'I was acutely aware that tackling a series of Venice paintings came with dangers. Cliché of course, a sense of unoriginality, but most importantly with the very real threat of

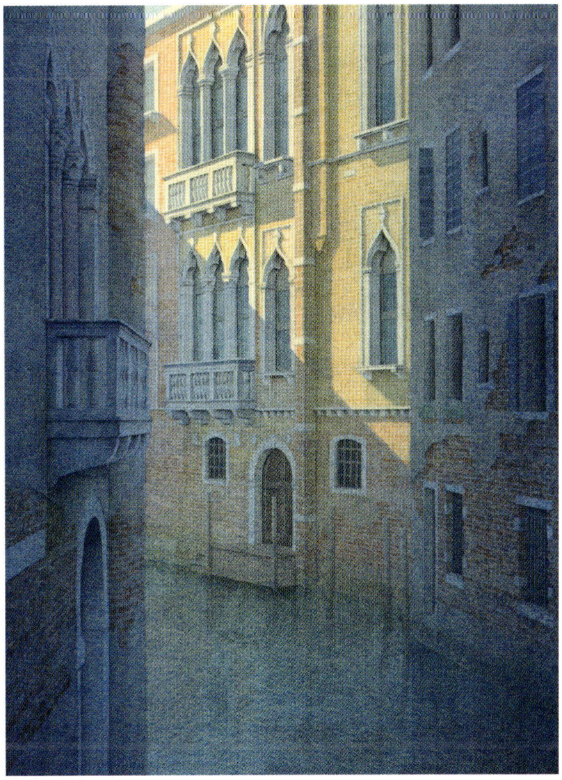

Palazzo Soranzo van Axel

Watercolour 2025

21.5 x 17 ins | 54 x 43 cm

L'alba a Venezia

Watercolour 2025

30 x 22.5 ins | 76 x 57 cm

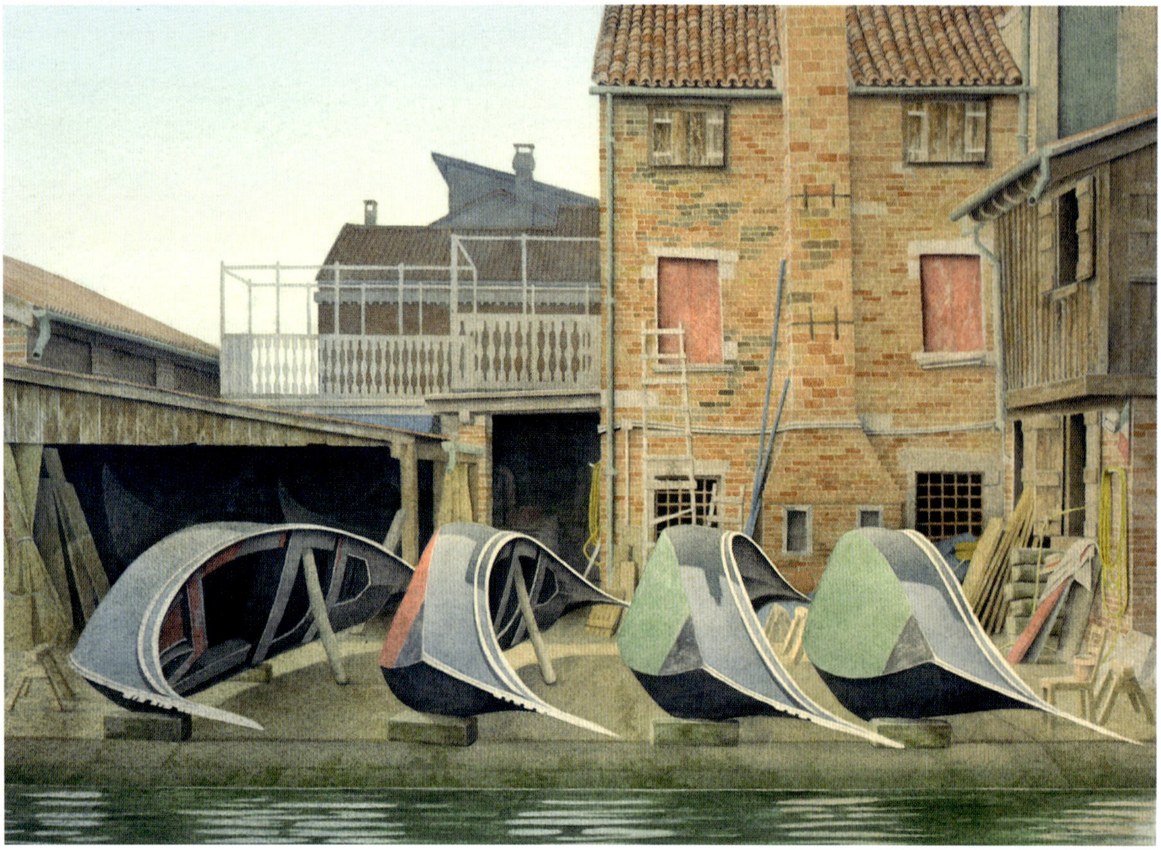

Venetian Boatyard

Watercolour 2025

18 x 26 ins | 46 x 66 cm

being ridiculed when compared to the great watercolourists of the past: Turner, of course, but also Sargent's and Ruskin's beautiful en plein air works, to name just three.

'I wanted to get under the skin of Venice, or as I have termed it, behind the mask. I like to get up really early there – 5am – to watch the great city wake up. In the early hours, the streets are deserted save for street cleaners, and photographers who are all patiently waiting to take exactly the same shot.

'What first took my breath away was how the rising sun began to light that great edifice, the most beautiful secular Gothic building in the world, the Doge's Palace. I have painted it several times and will probably paint it several times more.

'It was also in the early hours when I discovered what beauty there is in the canal reflections, before they get churned up by gondolas. And I also loved to discover the backstreet city, away from the sea of tourists that floods Venice between St Mark's Square and the Rialto.'

Back in the studio he sought to show the buildings of Venice in the way it had felt in those early hours – 'when I had those glorious buildings to myself, and with the morning light dancing its magic on the walls and water in the world's most beautiful city.'

And so, from scores of sketches and hundreds of photos, he takes out the mundane and ephemeral. 'We think of Venice for its great buildings, and its maze of canals, but there is so much clutter – street

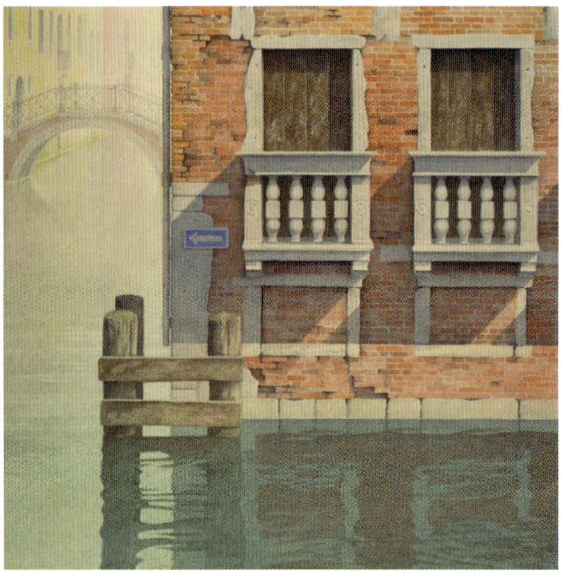

Senso Unico

Watercolour 2025

18.5 x 18.5 ins | 47 x 47 cm

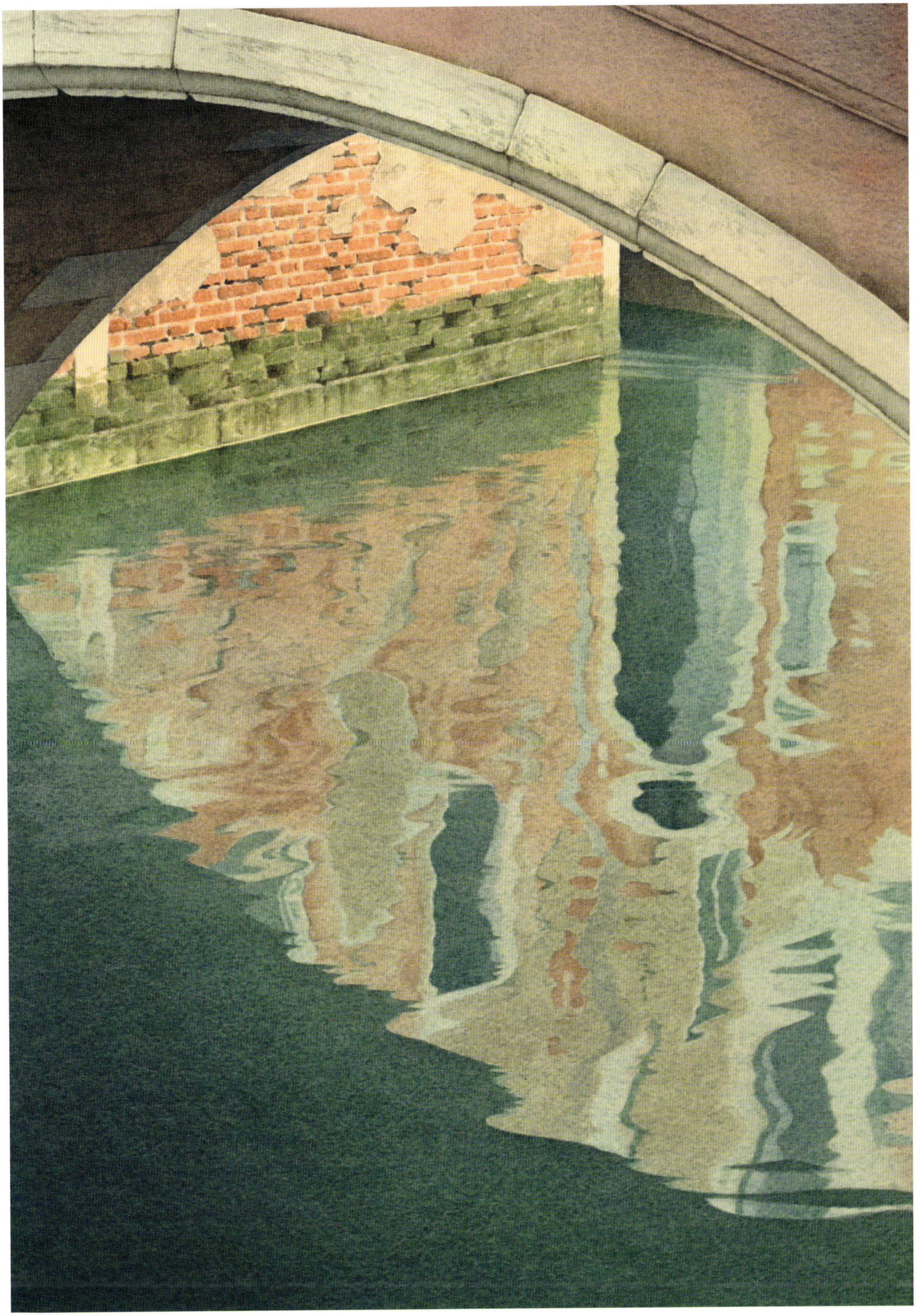

Sotto Ponte

Ubaldo Belli

Watercolour 2025

23.5 x 17.5 ins

60 x 44 cm

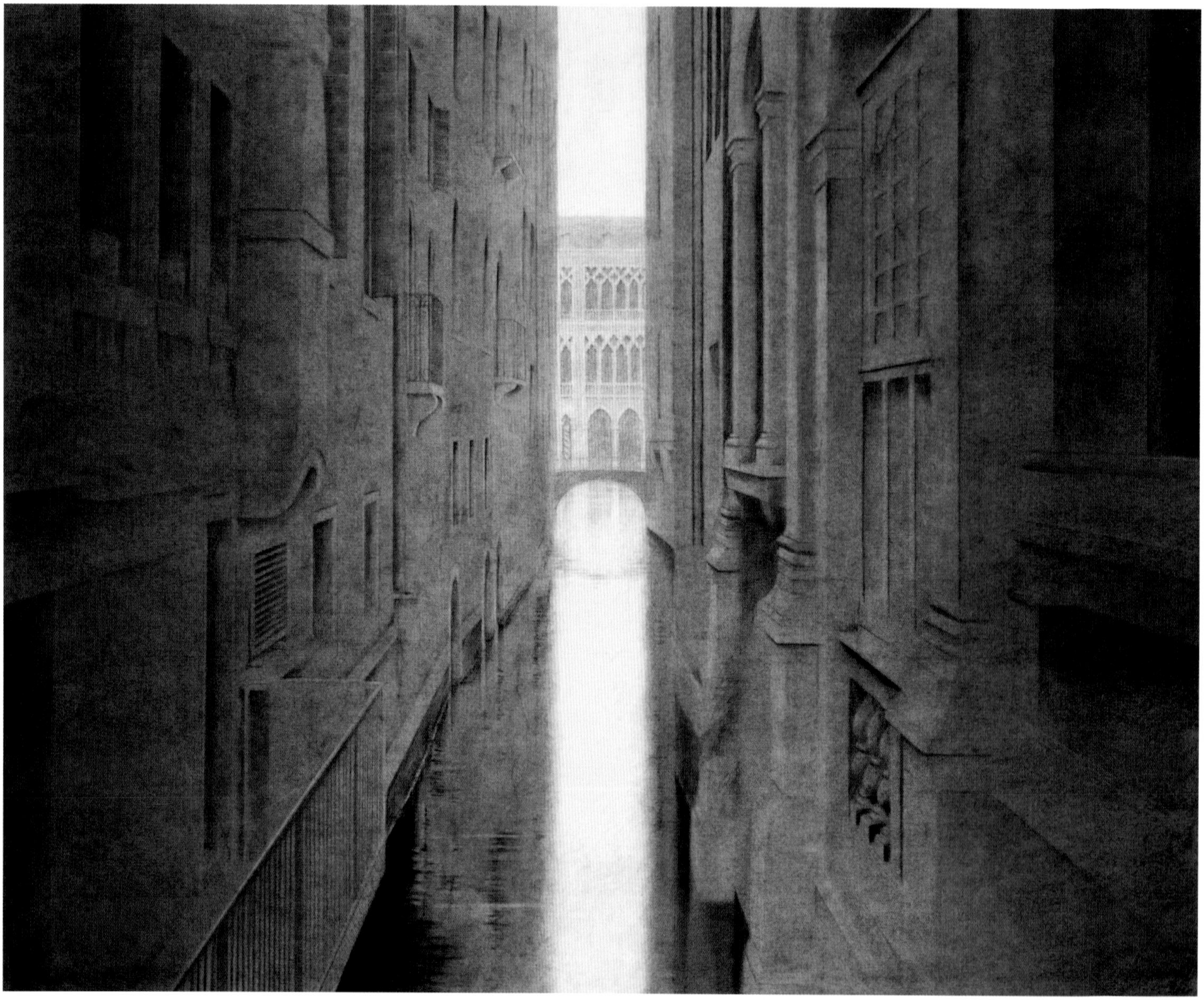

Behind the Mask

Charcoal 2024

32 x 39.5 ins | 81 x 101 cm

signs, rubbish bins – that I feel need to disappear.'

And in a city centre reduced to fewer than 50,000 residents swamped annually by as many as thirty million tourists, he will seldom paint a single human figure. 'There are too many people already, I don't want to add to them,' he says.

A 2026 *Behind the Mask, Visions of Venice* exhibition also launches a new collaboration with the Jonathan Cooper Gallery in Park Walk, Chelsea. This veteran London art dealer who has showcased myriad impressions of the natural world since the 1980s was immediately drawn to the work of Gerard Stamp.

'The quality is exceptional,' says Jonathan Cooper. 'His pictures are empty of people but not of content – they have an enormous presence. The colour and placing are great and the technique is immaculate. There are very few watercolourists who are really, really good and Gerard is one of them.'

Further plans for the future involve a focus on and spilling out from the second great building of the Norwich skyline – the royal castle commissioned by William the Conqueror and completed by his son, Henry I, in 1121. After centuries as a fortress, it became a jail and then a museum.

In 2013 Gerard staged a *Conquest* exhibition in the Norman building linked to a show for John Sell Cotman. And for an hour or two in 2022 he

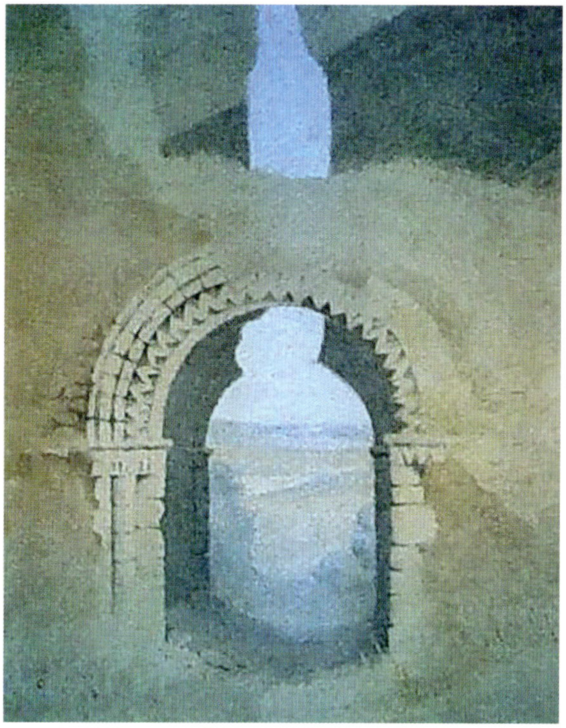

Bawsey Tower

Watercolour 2005

11.5 x 8.5 ins |29 x 21 cm

was allowed special access during a huge overhaul. The £25 million Norwich Castle Keep Project, finally unveiled to the public in the summer of 2025, sees all five medieval floors open to visitors for the first time. The majesty of the Great Hall is revealed in restored Caen limestone shipped from Normandy nearly a millennium ago.

Gerard donned hard hat for travels over scaffolding with his camera. The resulting large watercolour – presented to Norwich Castle and on show in the atrium – with grids of girders and a whole panoply of safety measures – underlines the peril and the miracle of medieval masonry.

The Restoration of a Royal Palace Norwich Castle

Watercolour 2022

30 x 30 ins | 76 x 76 cm

Norwich Castle Museum and Art Gallery

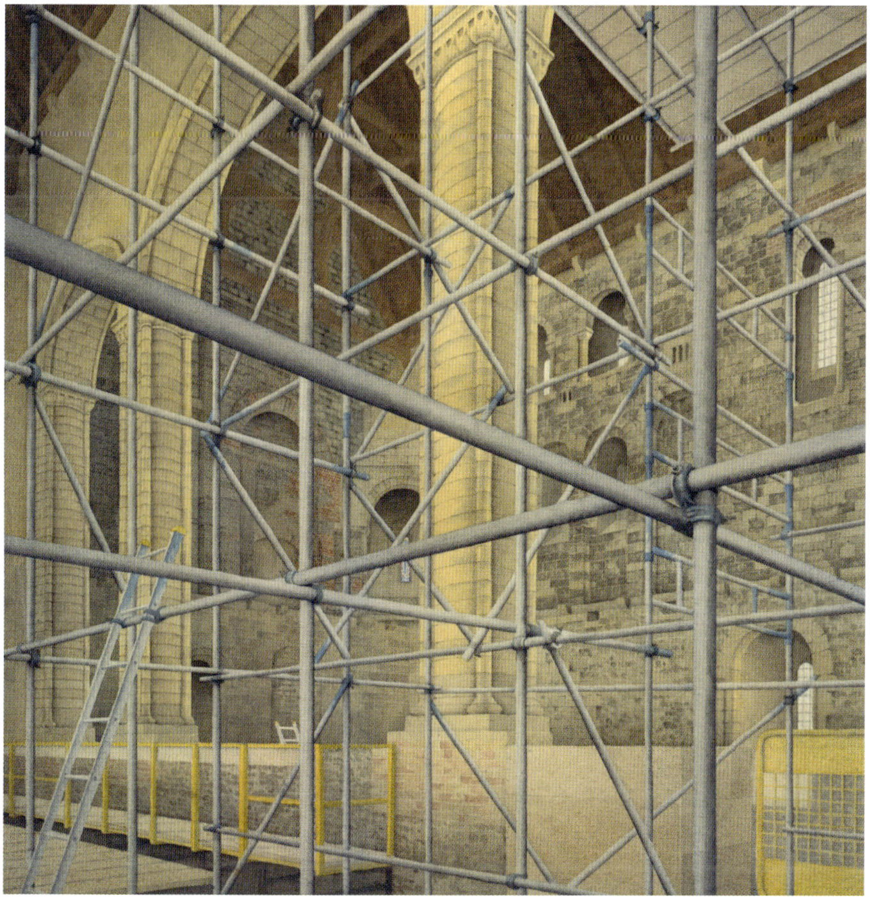

Now he plans to trace Norman architecture to its roots in Normandy. It's a plan taking shape since the *Monet and Architecture* exhibition at the National Gallery in 2018. 'When I saw the line of paintings of Rouen Cathedral, I had to sit down. I've never seen anything better than that.'

He wants to connect the great cathedrals of Rouen, Coutances, Bayeux and Evreux to Norwich and Canterbury, and then to trace a new line of ruination in country churches. 'I think the French are better at leaving ruins to be romantic than we are,' he says.

And, of course, there will be further trips to Venice. Whether at home or abroad, and tackling fresh subjects or old, Gerard Stamp keeps faith with the brotherly creed of Anti Ugly.

He concludes: 'We are living in an angry and uncertain world, and often a very frightening one. It is also a crowded world where, though there are wonderful exceptions, we endure much ugliness in art, in architecture, in urban planning, and in the relentless industrialisation of our rural landscape and seascape. Beauty is well overdue a revival.

'In a time of great change these buildings provide constancy for the soul and sanctuaries for the eyes. I paint them because they are beautiful.'

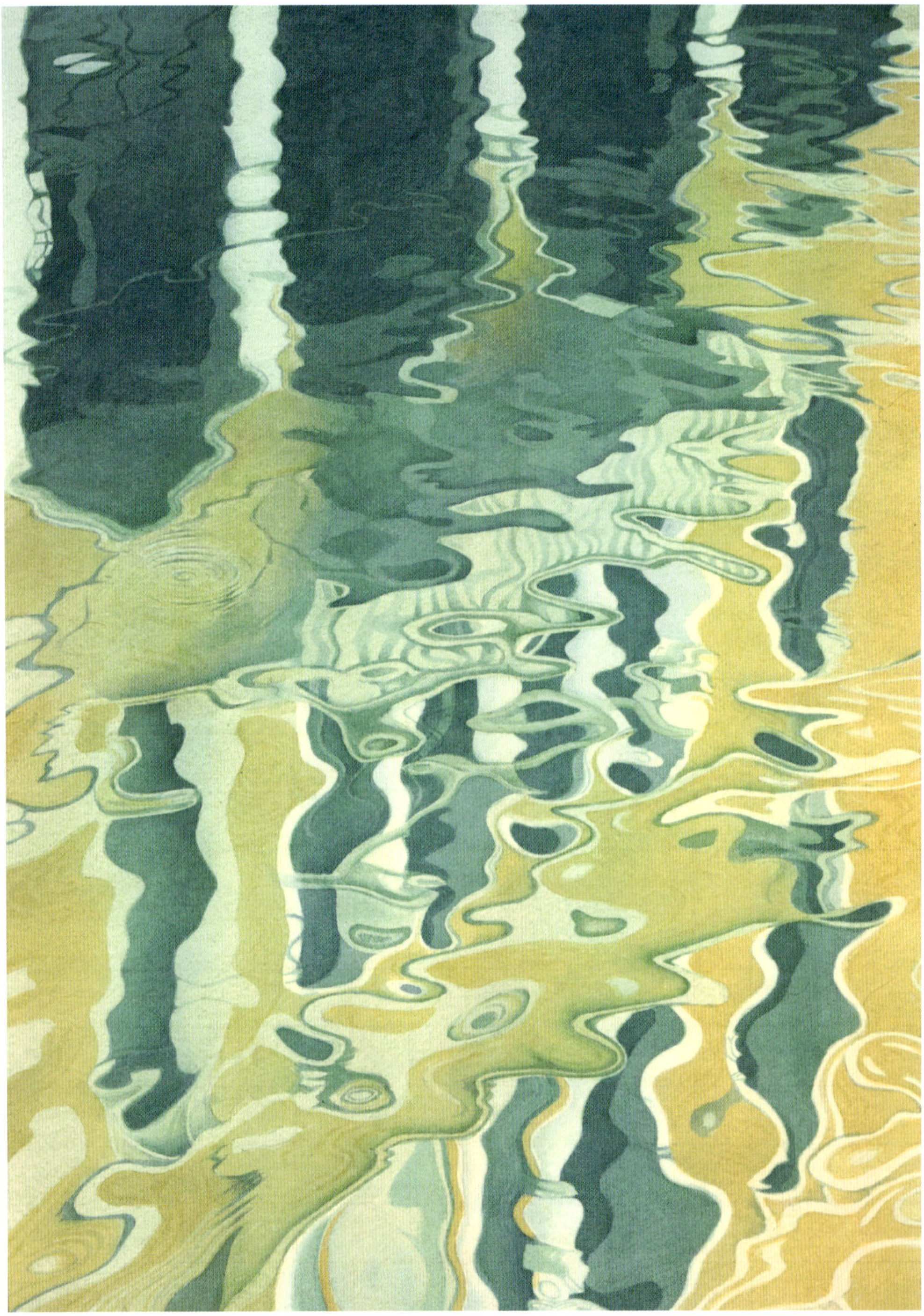

Venetian Watercolour I

Watercolour 2024

29.5 x 21.5 ins | 75 x 55 cm

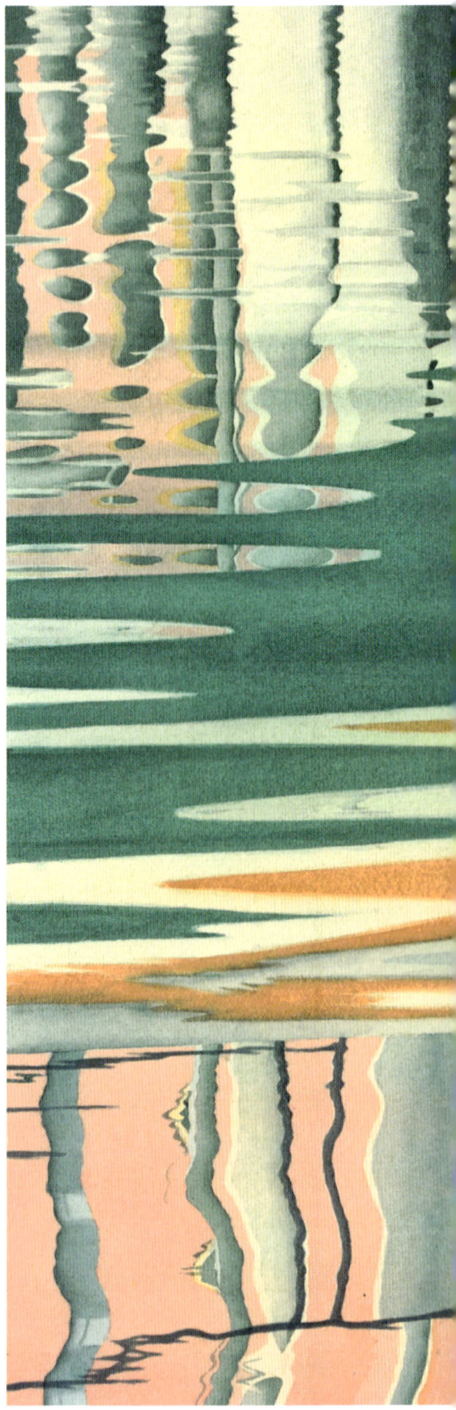

Venetian Watercolour II

Watercolour 2024

29.5 x 21.5 ins | 75 x 55 cm

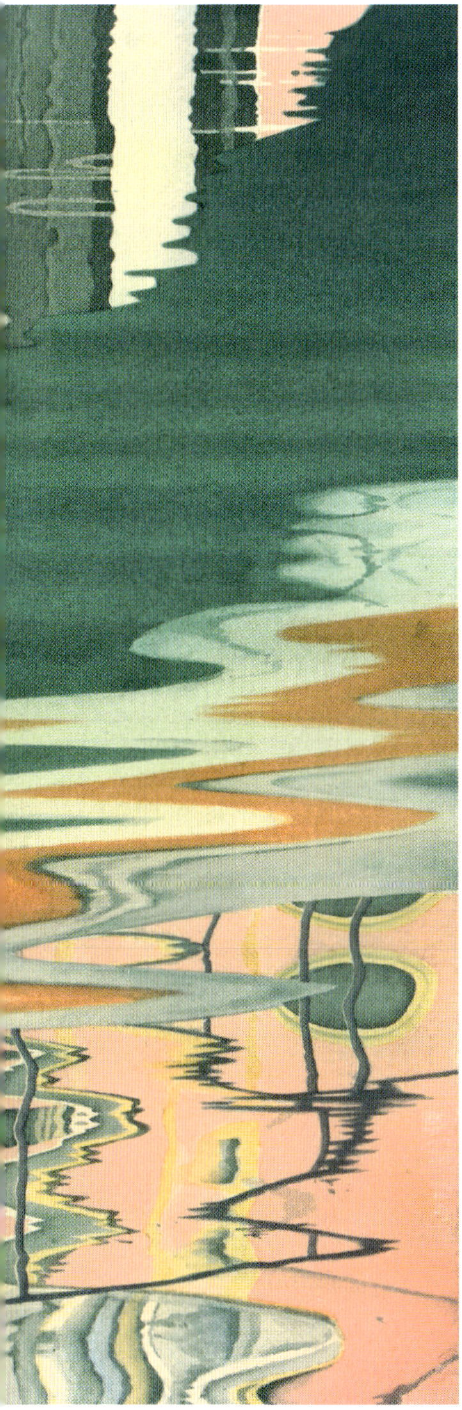

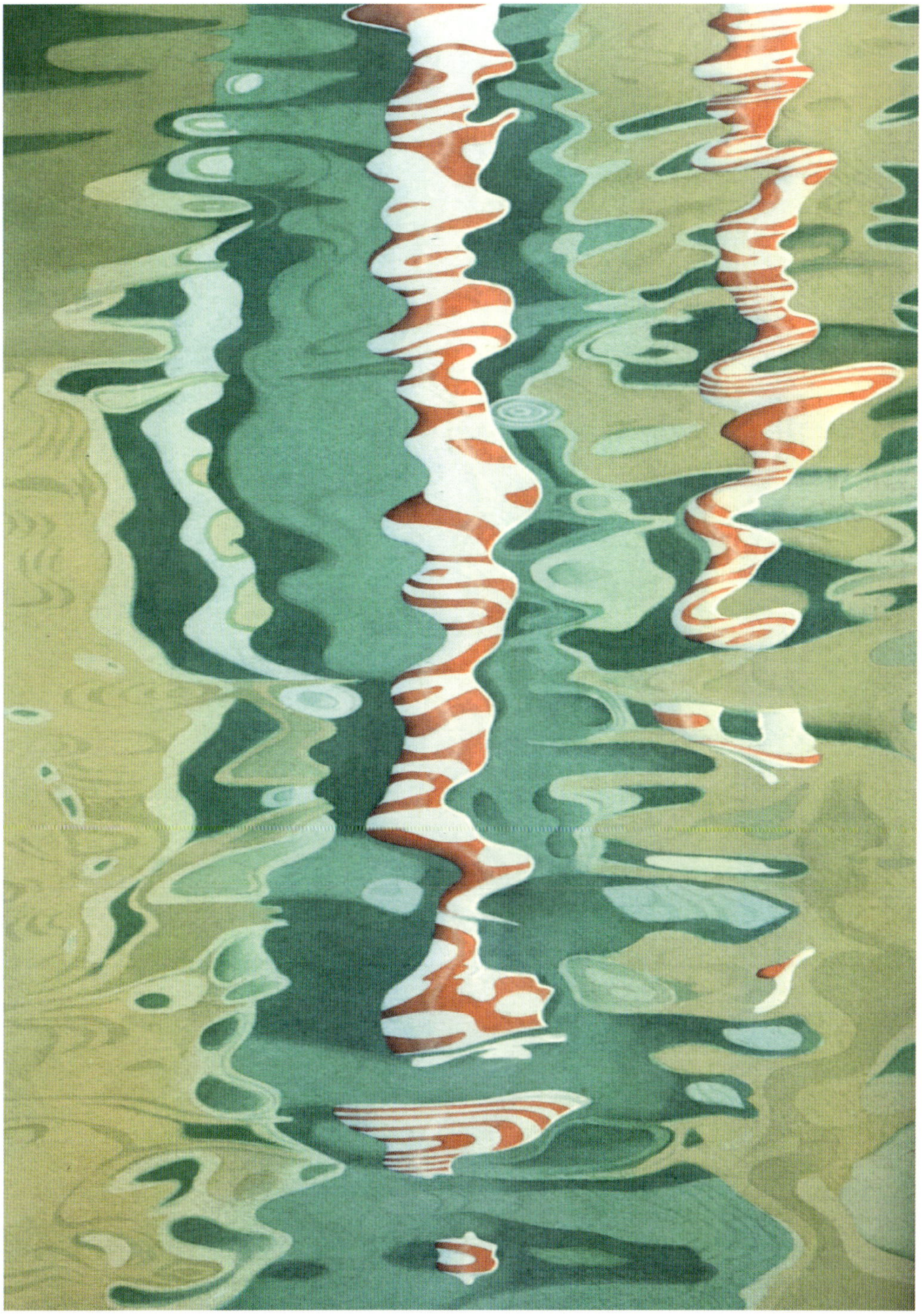

Venetian Watercolour III

Watercolour 2024

29.5 x 21.5 ins | 75 x 55 cm

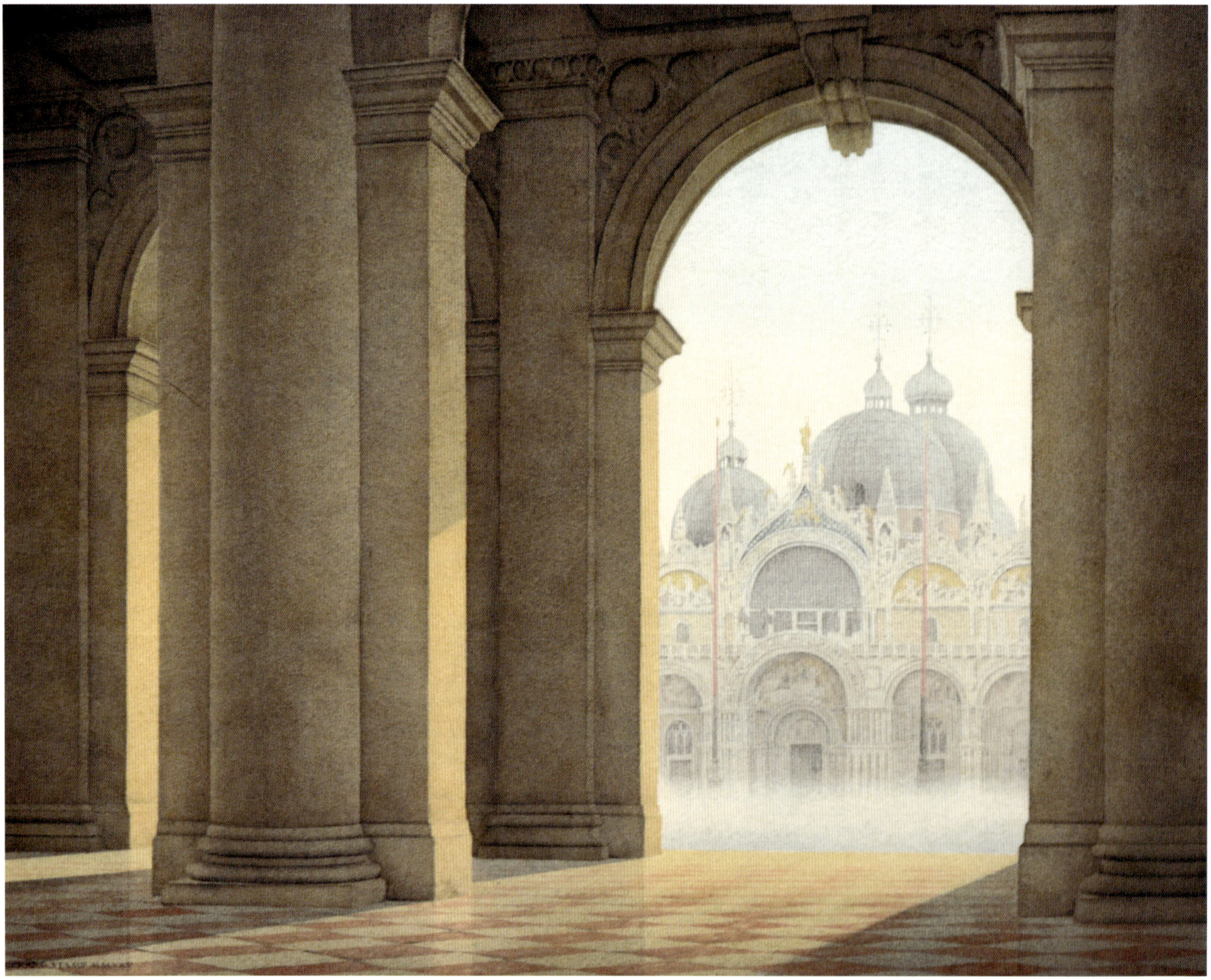

St Mark's Square

Watercolour 2024

25 x 32.5 ins | 64 x 83 cm

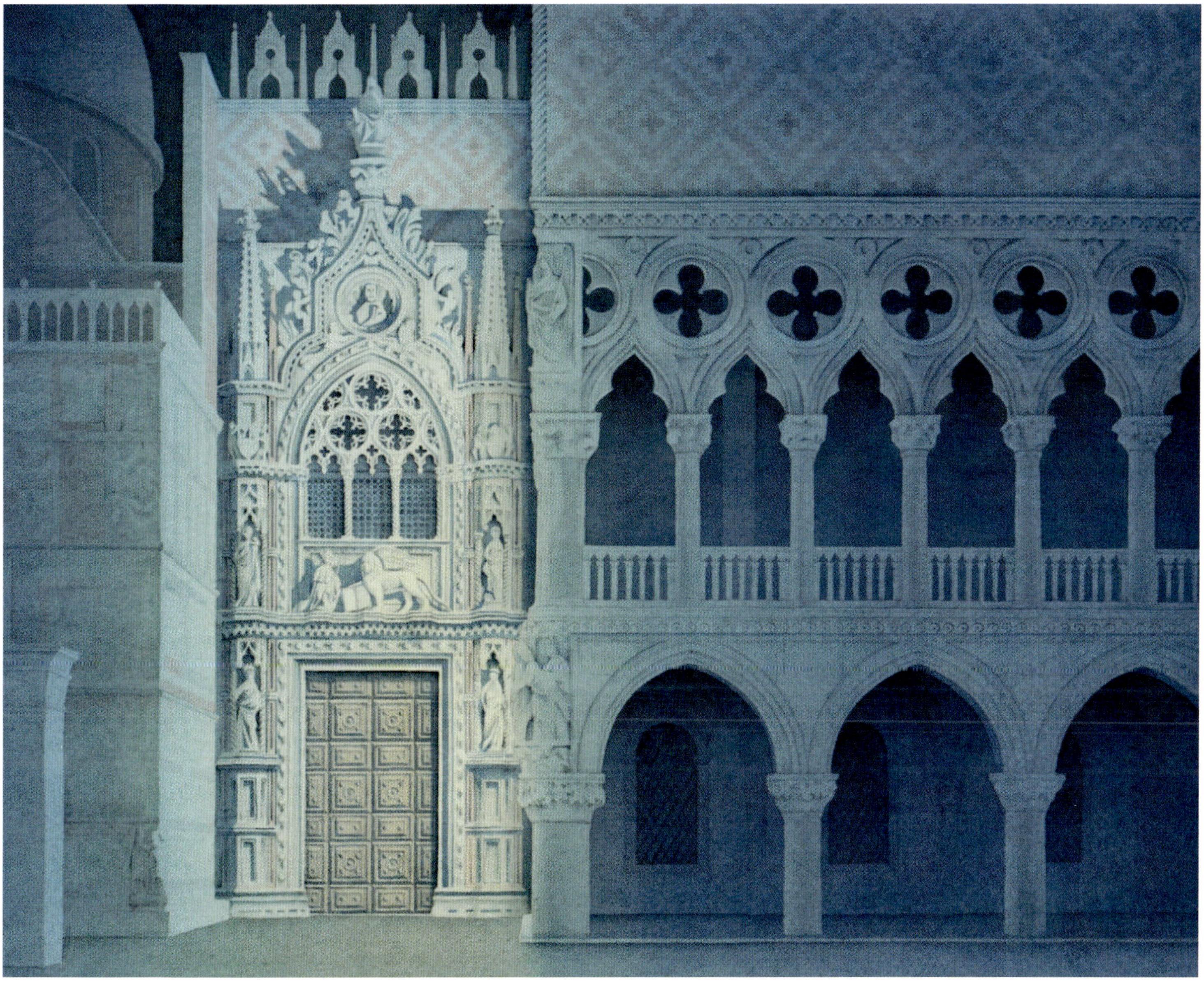

Floodlit Doge

Watercolour 2026

25 x 34 ins | 64 x 86 cm

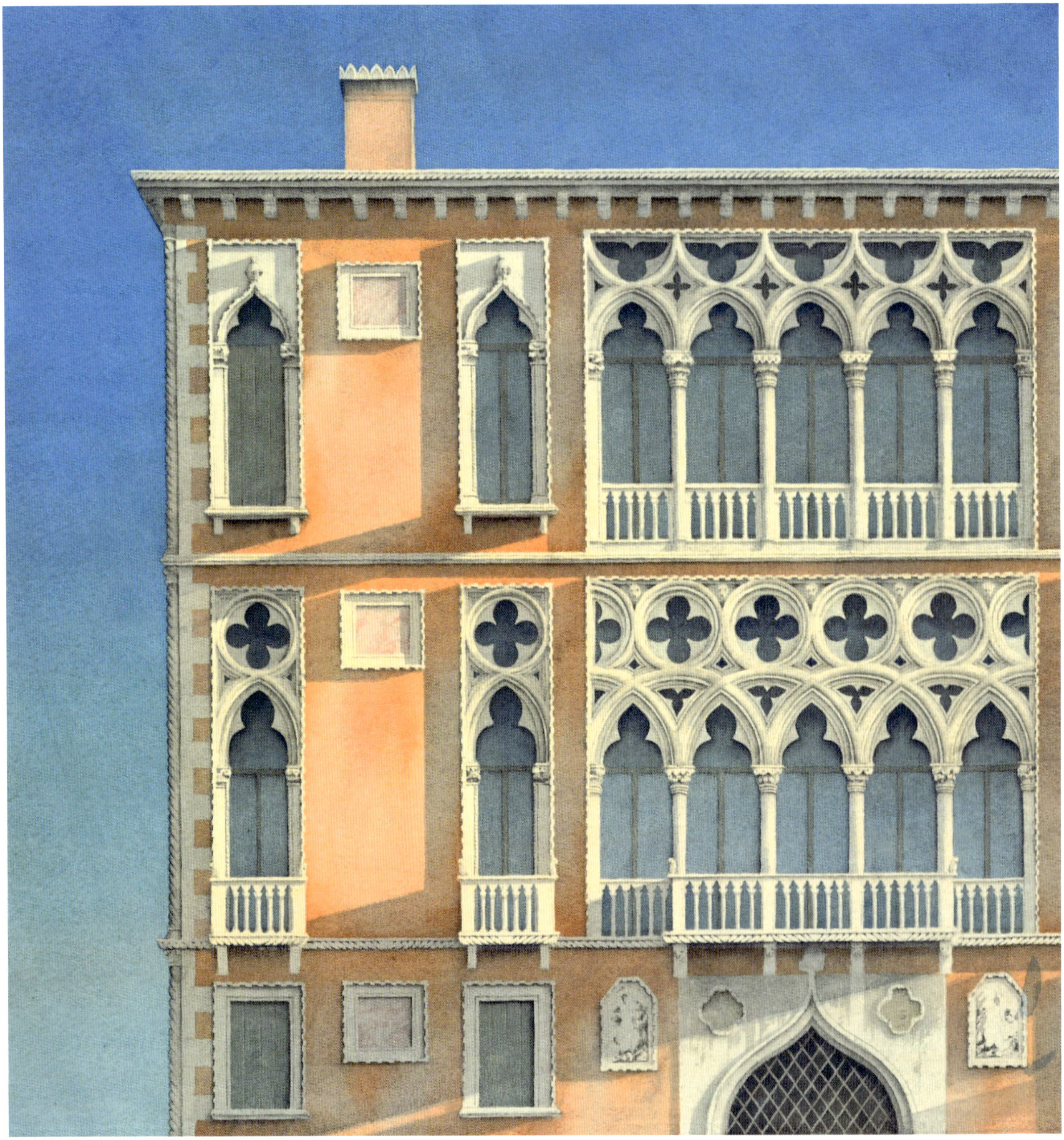

Venetian Windows I

Palazzo Cavalli-Franchetti

Watercolour 2025

25.5 x 26.5 ins | 65 x 67 cm

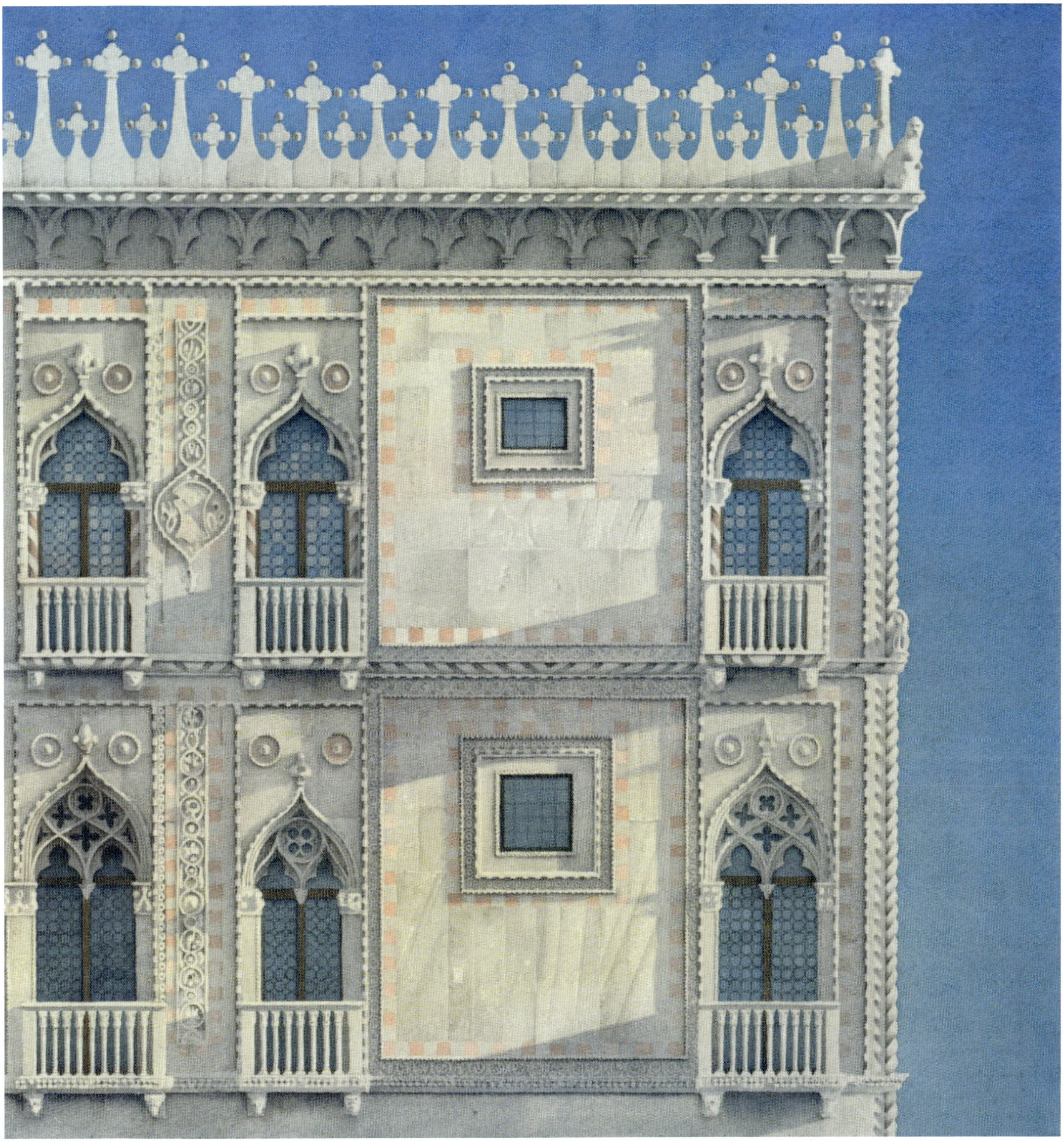

Venetian Windows II

Ca' d'Oro

Watercolour 2025

25.5 x 26.5 ins | 65 x 67 cm

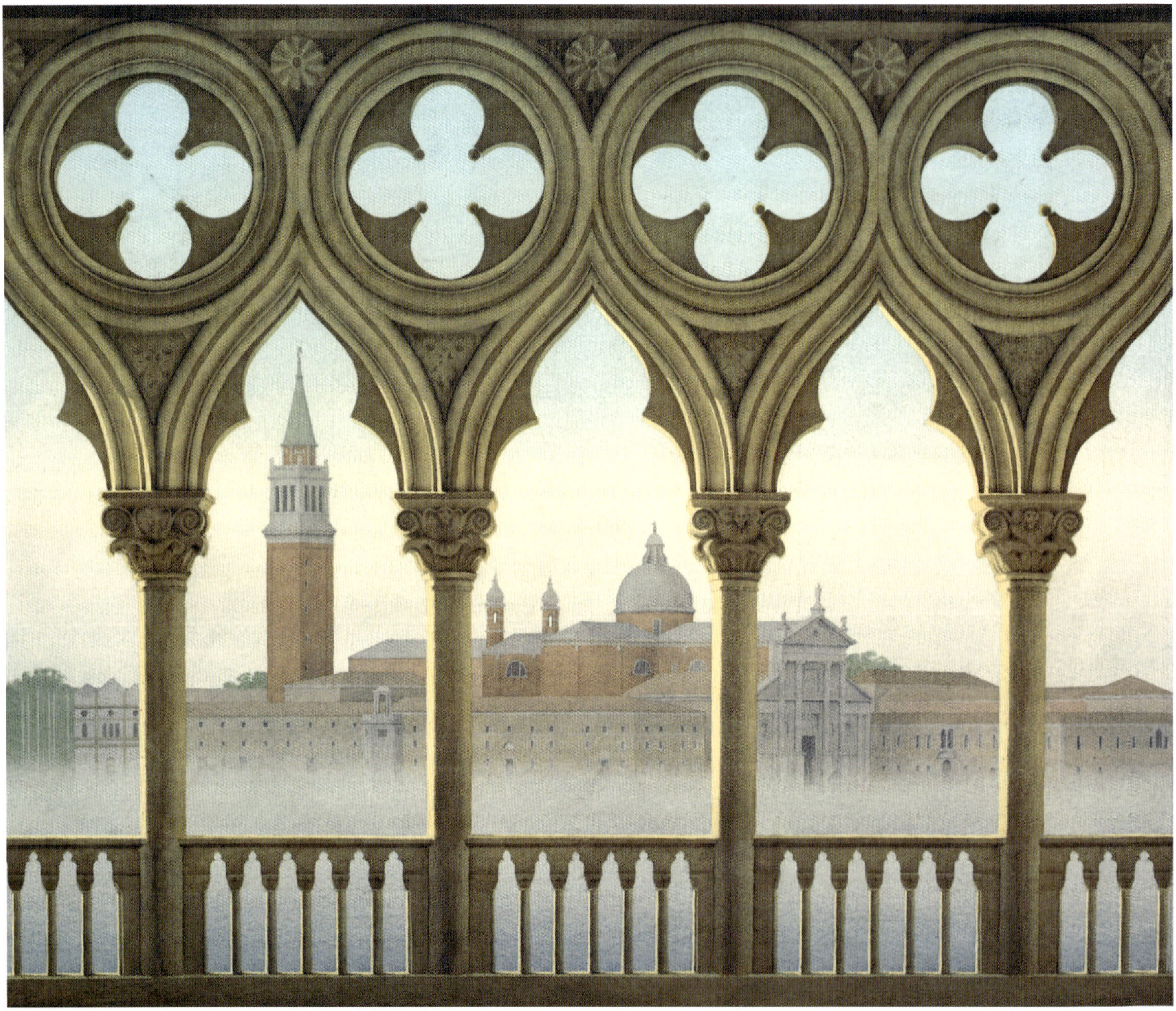

Balcone del

Palazzo Ducale

Watercolour 2025

28 x 34 ins | 72 x 87 cm

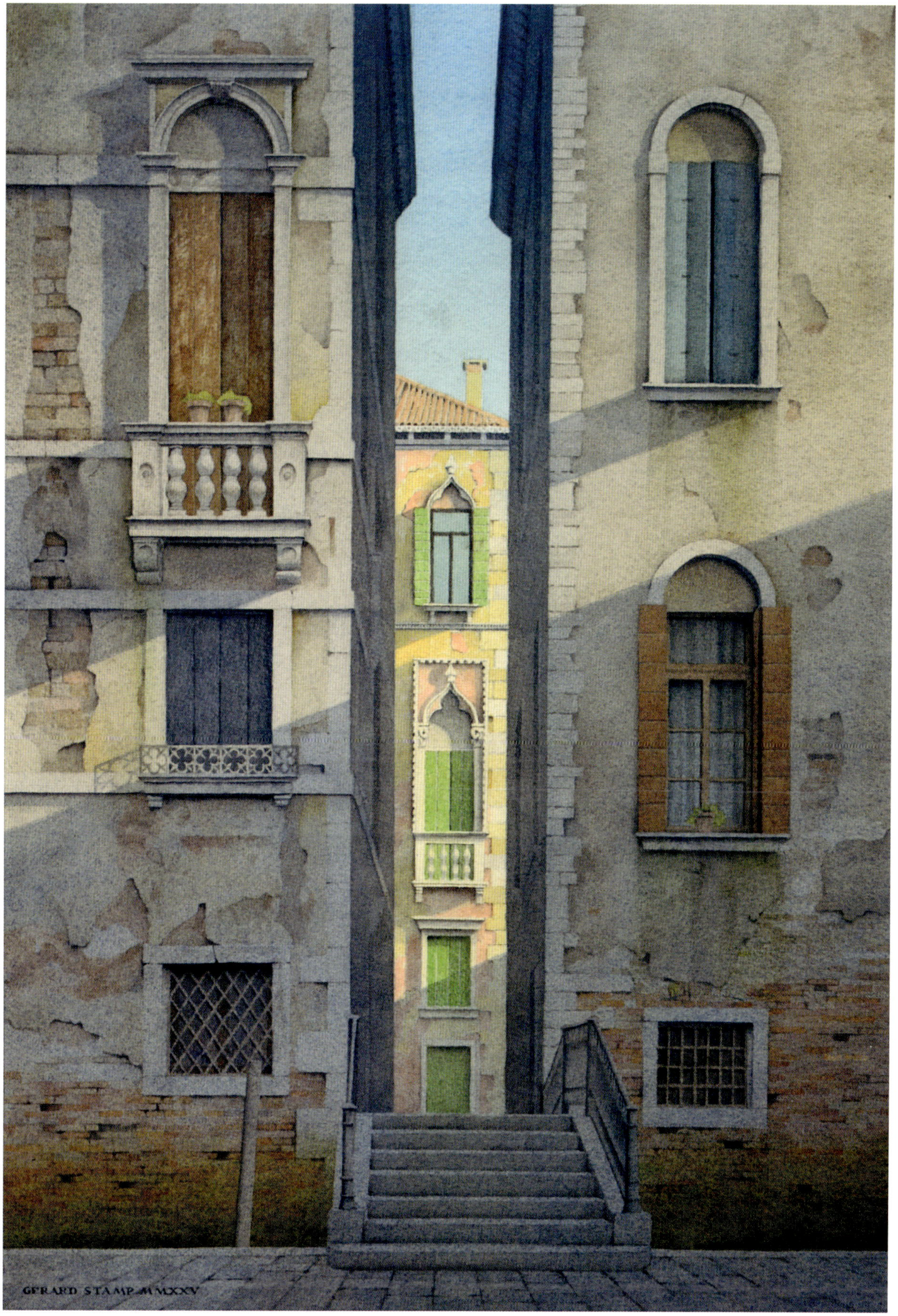

A Venetian Alley

Watercolour 2025

25 x 17.5 ins | 64 x 45 cm

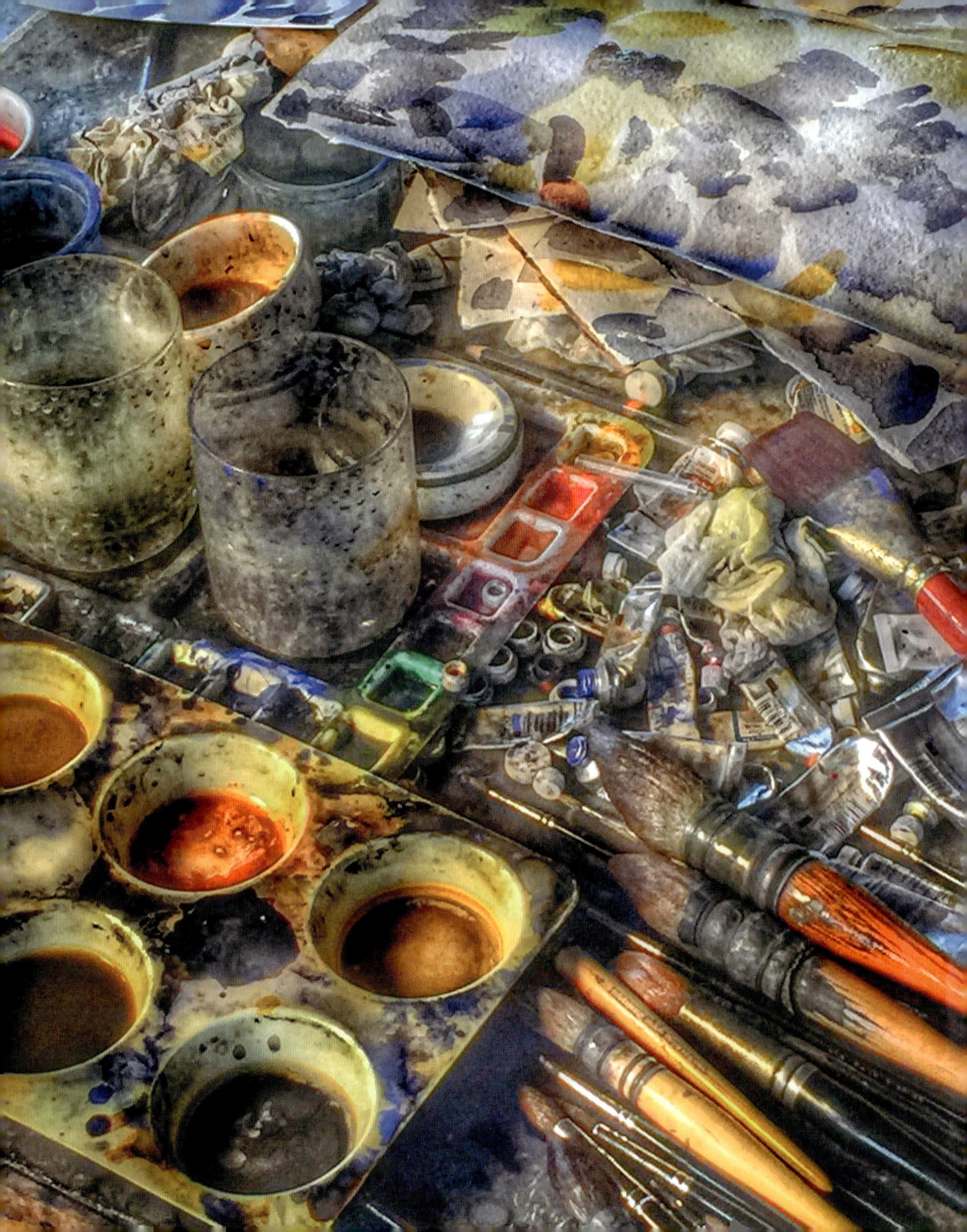

Afterword

How not to paint in watercolour

No other art medium seems to provoke more questions about technique than watercolour. None carries such a persistent reputation for being unforgiving, unpredictable and difficult to control. And certainly no other medium has spawned quite so many instructional books. (A quick search of one popular UK high-street bookseller revealed at least fifty titles aimed at beginners; goodness knows how many exist worldwide.)

The implication in many of these books is that there is a 'right' and a 'wrong' way to handle watercolour. Yet a glance at the works of, say, Ravilious, Melville, Turner and Sargent shows there are countless ways to use it. In truth, most of these books teach one thing: 'how to paint in watercolour *the way I do*'.

I've been asked about technique more times than I can remember, so here I'll describe the process I use to create a watercolour painting. As an example, I have taken photographs during the creation of a large painting, *Giorno del Bucato*. This is not a 'how-to' essay – quite the opposite. I don't recommend you try this at home, for reasons that will become clear.

My method was born out of a weakness. I love detail – whether in textures or in the technical bravura of faithfully representing a complex subject. The artists I admire (Cotman, of course, but also Caspar Friedrich, Frederick Griggs, Eric Ravilious, William Nicholson, or Gerhard Richter with his astonishing landscapes) all handle detail with mastery and apparent effortlessness. My early attempts were nothing of the sort: tight, stiff, more like technical illustrations, entirely lacking atmosphere. One late afternoon, after days spent on a particularly joyless effort, I became so frustrated that I threw it into a sink full of water and went home under a black cloud. That moment proved to be my epiphany.

In the early years I would sit and sketch en plein air, carefully recording details and colour notes. Too often, however, I would realise that if only I had been sitting a few feet to the left – or right – the composition would have been far better. These days, although I still make rough compositional sketches on site, I also take dozens of photographs and work out the final composition in the comfort of my studio. (These two pages from my sketchbooks – ten years apart – show what I mean.) Once the composition and the atmosphere – the 'feeling' – are clear in my

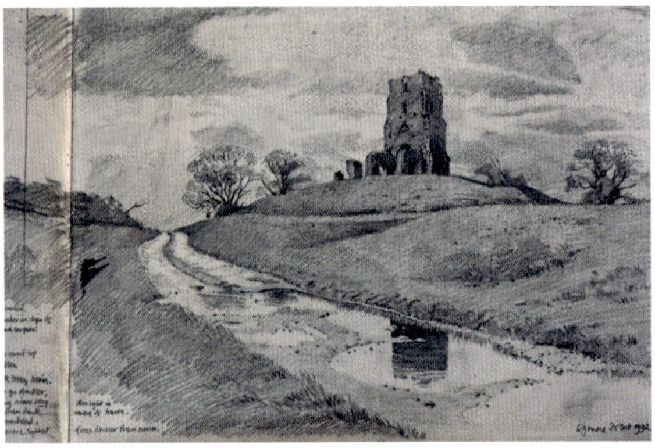

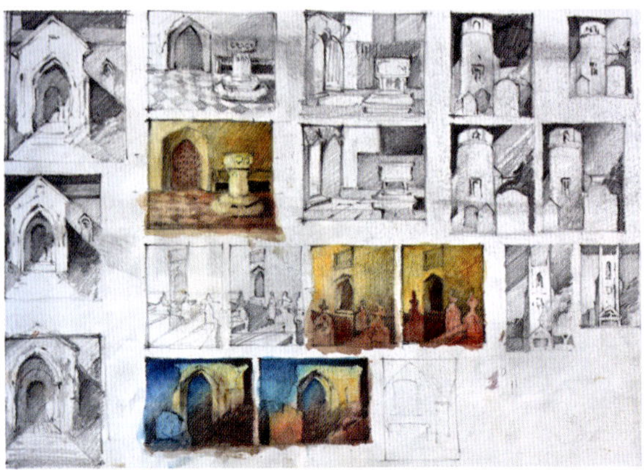

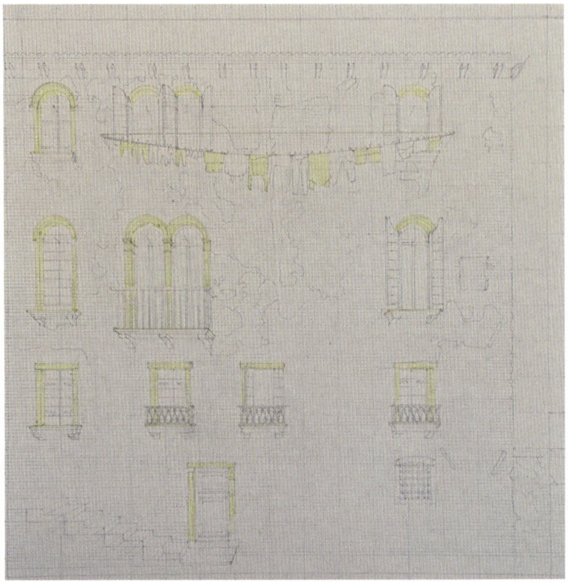

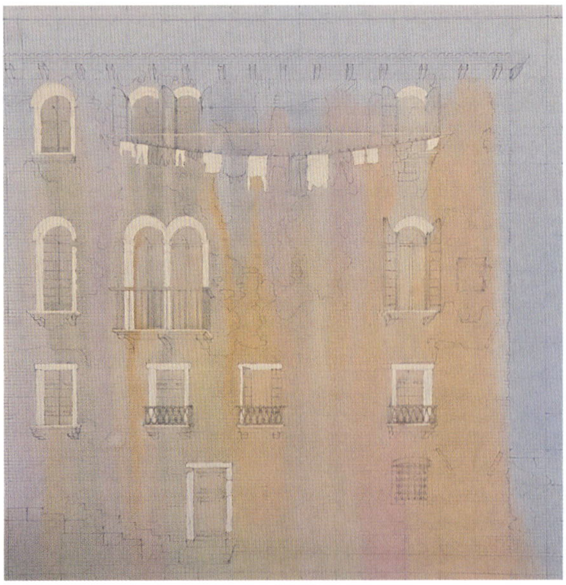

mind, I meticulously draw it out using a soft 3B pencil on stretched watercolour paper (Arches rough, extra heavy, 640gsm). Next, I wet the paper all over and lay down broad washes of colour, loosely indicating their eventual positions. This helps bind the painting together and, just as importantly, subdues that intimidating expanse of white paper. If I need to preserve highlights, I use stopping-out fluid. In this example I wanted the window surrounds and some of the washing line to be protected.

A word about paint. I use the best quality available, never the so-called 'student' paints, which are chalky and opaque. I never use white bodycolour; my highlights are always pure paper. Every wash – sometimes there are dozens – is transparent. My palette is limited to fewer than ten colours, all chosen for their transparency (Phthalo Blue, for instance, is very transparent; Cobalt Blue is semi-opaque). I never use black: my shadows and dark greys come from mixing Ultramarine Blue with Burnt Umber.

When the paper is dry, I begin building up detail and colour. Atmosphere can wait; this is the stage where I establish as much detail as I want to appear – however subliminally – in the finished painting. Depending on the subject, this is the longest and most meticulous part of the process, and possibly the most mechanical. Thank goodness for Radio 3.

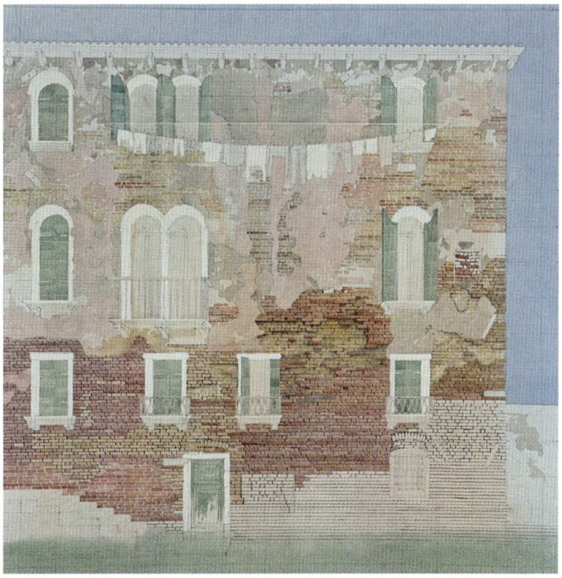

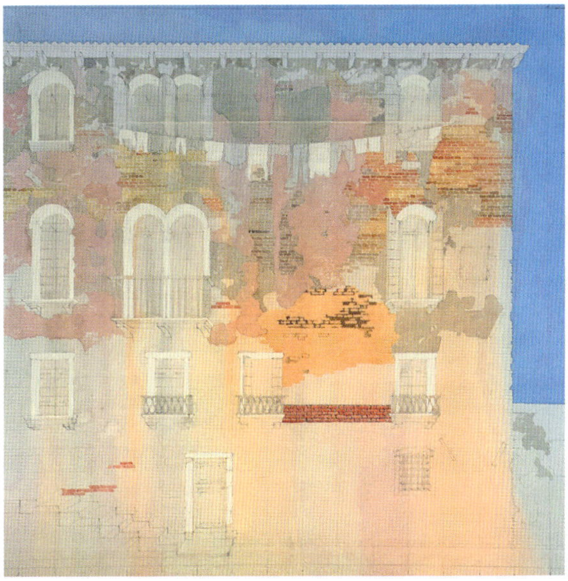

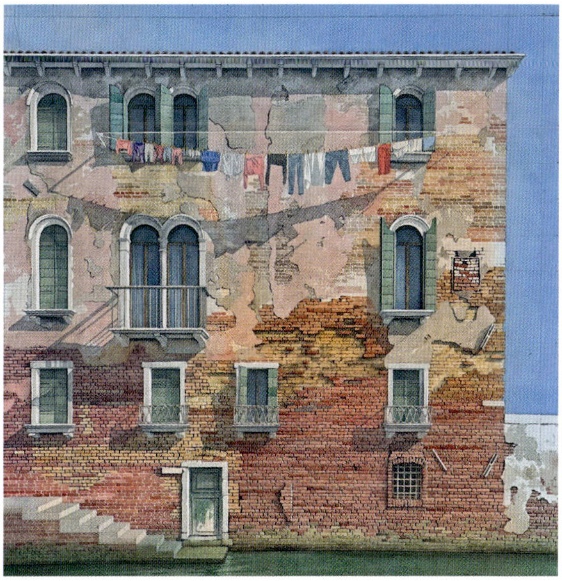

Now for the risky bit – the stage that surprises many people, and which I hesitate to recommend because I don't want to be blamed for the loss of

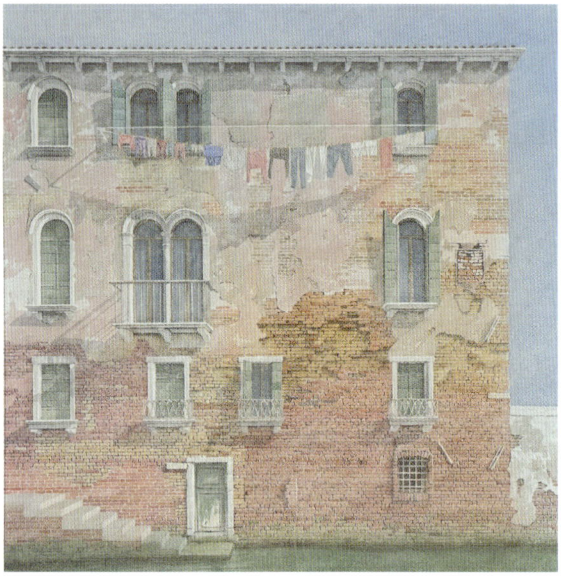

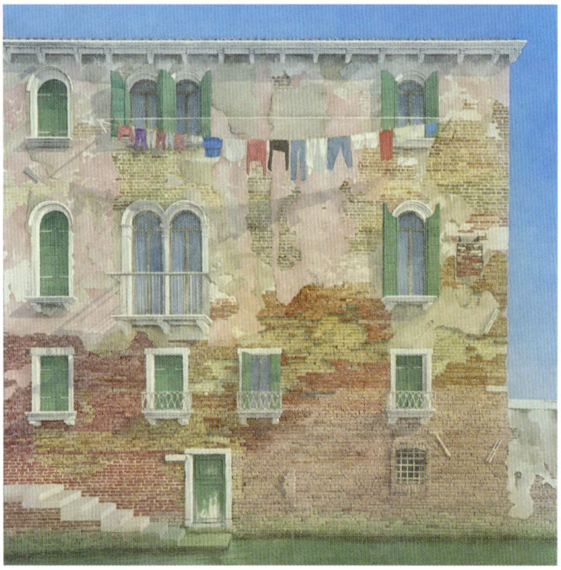

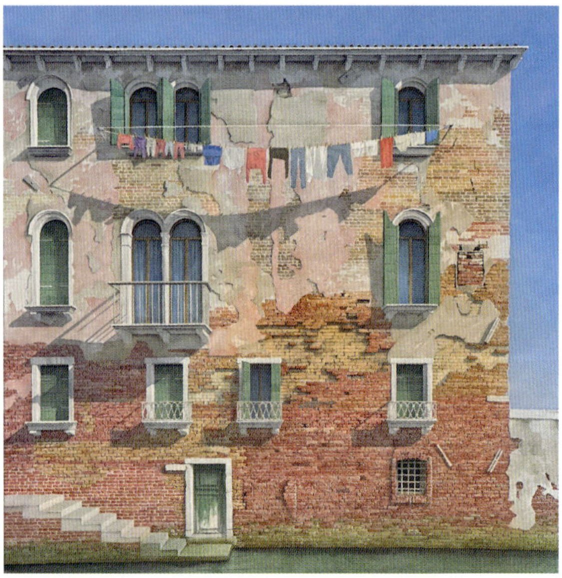

many hours of painstaking work. Remember that painting I left in the sink? The next day, nursing a mild hangover, I retrieved it. To my astonishment, everything I disliked had soaked away. I re-stretched the paper and worked on it again until satisfied. The little painting is reproduced on page 39.

More importantly, I realised what I needed to do from then on. Once a painting is bone dry, I completely saturate it with water and, using a wet sponge or large decorator's brush, vigorously wipe over the entire surface. This removes the surface paint, leaving only the stained paper beneath.

On rough paper, the paint lifts more from the raised areas, creating a pleasing texture. Any surviving pencil marks are rubbed out. What remains looks as though you are viewing the painting through tracing paper – softened, freed of tightness and hard edges. The danger, of course, is that too much may be lost.

Then comes the part I enjoy most: working back into the painting. I rebuild the shadows, rework details where needed, leave some areas untouched (such as the horizon on pages 66/67) and concentrate on my abiding obsession: the light.

Sometimes I will give the entire painting a unifying wash of Raw Sienna - I did here, but not before once again protecting some of the laundry with stopping-out fluid.

If necessary, I repeat the washing process. Things only go wrong when the paper begins to fail; push it too far and it turns to blotting paper. At that point, all is lost.

So there you have it. Next time someone asks me about watercolour technique, I shall suggest they buy this book.

Gerard Stamp, 2026

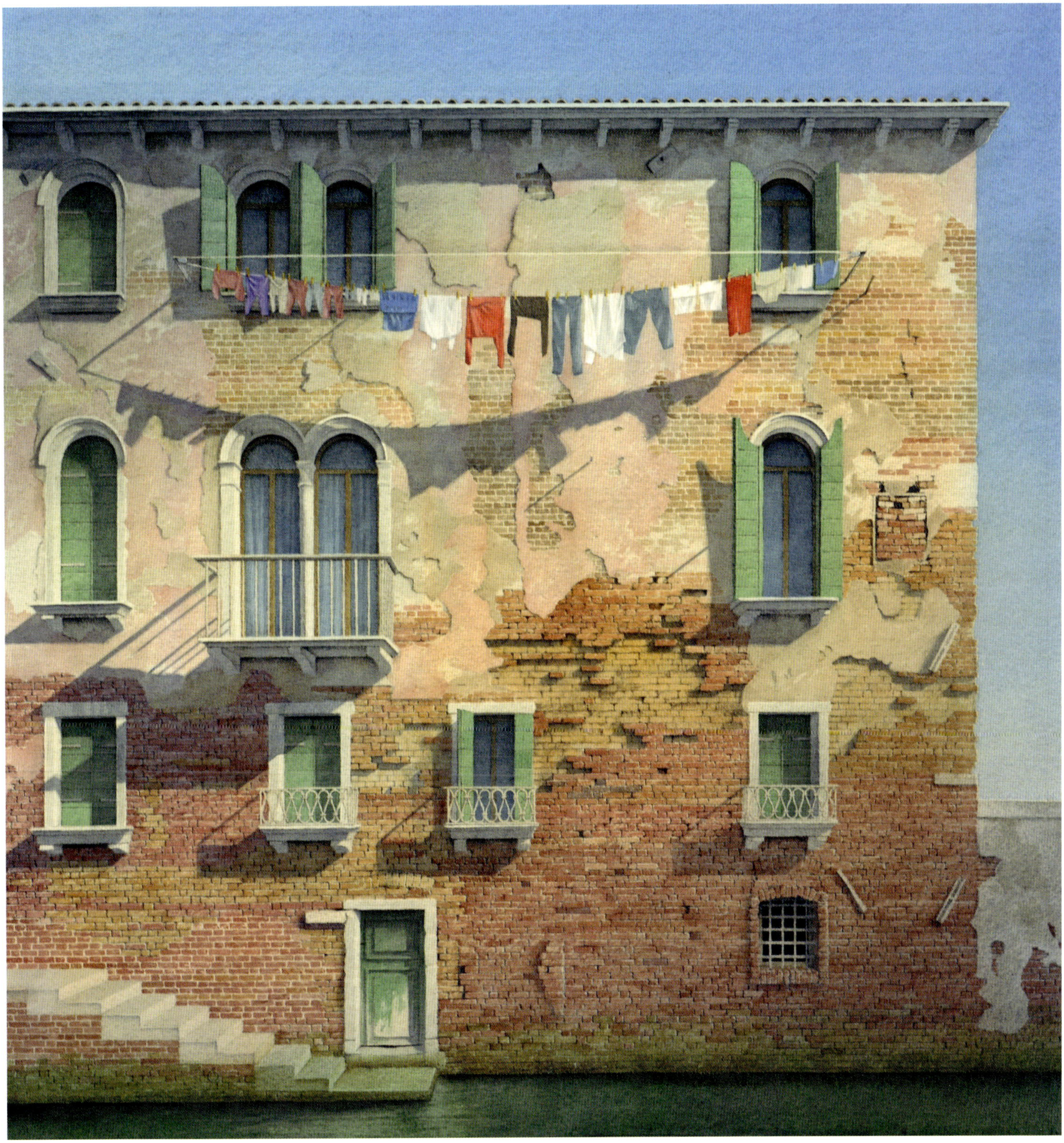

Giorno del Bucato

Watercolour 2026

35 x 34 ins | 89 x 86 cm

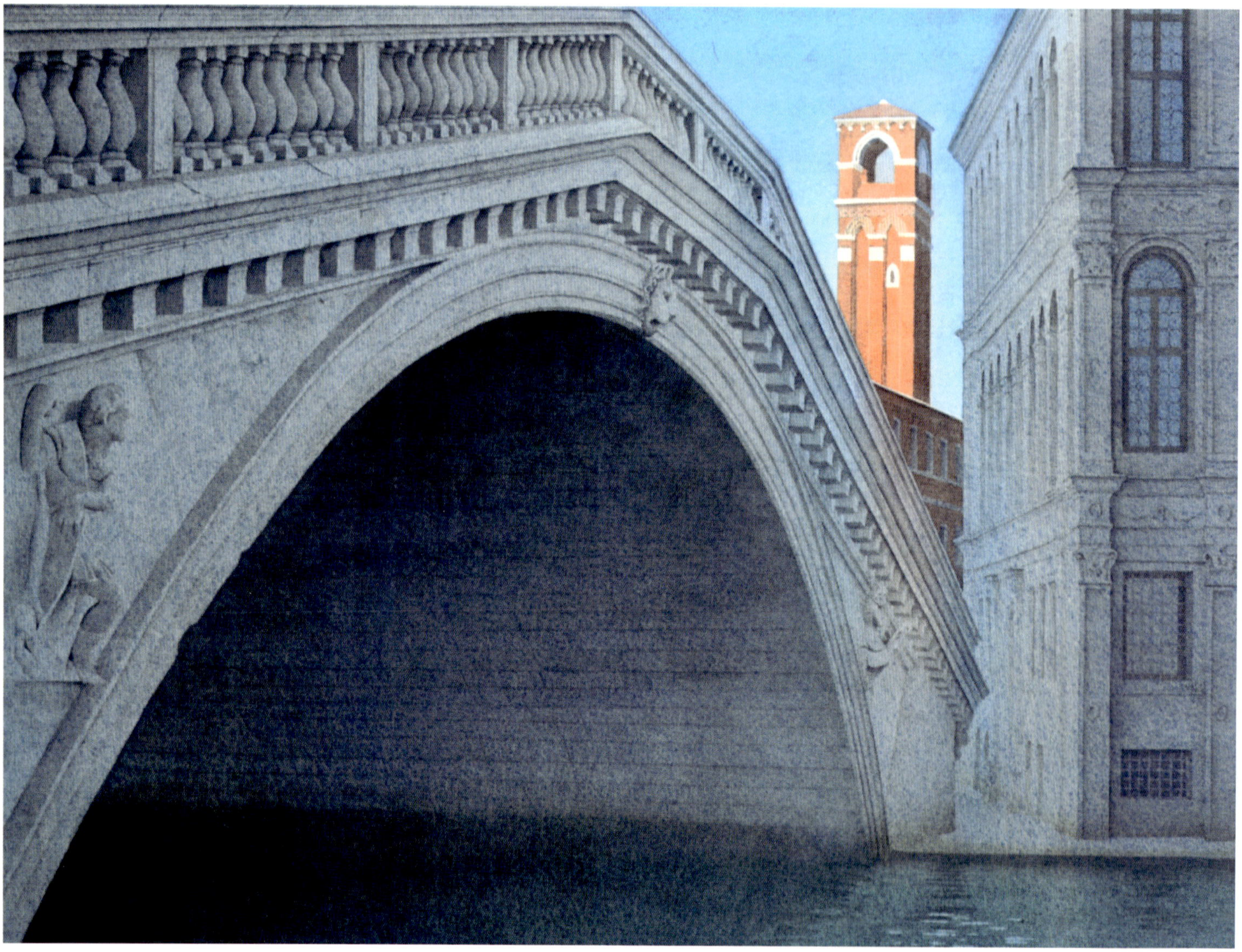

Rialto

Watercolour 2026

21 x 27 ins | 54 x 68 cm

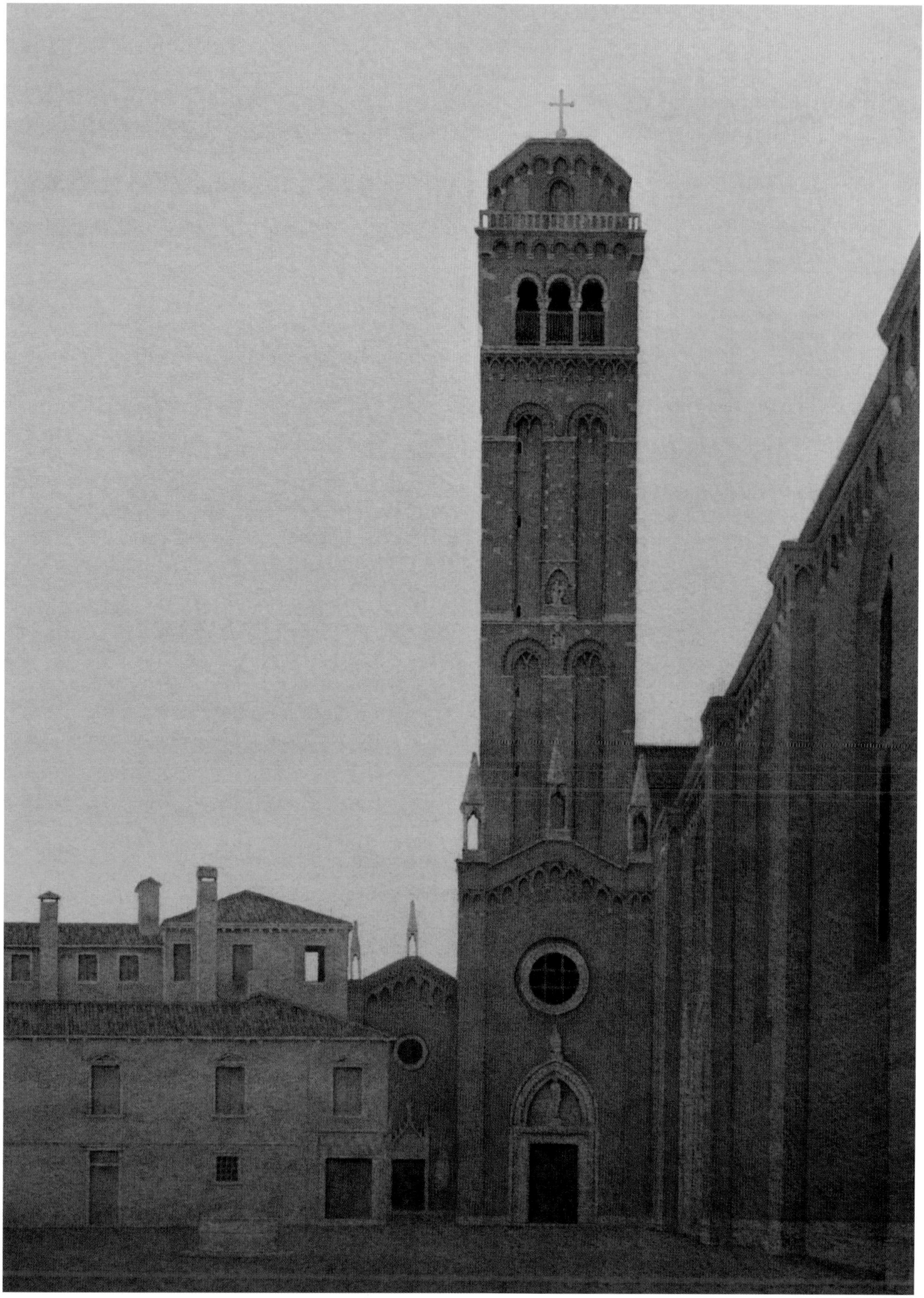

The Open Window

Watercolour 2026

25 x 18 ins | 53 x 46 cm

Index

Images in italics